Screening Schillebeeckx

SCREENING SCHILLEBEECKX

Theology and Third Cinema in Dialogue

Antonio D. Sison

Foreword by Robert J. Schreiter

SCREENING SCHILLEBEECKX

© Antonio D. Sison, 2006.

Foreword copyright © Robert J. Schreiter, 2006

First published in 2006 by
PALGRAVE MACMILLAN™
175 Fifth Avenue, New York, N.Y. 10010 and
Houndmills, Basingstoke, Hampshire, England RG21 6XS
Companies and representatives throughout the world.

PALGRAVE MACMILLAN is the global academic imprint of the Palgrave Macmillan division of St. Martin's Press, LLC and of Palgrave Macmillan Ltd. Macmillan® is a registered trademark in the United States, United Kingdom and other countries. Palgrave is a registered trademark in the European Union and other countries.

ISBN-13: 978–1–4039–7516–4
ISBN-10: 1–4039–7516–7

Library of Congress Cataloging-in-Publication Data

Sison, Antonio D.
    Screening Schillebeeckx : theology and third cinema in dialogue /
Antonio D. Sison.
        p. cm.
    Includes bibliographical references and index.
    ISBN 1–4039–7516–7 (alk. paper)
    1. Motion pictures—Religious aspects. 2. Motion pictures—Political
aspects—Developing countries. 3. Schillebeeckx, Edward, 1914– I. Title.

PN1995.5.S625 2006
791.43′682—dc22   2006044751

A catalogue record for this book is available from the British Library.

Design by Newgen Imaging Systems (P) Ltd., Chennai, India.

First edition: November 2006

10 9 8 7 6 5 4 3 2 1

Printed in the United States of America.

To Edward Schillebeeckx, the "happy theologian."
For the inspiration,
the respectful listening,
and the wise counsel—
"To Antonio, be also a 'happy theologian.' "

CONTENTS

Acknowledgments

I consider myself blessed to have had the incalculable experience of pitching tent in three continents in a span of six years. That said, I wish to give a modest tribute to the intercontinental "conspiracy of grace" that helped birth this book.

Philippines:
Kidlat Tahimik, independent filmmaker and nationalist, whose films taught me more about being Filipino than the history books I've read. And special thanks to him for granting me permission to use a screen capture from his film *Perfumed Nightmare*.

Christina Astorga and Victoria Parco, former colleagues at the Ateneo de Manila Theology Department, who were always helpful along the way.

Maryhill School of Theology in Manila for my early theological training.

Jose "Ka Joe" de Mesa for his insightful review of my research work.

Bo Sanchez and Shepherd's Voice Publications (SVP) for the unselfish support.

Reeya Lucero and Randy Aquino, true friends who were ready to help despite the geographical distance.

My parents, who inspire me with their guileless simplicity and honesty—Anthony Q. Sison, the good judge of San Carlos City, Pangasinan; and Josephine D. Sison, who became a barrister while rearing a brood of six. My biased virtual cheering squad: my siblings and their respective families. My sister Patricia Sison-Arroyo, the consummate multi-tasker, deserves credit for often volunteering to be my arms and legs on the other shore.

The Netherlands:
The Faculty of Theology of the *Katholieke Universiteit Nijmegen* (now *Radboud Universiteit Nijmegen*) for supporting my four-year doctoral programme. Toine van den Hoogen and Emille Poppe, who supervised my graduate research work. The late Emeritus Professor Theo Beemer for all our open-minded intellectual conversations.

Patrick Chatelion Counet, my "co-collaborator" in the Theology-Film dialogue.

Ingrid Diaz-Wolters and Gunther Sturms, who offered a ready helping hand throughout my Dutch residency.

United States:

S. Brent Plate of Texas Christian University for his intellectual generosity. Brent opened the door for me to contribute a chapter to the Palgrave Macmillan anthology *Representing Religion in World Cinema.*

Angela Ann Zukowski, MHSH, for her inspiring guidance, and her spirited team at the Institute for Pastoral Initiatives, University of Dayton.

The U.S. National Catholic Reporterís "Global Perspective" column, for giving me a platform where I could share my theological musings to a wider readership.

The gracious community spirit of the Missionaries of the Precious Blood (C.PP.S.). Special thanks to Ken Schnipke for his consistent nurturing presence; and Angelo Anthony, who has been an enthusiastic conversation partner. Current housemates Jerry Steinbrunner and Hugh Henderson of St. Mark's Parish, Cincinnati, for their care and generosity.

Joseph Grilliot, my co-candidate in formation, film buddy, and kindred spirit. Joe (and the Grilliot family) has been a blessing to me in more ways that I can count.

The Sisters of the Precious Blood, especially Alice Schoettelkotte; and the Precious Blood Companions, for their encouragement.

Last but certainly not least, Robert J. Schreiter, Professor of Historical and Dogmatic Theology, and current Vatican Council II Chair of the Catholic Theological Union, Chicago. Bob has been many things to me—editor, mentor, role model, the list goes on. I am deeply grateful.

FOREWORD

This book opens up for us an exciting intersection between cinema studies and theology in a way that few other books have done. The more common discussion of the interplay of these two disciplines correlates the themes that appear in the script of films with their counterpart in theological reflection. But Antonio Sison takes us to a different place. In his exploration of Third Cinema—a distinctive and challenging approach to film—he looks at how elements of style and cinematography relate to deep, fundamental turns in theology's exploration of how God yearns for and guides human liberation.

Third Cinema stands alone in its emphasis upon how the craft of filming can reflect the angle of vision of the poor and oppressed of the earth, see and experience their world, and how they shape that into their struggle for liberation. The films Sison explores in this book are sterling examples of this unique entry into the consciousness of the majority of the earth's population, a consciousness that is largely ignored by the wealthy and privileged of the world. This portal into the colonized imagination offers the viewer an unexpected and suggestive challenge to rethink and to reenact relationships with those who are oppressed and seek liberation.

But Sison does not stop there. He retrieves impulses and trajectories from theology that have been seldom entertained or followed. Edward Schillebeeckx, one of the great Roman Catholic thinkers of the last fifty years, is unique among European theologians. He has been a theologian who truly understands the struggles of the poor and oppressed of the world. As a result of this, he has been perhaps the foremost dialogue partner with those trying to understand the aspirations of those who suffer for their own liberation. Too often, as Sison points out so well, has his understanding of the saving power of God been domesticated and depoliticized by his colleagues in theology to make him safer for general consumption. His concept of Political Holiness charts out a terrain where people's encounter with God really does lead to a liberation from oppression.

What Sison does in this book is more than a bridging of the two disciplines of Cinema and Theology. His investigation illumines both in a new way, opening up vistas that will lure others into further exploration. We will not view the films informed by Third Cinema in the same way again, nor will we read theology that tries to grasp the movements of God in our world with the same, sometimes shop-worn expectations. This book is exemplary in showing what genuine interdisciplinary work can achieve. For both those who are interested in cinema and those who read theology, here we experience a conjunction that will lead us to previously unexplored territory. This book does pioneering work on both fronts. I urge readers to enjoy its remarkable insights and suggestions.

Robert Schreiter

Introduction

The Pentagon called for an important meeting in August 2003, predictably, to discuss anti-terrorist strategies. What was of peculiar interest about this meeting was that it was a special screening session for *The Battle of Algiers*, a film lensed by Italian filmmaker Gillo Pontecorvo in 1965. An example of a type of political film known as Third Cinema, "The Battle of Algiers" essays the 1954–1962 Algerian revolt against French occupation and gives ideological visibility to the guerilla-style bombings carried out by the Algerian Liberation Front (NLF) during the turbulent period. The privileged audience of about forty Pentagon officers, along with some civilian experts, huddled to screen Pontecorvo's film in the hopes of gaining more insight into the motivations and modalities of present day terrorist activities. The obvious lesson for the day: "know thy enemy."

I am not a big fan of the Pentagon's activities. Neither is Third Cinema, which casts a gimlet eye on the hegemonic tactics routinely conducted by the globe's rich and powerful. Yet, ironically, the Pentagon screening session unwittingly confirms the power of Third Cinema; the power to represent and mirror the sociopolitical realities of a Third World that continues to exist, though the zeitgeist would like to believe otherwise. That said, I am convinced that Third Cinema merits regardful consideration and, as in the case of my work, more serious theological attention.

Situated within the interdisciplinary efforts to bridge Theology and Cinema, I explore the ways in which the liberative project of Edward Schillebeeckx's eschatological perspective is crystallized in Third Cinema. Third Cinema occupies a special niche in Cinema Studies. It is the only major film theory that did not originate from a Euro-American milieu.[1] It is also the only type of political film that insists on a dedicated representation of the plight of Third World peoples who continue in the struggle to become agents of their own history in the postcolonial aftermath. Third Cinema is of undeniable value for Third World cultures because it serves as a custodian of subversive memory; a critical counterbalance to the wilful amnesia of dominant western cinema, which almost always insists on the primacy of entertainment value over all other considerations. Films from Hollywood, for instance, usually do not care to examine how the causal structures of social, cultural, and economic inequality impact on two-thirds of the global population. As long as there exists a lopsided global symbolic exchange that separates the metropolitan capitalist First World from its erstwhile colonies in the Third, there will always be a strong case for Third Cinema.

My choice of Third Cinema as a dialogue partner for theology is driven by reasons personal and strategic. Personal because I am not just a scholar committed to the interface of Theology and Film, I am a Filipino, a child of the Third World, in search of soul and story. The films I choose as case studies reflect a world I was born and raised in. By proximity, the title that has the most personal resonance with me is Kidlat Tahimik's *Perfumed Nightmare*. Tahimik is a cutting edge Filipino filmmaker who paints from the palette of revisionist historiography. For him, hindsight is 20/20. His *Perfumed Nightmare*, winner of the coveted Berlin International Film Festival Golden Bear in 1978 and a rare Southeast Asian example of Third Cinema, is a re-visiting of the Philippines' tortured history of multiple colonizations and a subversive filmic re-telling of a collective deep story of liberation. Being a member of the culture in question, I am an involved participant in Tahimik's postcolonial "exorcism." But in a wider sense, each of the chosen case study films confirms my membership in, and solidarity with, Third World cultures.

Strategic because I am convinced that the very stylistic signature of the films carry undeniable ideological weight and thus trigger the hermeneutical impulse. The key point for consideration is Third Cinema's lucid sociopolitical critique and liberative current, situated within the general rubric of "postcolonial struggle." Through the various elements of cinematic grammar, the films portray, in one sense or another, the collaboration of human and divine agency, while an innervating vision of emancipative praxis looms in the horizon. Here, the divine is identified with the marginalized culture, represented here in synechdoche by the film's protagonists, whose growing resistance and protest draw them to an alternative future of greater human flourishing. The filmic texts, as such, lay down a bridge for possible creative crossings with theology.

What emerges as a lucid and nuanced discursive framework for a deeper discussion of Third Cinema is Edward Schillebeeckx's eschatological perspective. The decisive link between salvation and liberation, an unmistakable touchstone of Schillebeeckx's later theology, has almost completely fallen below the radar of research works in

Systematic Theology. Schillebeeckx's later theology is always immersed in the concrete, historical situation and epistemologically grounded in human liberation. In a personal interview I conducted in the Dutch city of Nijmegen, Schillebeeckx himself affirms that "the liberation of human beings is the golden thread of my theology." I submit that the depoliticizing tendencies in the reception of Schillebeeckx's work represents a myopic reading of Schillebeeckx's later theology and an undervaluing of the continued intercultural relevance and impact of his thought on the Third World situation. From my own Third World optic, I see these tendencies as missed opportunities; the inordinate muting of the prophetic-liberating voice of Schillebeeckx as a credible and significant western mouthpiece for marginalized peoples who are still in the process of finding their own voice amid dehumanizing sociopolitical realities.

I believe that *Screening Schillebeeckx: Theology and Third Cinema in Dialogue* will prove to be mutually enriching for both Systematic Theology and Cinema Studies. While theology can offer a unique critical perspective in the study of film, film can stimulate theology to reflect on its questions in new, creative ways.

I configure the book in three cumulative moments:

Cinematic Principle. In the "Cinematic Principle," the first moment of my methodological triptych, I discuss the concept of Third Cinema, briefly tracing its history as a Latin American political and aesthetic movement in the late 1960s, and then clarifying its later development as a critical theory of film. Third Cinema is posited on ideologically determined stylistic codes, and because artistic choice connotes ideological choice, a consideration of cinematic style is constitutive for Third Cinema critical theory. Pertinently, I analyze various case studies of Third Cinema, first exploring the context of the national from three continents—Cuba's *The Last Supper* (Latin America), Senegal's *Xala* (Africa), and the Philippines' *Perfumed Nightmare* (Asia); and then navigating through Third Cinema's current expanded sense, a virtual geography of Third Cinema—*Romero*, *Bread and Roses*, *Divine Intervention*, *Hotel Rwanda*, and *Motorcycle Diaries*. With Third Cinema critical theory as my hermeneutical key, I unpack the artful layering of stylistic options—mise-en-scène, cinematography, camera angling, editing, and sound—and validate how they work to paint an alternative, emancipative sociopolitical vision. I thus examine the ways in which the case studies exemplify an "aesthetic of liberation."

Theological Principle. In the second moment, which I designate as "Theological Principle," I situate Schillebeeckx's eschatological perspective within the rubric of Political Holiness. I build the theological discussion around the liberative stream of Schillebeeckx's later theology as expressed in cogent topics—the Quest for the Elusive Humanum, the Ecumene of Suffering, Christian Salvation and Sociopolitical Liberation, the Praxis of the Reign of God, Eschatological Salvation, Negative Experiences of Contrast, and Political Love and Holiness. Schillebeeckx's advocacy of political holiness as the new praxis-oriented mysticism breaks open his liberative stance toward the Third World as it continues to make sense of the myriad scars of colonial trauma and the pervading situation of massive global inequality.

Creative Crossings. In the third and final moment, "Creative Crossings," I explore the points of convergence between the cinematic principle and the theological principle, following a two-tiered structure.

First, I establish the epistemological resonances between Schillebeeckx's later theology and Third Cinema. I argue that a more regardful consideration of the practical-critical soteriological base of Schillebeeckx's eschatology offers a parallel connection with the liberative propositions that undergird the Third Cinema project. The clarification of this epistemological link serves as the ground principle from which I posit a second level of convergence.

A creative examination of what I perceive as the crystallization of Schillebeeckx's conception of political holiness in the stylistic options embodied in Third Cinema. Grounded on the close correspondence between the epistemological project of Schillebeeckx's later theology and Third Cinema, I discuss the ways in which the main threads of Schillebeeckx's eschatological perspective find cinematic expression in the case studies. What I propose as the methodological and conceptual bridge is Third Cinema critical theory, which, as I discuss earlier, is posited on the use of stylistic strategies to foreground the Third World quest for liberation and equality. I pay attention to what I would describe as the "creative crossings" between the two principles through the mediation of Third Cinema stylistic strategies.

In this creative and open-minded exploration, I argue for the primacy of cinematic style as the locus for a theological hermeneutic of film over the prevailing practice of extracting the religious dimension out of the more thematic, literary bases of film. What is at stake here is the recognition of cinema as an art form with its own grammatical signature—cinema as cinema.

Cinema as Cinema: The Significance of Stylistic Examination

The locus of the Theology-Cinema dialogue has often been exclusively foxholed in the thematic and literary bases of film. The area of primary importance, that of cinematic style, continues to be accorded minimal value and attention. As such, cinema is not examined on its own terms and is treated as though it were a mere appendage to literature. I cannot overemphasize this point because the unique proposition of this work is that over and above the overriding preoccupation with thematic and other literary elements, a more serious regard for style offers a distinctly cinematic approach to the Theology-Cinema confluence. Michael Bird makes a similar assertion in "Film as Hierophany," the essay he wrote for his own editorial collection, *Religion in Film*. Drawing from Paul Tillich's analysis of religious art,[2] he argues as follows:

> While many films have portrayed ostensibly religious subjects, these films have often erred precisely in their disregard for the medium's stylistic virtues. Rather than the "biblical blockbusters" and insipid trivialities that are frequently offered under the guise of "religious films," what is required in a cinematic theology is a consideration of how the *style* of film can enable an exploration of the sacred.[3]

I find it ironic that while Bird rightly laments the chronic oversight in the Theology-Cinema landscape, his own essay in the collection, an exploration of the religious perspective palpable in the works of Swedish auteur Ingmar Bergman, skirts the very key question he deems as essential: style. I find it doubly surprising that Bird overlooks the matter of style in the Bergman filmography—which includes seminal, paradigmatic examples of cinematic style such as *The Seventh Seal* (1957), *Wild Strawberries* (1957), *Persona* (1966), and *Cries and Whispers* (1972)—as one of the master filmmaker's major contributions is his original stylistic signature which has even been etched linguistically in the adjective "bergmanesque." Neither is cinematic style addressed in any of the other essays in *Religion in Film*. A recent book entitled *Robert Bresson: A Spiritual Style in Film* by Joseph Cunneen backs down on the promise of its title. He uses the term "style" in a general, uncritical sense, and thus, fails to offer a sufficient examination of how Bresson's stylistic options work to communicate religion or spirituality.[4] Cunneen's book, as many others preceding it, underconceives what may have been an opportune engagement with the grammar of film, thus, assuring its inclusion in the continuum of works on the Theology-Cinema confluence that perpetuate a blackout on the central question of style.

Exceptions do exist. To my knowledge, there are two noteworthy scholarly efforts that attempt to bridge Theology and Cinema through stylistic analysis. The first is Paul Schrader's *Transcendental Style in Film: Ozu, Bresson, Dreyer*,[5] which directly navigates through the elements of camerawork, acting, and editing in the films of Yasujiro Ozu, Robert Bresson, and Carl Theodor Dreyer, and examines how they become evocative of a patterned "transcendental style." Schrader is clear in his focus, qualifying at the outset that his work is not about religious film, that is, the general ways in which religious themes of films have been discussed or the ways in which the religious sensibilities of audiences have been triggered through a cinematic experience. "It is only *necessarily* a style."[6] The second example is Peter Fraser's *Images of the Passion: The Sacramental Mode in Film*, an analysis of Christian liturgical patterns through a close reading of selected films. Fraser examines films belonging to the religious genre that convincingly mirror the passion of Christ, a direction taken by not a few works in the Theology-Cinema area. What is decisive in Fraser's work, however, is that it pays due attention to the stylistic devices upon which the concept of the passion is cinematically rendered.[7] For Fraser, as for Schrader, a consideration of style is constitutive for the Theology-Cinema dialogue, as such, cinema is analyzed and debated as cinema, not as a mere adjunct to literature. These two exemplary works, however, remain as isolated islands afloat in an ocean of scholarly input concentrating exclusively on thematic and literary explorations.[8]

The same holds true in the more specific area of Theology-Political Cinema where a gaping lacuna awaits to be filled—establishing the link between emancipative theology and political, socially relevant cinema through a consideration of cinematic style. This dearth becomes quite apparent in one book, which is considered as the best known work on this area—Neal Hurley's *Reel Revolution: A Film Primer on Liberation*. Hurley draws from the resource that sheer gravity already serves on a platter, the use of Liberation Theology as referential framework in the analysis of political cinema. Covering a diverse sampling of politically resonant films from Eisenstein to Chaplin, *Reel Revolution* had made a notable, initial contribution to the Theology-Political Cinema discussion. It is, however, a work predicated entirely on an investigation of thematic and plot elements. He maps the thoroughly thematic concern of his work when he asserts, "Liberation is a serious *theme* and deserves more sober and sustained analysis and study than it has commanded in the past."[9] Indeed, liberation is a serious and relevant theme that warrants scholarly attention but the sustained analysis and study it commands needs to be angled toward the question of how this theme is worked-out in cinematic style. Like the majority of the works within the Theology-Cinema dialogue, stylistic examination is the missing link in Hurley's equation. As a case in point, Hurley devotes a chapter on Latin American Cinema and discusses Solanas and Getino's *La hora de los hornos* ("The Hour of the Furnaces"/Argentina, 1968), the seminal Third Cinema film noted precisely for its revolutionary style, strictly in thematic terms. Cinematic style, quite regrettably, had fallen below the radar of Hurley's project.

As this book niches into the Theology-Political Cinema confluence, I argue that the "reel revolution" as conceived by Hurley remains pallid and insubstantial sans a serious consideration of the mediation of cinematic style.

I am optimistic that *Screening Schillebeeckx: Theology and Film in Dialogue* would evince a single but meaningful step in the right direction.

Cinematic Principle

The Concept of Third Cinema

All films are political, but films are not all political in the same way.

Mike Wayne's on-target thesis in his book "Political Film: The Dialectics of Third Cinema"[1] sets the agenda for this chapter, for indeed, politically leavened films have always contributed to the overall landscape of world cinema. Easily, a number of titles come to mind—*Bronenosets Potyomkin* (Eisenstein/Russia,1925), *Ladri Bicyclette* (de Sica/Italy, 1947), *Pather Panchali* (Ray/India, 1955), *Apocalypse Now* (Coppola/United States, 1979), *The Killing Fields* (Joffe/United Kingdom, 1984), *Schindler's List* (Spielberg/United States, 1993), *Erin Brockovich* (Soderberg/United States, 2000) or even the fairly recent hit *Jarhead* (Mendes/United States, 2005), just to mention a few. But the key question begs for clarification: What constitutes Third Cinema and how does it differ from other films of the political genre? I seek to provide answers to this question by tracing the evolution of Third Cinema from its original conception to its present stage of development.

This chapter unfolds in three parts. The first deals with the inception of Third Cinema as a radical, politically driven creative movement in Latin America in the 1960s, focusing on the classical manifestos outlined by filmmakers Fernando Solanas and Octavio Getino vis-à-vis similar programmatic statements by kindred filmmakers of the region. The second explores the growth of Third Cinema as a systematic critical theory attributed largely to the groundbreaking work of African film scholar Teshome Gabriel. The third and final section surveys Third Cinema in its current evolutionary turn toward expansion, greater inclusiveness, and continued relevance.

Cinema as a Gun: Latin American Guerilla Cinema

The film *La Hora de las Hornos* ("Hour of the Furnaces," 1968), a subversive, political documentary produced by the Argentinian alliance of filmmakers known as *Grupo Cine Liberacion* and directed by members Fernando Solanas and Octavio Getino, marked the birth pangs of a radical cinema of colonial resistance. The film was produced in a volatile atmosphere, a period when Latin America and the rest of the Third World were burdened with underdevelopment and cultural dependency paralleled by the swelling of militant movements and organized protests.[2] Cautious of the restrictive atmosphere following the post-Peron military coup of 1966, the film was shot surreptitiously with the aid of the cadres of the Peronist Movement and completed in Italy. *La Hora de los Hornos* was for its filmmakers a "film act," referring to its radical digression from the conventional conception of cinema. Some of the revolutionary features of this film act include the submission of the film project to the critique of the Argentinian working class whose inputs formed the basis for a series of revisions.[3] Authorship then was decentered and took on a collective dimension. There is also the "openness" of the text structure itself which solicits a more participatory involvement from the audience. For instance, the film ends with the provocative text that reads—"Now it's up to you to draw conclusions, to continue the film. You have the floor."[4] Defying closure, *La Hora de los Hornos* shifts the onus to the audience, now tasked to extend the film into the context of their real lives, "Thus *Hour* engraves its ideas on the spectator's mind. The images do not explode harmlessly, dissipating their energy; fusing with ideas, they detonate in the minds of the audience."[5]

La Hora de los Hornos represented, at one and the same time, political militancy and artistic experimentation. The final cut is a convergence of a wide range of eclectic styles "from didacticism to operatic stylisation, direct filming to the techniques of advertising, and incorporating photographs, newsreel, testimonial footage and film clips—from avant-garde and mainstream, fiction and documentary,"[6] interwoven into a trilogy described as "a militant poetic epic tapestry."[7]

In 1969, Solanas and Getino drafted a caustic manifesto entitled *Hacia Un Tercer Cine*—"Towards a Third Cinema: Notes and Experiences for the Development of a Cinema of Liberation in the Third World." Quickened by their engagement with the production of *La Hora de los Hornos*, the Argentinian filmmakers criticized the impact of colonialism on Third World cultures and detailed its repercussions for cinema:

> Until recently, film had been synonymous with spectacle or entertainment: in a word, it was one more *consumer good*. At best, films succeeded in bearing witness to the decay of bourgeois values and testifying to social injustice. As a rule, film only dealt with effect, never with cause; it was a cinema of mystification or anti-historicism. It was *surplus value* cinema. Caught up in these conditions, films, the most valuable tool of communications of our times, were destined to satisfy only the ideological and economic interests of the *owners of the film industry*, the lords of the world film market, the great majority of whom were from the United States.[8]

The manifesto presents the argument that cinema had been depoliticized and commodified by the prevailing consumeristic economic order and served only to benefit the key players of the dominant film industries, mainly, that of the United States or, simply put, Hollywood. As such, a large majority of films were thoroughly infused with the key values of the "owners" of the global film market and were thus mere commodities produced for their entertainment value. Commensurately, the cinematic input of the Third World was driven to oblivion.[9] In the light of this scenario, Solanas and Getino proposed a cinema that would, in its filmmaking practice and aesthetic choices, represent the Third World struggle for liberation.[10]

"Third Cinema," the term coined by the two Latin American filmmakers, is rooted in the notion of the "Third World." The wordplay deliberately carries the connotations of its root term as the Third World refers to the lowest rung of the Theory of Three Worlds used by China in the 1955 Bandung Conference of the Non-Aligned Movement. The theory maintains that the base of the global pyramid is occupied by the underdeveloped countries, the most feeble runners in the blistering global socioeconomic race.[11] Third World nations belong neither to the industrialized capitalist world (First World), nor the industrialized communist bloc (Second World) and have thus been classified as "non-aligned." The concept of the Third World is imbricated in the issues of colonialism and racism, "for the 'Third World' refers to the colonized, neocolonized, or decolonized nations and 'minorities' whose structural disadvantages have been shaped by the colonial process and by the unequal division of international labor."[12] Notwithstanding the demise of the Second World in 1989, "Third World" is still considered as a valid descriptive term for the prevailing social condition of structural exploitation and impoverishment that continue to burden many countries in the face of globalization.[13]

It is instructive to note, however, that no matter how indebted Third Cinema is to the concept of the Third World, the category does not so much allude to the geographical origins of a given film or a specific genre. Rather, the notion of Third Cinema is indicative of a film's dedication to an authentic representation of Third World peoples who struggle to become agents of their own history in the postcolonial aftermath:

> What determines Third Cinema is the conception of the world, and not the genre or an explicit approach. Any story, any subject can be taken up by Third Cinema. In developing countries, Third Cinema is a cinema of decolonisation, which expresses the will to national liberation, anti-mythic, anti-racist, anti-bourgeois, and popular.[14]

Solanas and Getino draw the difference between Third Cinema and other forms of cinema necessarily classified as:

- First Cinema, which refers to industrial or commercial cinema epitomized by Hollywood. First Cinema functions to perpetuate the message of the dominant ideology through its imagery, subject matter; and its mode of production, distribution, and exhibition;
- And Second Cinema, which is mainly represented by European auteurist cinema but also including art cinema, American independent cinema, and the various new wave cinemas. Although it may be sociopolitically subversive, for instance, in its resistance to censorship and state power, Second Cinema still works within the limits set by the prevailing system. Echoing the words of French auteur Jean-Luc Godard, Solanas and Getino describe auteurist cinema as "trapped inside the fortress" and thus incapable of catalyzing meaningful social change.[15] "At best, it can be the *'progressive' wing of Establishment cinema.*"[16]

Third Cinema is presented as a radical alternative to First and Second Cinemas.

It is important to stress that as explicated in the above classification, First, Second, and Third Cinema do not correspond to the First, Second, and Third Worlds. The three categories of cinema as proposed by Solanas and Getino represent a kind of virtual geography. The conceptual dependence on the Theory of Three Worlds is not a wholesale appropriation; it is confined only to the analogy of the term "Third Cinema" with the "Third World." While this may seem contradictory, the two Argentinians substantiate the demarcation when they cite supra-geographical examples of Third Cinema, "Newsreel, a US New Left film group, the *cinegiornali* of the Italian student movement, the films made by the *Etats Generaux du Cinéma Français*, and those of the British and Japanese student movement."[17]

The two-pronged concern of Third Cinema[18] according to the Argentinian manifesto are as follows:

• Disavowal from the filmmaking conventions and principles of Hollywood. National cinemas of the Third World had been practicing mere mimicry of politically benign traditional film concepts that serve to perpetuate Hollywood conventions and biased Western consciousness. The only plausible way left for the filmmaker is to work completely outside of the dominant system. The epic film *War and Peace* (Bondarchuk, Russia 1968) is cited as an example of a cinematic opus thoroughly molded by the propositions of Hollywood.

• Acknowledgement of the need for film to present an unequivocal political and ideological stand against imperialism and class inequalities. Just as Hollywood presents a politically lopsided equation heavily in favor of the First World perspective, so is Third Cinema inversely one-sided as it represents the perspective of the Third World, precisely what Hollywood has repressed. Film must "mobilize, agitate, and politicize, to arm them (the people) rationally and perceptibly."[19] and to disturb the sociocultural status quo.

The manifesto proposes an alternative filmmaking practice described as "guerilla filmmaking," a radical notion of film production akin to the collective endeavor that ensued in the making of *La Hora de los Hornos*.

> Guerilla filmmaking proletarianizes the film worker and breaks down the intellectual aristocracy that the bourgeoisie grants to its followers. In a word, it *democratizes*. The filmmaker's tie with reality makes him more a part of his people. Vanguard layers and even masses participate collectively in the work when they realize that it is the continuity of their daily struggle. *La Hora de las Hornos* shows how a film can be made in hostile circumstances when it has the support and collaboration of militants and cadres from the people.[20]

Moreover, Solanas and Getino argue against the dualism between art and politics which in their view, reflect discordant class interests—"that of the rulers and that of the nation . . . *our* culture and *their* culture, *our* cinema and *their* cinema."[21]

The combative, revolutionary tone and agenda of the Argentinian manifesto reflects the paradigm of decolonization proposed by Afro-Carribean thinker Frantz Fanon in his 1961 work *The Wretched of the Earth*. Considered as Fanon's most important political book,[22] *The Wretched of the Earth* is a powerful treatise on the political development of Third World countries. The liberation movements in Algeria and Africa provided inspiration for Fanon's thesis that decolonization is a process of seizing freedom through a liberation struggle.[23]

> In decolonization, there is therefore the need of a complete calling in question of the colonial situation. If we wish to describe it precisely, we might find it in the well known words: "The last shall be first and the first last." Decolonization is the putting into practice of this sentence. That is why, if we try to describe it, all decolonization is successful.[24]

Re-appropriating Fanon's arguments for Third Cinema, Solanas and Getino insist that art and cinema must first and foremost play an emancipatory role—as virtual revolutionary weapons in the struggle for liberation. As such, "The camera is the expropriator of image-weapons; the projector, a gun that can shoot 24 frames per second."[25] The notion of "cinema as a gun" ratifies Fanon's viewpoint that there is a need to extinguish aesthetics from society for only then can culture, cinema and the concept of beauty be decolonized and truly owned by Third World peoples. "Ideas such as 'Beauty itself is revolutionary' and 'All new cinema is revolutionary' are idealistic aspirations that do not touch the neocolonial condition, since they continue to conceive of cinema, art, and beauty as universal abstractions and not as an integral part of national processes of decolonization."[26] In the argument of Solanas and Getino, the concept of Third Cinema as an emancipatory weapon provides a contributory kinetic dissonance that projects a larger utopic vision that of imagined communities liberated and decolonized:

> The anti-imperialist struggle of the peoples of the Third World and of their equivalents inside the imperialist countries constitutes today the axis of the world revolution. Third Cinema is, in our opinion, the cinema that recognizes in that struggle the most gigantic cultural, scientific, and artistic manifestation of our time, the great possibility of constructing a liberated personality with each people as the starting point—in a word, the decolonization of culture.[27]

Parallel manifestos reverberating a thesis similar to that of Solanas and Getino emerged elsewhere in Latin America. In Cuba, Julio Garcia

Espinosa authored *Por un Cine Imperfecto* ("For an Imperfect Cinema," 1969), a manifesto rejecting the technological polish characteristic of North American and European cinema. Although differing in context, Espinosa's programmatic thesis shares the Argentinian manifesto's suspicion and criticism of the aesthetic "perfection" of First World cinema, which functions only to perpetuate passive consumption from the audience. Espinosa calls for an "Imperfect Cinema" rooted in the traditions of genuine popular art, which considers audiences as participatory co-authors and not mere consumers:

> Popular art has always been created by the least learned sector of society, yet this uncultured sector has managed to conserve profoundly cultured characteristics of art. One of the most important of these is the fact that the creators are at the same time the spectators and vice versa. Between those who produce and those who consume, no sharp line of demarcation exists.[28]

The Imperfect Cinema proposed by the Cuban manifesto is no longer bound by the "predetermined taste" set by commercial cinema. Rather, it seeks to address the critical question, "What are you doing in order to overcome the barrier of the cultured 'elite' audience which up to now has conditioned the form of your work?"[29]

Almost a decade later, Bolivian filmmaker Jorge Sanjines argued along similar lines in "Problems of Form and Content in Revolutionary Cinema (1978)." Sanjines proposes a Revolutionary Cinema representative of the struggles of the peasantry who are the central characters in the cinematic quest for cultural recovery. The manifesto underscores the significance of the "collective protagonist," a concept predicated on the argument that individual histories merit filmic representation "when these have meaning for the collective, when these serve the people's understanding, rather than that of one individual, and when they are integrated into history of the collective as a whole."[30]

Other Latin American declarations aligned with the aforementioned classical manifestos include Fernando Birri's "For a Nationalist, Realist, Critical and Popular Cinema" (Argentina, 1984), Tomas Gutiérrez Alea's "The Viewer's Dialectic" (Cuba, 1988) and Espinosa's reflection of his own 1969 manifesto "Meditations on an Imperfect Cinema . . . Fifteen Years Later" (Cuba, 1984). It is instructive to note that the movement for a militant cinema in Latin America, while inscribed with a similar thematic and aesthetic vision, was not a unified, spontaneous project.[31] However, much of the ideas embodied by these manifestos have factored into the omnibus concept of Third Cinema.[32]

Bound by its particular historical and political context, Third Cinema in the classical manifesto drafted by Solanas and Getino, and in the various declarations emanating from Latin America, is a cinema that is unapologetically partisan, passionately angry, anti-aesthetic, and utopian.

Teshome Gabriel and the Aesthetics of Liberation

While the militant arguments of Solanas and Getino designate Third Cinema as a weapon hostile toward the dominance of Hollywood and Western culture, Ethiopian scholar Teshome Gabriel proposes a careful methodological approach, an earnest effort to develop a critical theory of Third Cinema. Gabriel's 1979 groundbreaking work *Third Cinema in the Third World: The Aesthetics of Liberation* is credited as the first scholarly attempt to establish a Theoretical and Critical inquiry into Third Cinema. His later critical essays "Towards a Critical Theory of Third World Films" and "Third Cinema as Guardian of Popular Memory: Towards a Third Aesthetics" are likewise considered as important critical contributions to the Third Cinema discussion. The subsequent section explores the Theoretical and Critical propositions of Gabriel's work.

Theoretical Context

Kindred with the earlier polemics of Solanas and Getino, Gabriel constructs his theoretical propositions from the basic framework provided by Frantz Fanon's *The Wretched of the Earth*. In this seminal book, the African postcolonial theorist proposes three phases of decolonization as applied to postcolonial literature—the Assimilation, Remembrance, and Combative phases—with each level representing a positive movement toward the recovery of national identity and culture.[33] In two occasions, first, in the book *Third Cinema in the Third World: An Aesthetics of Liberation*[34] and later, in the essay "Towards a Theory of Third World Films,"[35] Gabriel reappropriates Fanon's genealogy to interpret the development of Third World Films:

Phase I: The Unqualified Assimilation. The uncritical acquiescence to the concepts, propositions, and values of the dominant culture, the

Hollywood template of conventional cinema. In this phase, cinema is infused with entertainment value and motored by a vigorous profit motive.

Phase II: The Remembrance Phase. The direction taken by National Third World Cinemas to re-root into their respective indigenous folkloric heritage thus representing a thematic break from First Cinema but still retaining the dependency on conventional film language. Among the cinematic works cited by Gabriel[36] in this stage are Ousmane Sembene's *Mandabi* (Senegal, 1969), a film about a traditional man overwhelmed by modernity and progress, and Glauber Rocha's *Barravento* (Brazil, 1962), an ethnographic study of folklore and mysticism.

Phase III: The Combative Phase. The emergence of decolonization of culture and liberation resonant with Julio Garcia' Espinosa's notion of an "Imperfect Cinema,"[37] Phase III is characterized by an industry that is truly national and popular. Films that have matured into this phase are lucid and honest representations of the lives of the people of Third World, thus, are considered as having actualized the idea of Third Cinema. Production-wise, this entails working within the available resources of the developing world where technical and artistic perfection cannot be the end in view.

Gabriel stops short of drawing a neat, categorical link between Fanon's three stages and the notion of a First, Second, and Third Cinema, although the parallels are undeniable.[38] Also notable here are Gabriel's less dogmatic criteria for a film's inclusion into Third Cinema proper. While Solanas and Getino underscore the weightiness of "collective authorship" as a benchmark for Third Cinema, Gabriel reinterprets the criterion by considering a broader selection of films qualifying for the third stage. Works marked by individual authorship but nonetheless contexted in the values of collectivity make the cut in Gabriel's classification. Such films, aptly representing Auteurist Cinema, would have easily fitted into Solanas and Getino's conception of Second Cinema. Furthermore, Gabriel disqualifies any strict schematicism when he points out the fluid interstices between phases. He identifies films such as Sembene's *Xala* (Senegal, 1974) as occupying the "grey area," the transitional stage between Phases II and III—"The importance of the grey areas cannot be over-emphasized, for not only do they concretely demonstrate *the process of becoming* but they also attest to the multi-faceted nature of Third World cinema and the need for the development of new critical canons."[39]

Text, Reception, and Production

Having clarified his theoretical points of reference, Gabriel moves on to his critical project by introducing yet another triad, that of Text, Reception, and Production. This three-point "analytic construct" provides for a further "integrative matrix within which to draw out from the Third World's cultural history."[40] Below are clarifications of each component as defined by Gabriel:[41]

Component 1: Text. Gabriel defines "text" from a cultural studies approach—the intersection of codes and sub-codes; the chief thematic and formal characteristics of existing films and the rules of that filmic grammar and the transformational procedure whereby new "texts" emerge from old.[42]

Component 2: Reception. The concept of "Reception" is posited on the idea that "the meanings of a text are always shaped by the historical circumstances of reading or viewing at a particular moment."[43] For Gabriel, the core argument of Reception Studies is the active interrogation of images by the audience versus the passive consumption of films. The issue of alienated and non-alienated identity and the ideal/inscribed or actual/empirical spectatorship illustrates this component of critical theory.[44]

Component 3: Production. Representing one of the three branches of the film industry (the two others being Distribution and Exhibition), "Production" refers to the process of creating the film.[45] Gabriel views production as the social determination where the wider context of determinants informs social history, market considerations, economy of production, state governance and regulation. Here, the larger historical perspective, the position and the institution of indigenous cinema in progressive social taste, are contexted.

Gabriel finds in these three components of Critical Theory a clarifying template, a prism from which to describe and problematize the aforementioned three distinct phases of Third World Film Culture where the operations of Text, Reception, and Production come to play in varying hues.

On the level of "Unqualified Assimilation" (Phase I), Text simply reflects the status quo, that is, the filmic grammar predominant in mainstream Western cinema. The uncritical mimicry characteristic of the textual component impacts on the area of Reception where, in a case of "alienated identity," the spectator is unable to see an authentic image of himself/herself in the filmic text. The perpetuation of the status quo branches further into the area of Production where the actual processes involved in filmmaking are controlled by the dictates of industry studio systems.

Applied to the "Remembrance Phase" (phase II), Text may be described as thematically indigenized but still enmeshed in the artifice of conventional formal elements and style. The Reception angle would be characterized by a "diluted traditional identity" where the viewer finds in the text trace elements of folklore and mythologies enough to trigger memory. A decentering of the cinema as an institution marks the area of Production as the effort toward self-determination becomes apparent.

A fuller integration of the three components of critical theory occurs in the "Combative Phase" (Phase III). In the area of Text, the rules of grammar have been broken by the overriding formal and the-matic vision; alternative film language and new codes emerge. Because decolonization and human liberation are brought to light in an authentic cultural landscape, the viewer as subject comes into sharper focus and alienation no longer sets in. Production then reaches a level where a dynamic new institution of filmmaking is able to cater to Third World educational and socioeconomic interests.

Gabriel tests his theoretical propositions further by elaborating on the influences of social factors on the critical components as they are worked out in the cinemas of the Third World in contrast to the First World. "I contend that the confluence obtained from the interlocking of the phases and critical constructs reveal underlying assumptions concerning perceptual patterns and film viewing situations."[46] One illustrative example Gabriel presents is the case of *Der Leone Have Sept Cabezas* ("The Lion Has Seven Heads"/Rocha, Brazil 1973). Western critics received the film as a curio of clichéd images in an astigmatic oversight of the real point unfolding onscreen—the unending antiimperialist struggle from Che Guevara to Amilcar Cabral, and beyond.[47] Gabriel attributes the difficulties in the area of reception to the "unequal exchange" between the Global North and South. This phenomenon certainly includes an unequal "symbolic" exchange, spawned largely by the omnipresence of American popular culture. In his essay " 'No Commodity Is Quite So Strange As This Thing Called Cultural Exchange': The Foreign Politics of American Pop Culture Hegemony," Reinhold Wagnleitner details how the United States has become "the most visible and audible country in world history":

American symbolic power has reached such proportions that it is often overlooked, as if it were a natural part of international environment. Of course, the sway of soft power has reached the highest degree of subtlety and finesse when an ideological, semiologic, and symbolic superiority is installed as quasi-natural, while in reality it rests on economic, commercial, military, and financial power.[48]

The barefaced reality remains: the poorest, most underdeveloped countries emblematize cultures that are almost always the least noticed and represented in the global community. This cultural asymmetry finds expression in the mainstream cinema experience where audiences who have been thoroughly weaned on Hollywood consider dominant filmic conventions as normative givens. In its contestation of mainstream cinematic options, Third Cinema ousts Western viewership from the front row seat of being the "privileged decoder" and "ultimate interpreter of meaning." The standard critical principles set by classical film scholarship then become unsatisfactory when applied to the Third World cinematic experience, which is, Gabriel insists, "moved by the requirements of its social action and contexted and marked by the strategy of that action."[49]

The Link Between Style and Ideology

Does 'style' by itself bear an ideology?
Does the ideology of a work transcend style?
Does change in style manifest an ideological shift?

David Bordwell and Kristin Thompson

Guided by the tenor of these questions, Gabriel launches his critical inquiry into Third Cinema in *Third Cinema in the Third World: The Aesthetics of Liberation*.[50] He draws up a list of recurring themes in Third Cinema—the issues of class, religion, gender, and culture, explaining in brief how each theme inevitably factors into Third World sociocultural expression. In the area of culture, for instance, Gabriel notes how music plays a significant role in the lives of colonized peoples. A film such as *Venceremos* (Caskel, Chile 1970) is a case in point; the Third World film is told entirely in song. Moreover, musical themes and lyrics provide commentary from the point of view of the colonized who become the privileged interlocutors of the film as in the case of Sembene's *Mandabi*. The Ethiopian film theorist is quick to add, however, that his differentiation of Third Cinema along "thematic lines" is employed for the sole purpose of analysis and discussion. In Third Cinema, thematic elements are not neatly compartmentalized but interwoven. Inasmuch as various themes surface in any given cinematic work, Gabriel notes that it is the unifying theme of "oppression" that will always remain a core constant in Third Cinema.

Gabriel proceeds to investigate the link between style and ideology, contending that "A study of style alone will not engender meaning . . . . Style is only meaningful *in the context* of its use—in how it acts on culture and helps illuminate the ideology within it."[51] While style is not reserved for any particular ideology, it provides an important key to unlocking the ideological underpinnings of a film. Here and in subsequent discussions, Gabriel employs an elucidating methodical device—he sets against each other intercomparable examples of Third and First Cinema. Gabriel is careful to note that the straightforward comparative approach he employs is meant "to provide us with an initial understanding of the relationship between film style and ideology."[52] I find it important to make this qualification primarily because of some possible overlapping areas between Third Cinema and Second Cinema stylistic strategies that could work to contradict Gabriel's comparative approach. An apparent example would be Sergei Eisenstein's *Strike* (Russia, 1924), which may not, strictly speaking, fit into the specific Third Cinema ideological orientation but whose stylistic choices are no less ideologically determined along a similar liberative trajectory. Eisenstein's stylistic signature, in fact, has been noted as one of the precursors of Third Cinema.[53] His employment of montage, for instance, is directed toward the move for social change.[54] As how it might appear, *Strike* could be classified as Second Cinema and compared with a Third Cinema example on the basis of Gabriel's approach and a blurring of boundaries is sure to surface at many points. Although I do mention a point of convergence between the editing strategy known as a "nondiegetic insert" in *Strike* vis-à-vis *Perfumed Nightmare* in the next chapter, I do not intend to elaborate on the intricacies of Eisenstein's style as against Third Cinema. The relevant point to make is that for Gabriel, the comparative approach is an illustrative tool to trace the link between Third Cinema stylistic strategies and an ideology of Third World liberation. Nowhere does he present it as a comprehensive and definitive methodology for an analysis of style in Third Cinema in comparison with First and Second Cinema.

One such illustrative comparison includes two divergent portrayals of the same subject—South Africa. The title *Journey to the Sun* (South Africa, 1975) by the South African Tourist Bureau portrays South Africa as an idyllic Shangri-La, replete with paradisial wildlife and friendly locals. In one scene, footage of exuberant native dancers are intercut with exotic dancing birds in a zoo. Gabriel dissects the ideological undercurrent of this sequence, pointing out that apartheid South Africa does keep native South Africans in an "analogous zoo." On the other hand, the film, *Last Grave at Dimbaza* (Mahomo, South Africa, 1975) presents the gritty side of South Africa, the oppressive conditions of black South Africans who have been made prisoners in their own homeland by their colonizers. In this case, the human zoo that is South Africa is lucid and apparent. The use of statistical information adds intensity to the physical reality presented on screen and when South African whites are featured, they are always presented in soft-focus, suggesting that reality as the colonizers see it, is a delusion— a dream world of their own conjecture and fabrication. Gabriel elaborates on the comparative analysis by charting the differences between the two given films on the basis of the formal elements of Film Analysis. A comparison of "Camera Style" is one such element considered by Gabriel.[55] Through the employment of this comparative approach, Gabriel is able to clarify his argument that the optic of Third Cinema sees filmic style as ideologically determined. Style in and of itself is not ideology, rather, "ideology is the 'base' and style the superstructure, autonomous, but linked symbiotically with ideology."[56] He adds a validating detail to his argument by recalling a remark made by Bertolt Brecht—"When art reflects life, it uses special mirrors."

I find it useful here to delineate the concept of style implicit in Gabriel's thought by drawing from aesthetic philosopher Noel Carroll whose approach to stylistic analysis is bent toward a "functional account" of film form (a term he uses synonymously with film style). According to Carroll, "the form of the film comprises the collection of formal choices that enable the realization of its points or purposes."[57] Stylistic or formal options in a film are always "functional contributions" to the film's purposes. Hence, film form is generative; formal elements work together to secure and advance the purposes of the film. Since some conception of the film's purpose is necessary in the functional account, "interpretation" becomes an essential adjunct process in formal analysis. Carroll favors the functional account of film form over the exhaustive "descriptive account" which "classifies any relation among elements of a film as an instance of film form, irrespective of any principle of selection."[58] While the latter promises to be comprehensive, it proves too broad to be useful largely because stylistic analysis has a strong propensity to be selective and explanatory; it does not cover every relation in the total web of elements in a film. Gabriel's argument that the relevance of style in Third Cinema is predicated on the context of its use fits onto the footprint of Carroll's functional account. To reiterate, Gabriel conceives of Third Cinema as "moved by the requirements of its social action and contexted and marked by the strategy of that action." Style then, as explicated clearly in Gabriel's comparative analysis, works meaningfully "in the context of its use." In the notion of Third Cinema, the purpose of film is always to critically map the Third World experience and the ideological ramifications that experience signifies. For Gabriel as for Carroll, film form follows function.

Manipulation of Space and Time in Third Cinema

In his essay "Towards a Critical Theory of Third World Films,"[59] Gabriel expounds on how the aspects of Space and Time are manipulated in Third Cinema in a manner divergent from what is common fare in mainstream, First Cinema. Whereas Hollywood opts to manipulate Time much more than it does Space, Third Cinema does the reverse; it has a predilection for Spatial manipulation. Gabriel notes that Third Cinema emanates from oral folk tradition where Time is allowed to unfold at its own pace and is not hastened. Time in the Western conception is commodified—"time is art, time is money, time is most everything else."[60] A deliberate, contemplative pacing will most likely be viewed by First Cinema in negative terms, in the anticipated ennui and impatience of its audience. There arises then the need to "cheat" natural time through editing strategies.

Gabriel enumerates a number of cinematic practices typical of how Third Cinema negotiates Time and Space in a way that would seem excessive for First Cinema:

The Long Take. It is fairly common in Third Cinema to employ the uninterrupted long take, a shot that continues for a relatively long duration of time before the transition to the succeeding shot;[61] and a seemingly redundant reprisal of scenes and imagery. Gabriel notes that this predisposition approximates the Third World audience's deliberate, unhurried sense and rhythm of life. In like manner, Third Cinema's preference for lingering wide-angle shots emphasizes the viewer's keen sense of community and her link with nature. Such strategies are not uncommon in First and Second Cinema but they are used for a different agenda, that of conveying existential alienation from self and nature as in Jean-Luc Godard's *A bout Souffle* (France, 1960) and Francois Truffaut's *Les Quatre cents coup* (France, 1959).

Cross-cutting. The use of the editing strategy that "alternates shots of two or more lines of action occuring in different places, usually simultaneously,"[62] or what is known as cross-cutting, is frequently used in Third Cinema to explicate the clash of ideologies. The same strategy is not uncommon in First and Second Cinemas mainly to present the positive-negative polarity between antagonists; a device to build suspense and not to explore in any depth the imminent ideological considerations of the collision.

The Close-up Shot. Widely employed in Western Cinema to underscore individual psychology, the close-up shot is sparsely used in Third Cinema. When it finds a role in Third Cinema practice, the close-up shot often serves an informative purpose that has to do with an ideological, rather than a psychological, issue. Gabriel contends that the employment of this camera framing strategy, especially when the scale of the object/character shown is relatively large to highlight individual isolation, would seem unnatural in Third Cinema for the following reasons[63]: (a) it calls attention to itself; (b) it eliminates social considerations; (c) it diminishes spatial integrity.

The Panning Shot. Panning refers to a type of camera movement where the camera body moves either to the left or to the right on a stationary tripod, producing an onscreen horizontal scanning of Space.[69] For the reason that it maintains integrity of Space and Time, the panning shot tempers the necessity for frequent editing. Gabriel observes that the narrative value of the panning shot in Third Cinema lies in its redefinition of the Time concept. Rather than presenting Time as rigidly linear and chonological, Time here is seen as coexisting with Space.

The Concept of Silence. Moments of silence figure noticeably in Third Cinema. Unlike the Hollywood bombardment of dramatic musical scores and sound effects that deliberately pull at the heartstrings, the "sounds of silence" in Third Cinema offers the viewer more opportunities for reflection and, in the context of the long take, evinces a "suspension of judgment."

The Concept of "Hero". The portrayal of a self-transcending "hero" character is a consistent feature of film narrative. A recent Best Picture winner of the American Academy Awards, *Gladiator* (Scott, United States 2000), belongs to a long line of films that champion an outstanding individual whose exploits impact on the course of history. The hero concept is no stranger to Third Cinema but it is used for very different reasons. Hero characters in Third Cinema are not made to rest on their laurels, in fact, it is likely that they will be killed off unceremoniously. Gabriel explains that in contrast to dominant cinema, "wish-fulfillment through identification" is not the agenda of Third Cinema, "collective engagement" is. Thus, "the individual 'hero' in the Third World context does not make history, he/she only serves historical necessities."[65]

I reemphasize that Gabriel does not claim to have mapped dogmatic demarcations between the aesthetic standards of Third Cinema versus Western Cinema. What he endeavors to illustrate are the respective aesthetic *tendencies* linked with the filmmaking practices of the types of Cinema in question. It is clear that while Cinema has European and American origins, Third Cinema is reappropriating the tried and tested conventions of the medium so that they serve the discursive purpose of laying bare the plight of the Third World. As such, the aesthetic decisions that have resulted from this ideologically determined consideration validate the argument that Third Cinema film makers openly engage with the medium but, manifestly, on their own terms. According to Gabriel, these terms are largely defined by the resonances of oral folk tradition clearly discernible in Third Cinema.

Third Cinema and Popular Memory

According to Gabriel, Third Cinema may be of varying types, depending on the prevailing social order of its context. He notes that the strident "cinema as a gun" akin to the seminal Latin American conception, continues to exist where a more revolutionary agenda calls for it, that is, Palestinian Cinema. In other regions, postcolonial filmmakers and progressives from the West have moved to the cultural front where there is greater emphasis on clarifying the role of Third Cinema as custodian of popular expression, for example, Ousmane Sembene of Senegal. In any case, there is a central strategy that unites Third Cinema—the rediscovery and quickening of "popular Memory."

In Third World countries still recovering from the aftermath of colonization, the unearthing of folkloric oral traditions[66] conveniently silenced by the official versions of history is a self-reflexive key to identity and emancipation. True to the Western schema of "rationality," the official versions of history awarded privileged status to the written text and in the process, marginalized "oral historiography," the very dynamics of indigenous folklore. Thus, Gabriel argues that popular memory has a crucial "rescue mission":

> Because the promise of freedom and the recovery of autonomy of identity lingers in memory, folklore offers an emancipatory "horizon"—a

> liberated and alternative future. In a world where "logic" and "reason" are increasingly being used for "irrational" purposes and aims, folklore attempts to conserve what official histories insist on erasing. In this sense, folkloric traditions of popular memory have a rescue mission. They wage a battle against false consciousness and against the official versions of history that legitimate and glorify it.[67]

Inasmuch as popular memory plays a crucial role in the postcolonial quest for emancipation, Gabriel clarifies that it does not amount to an escapist regression to the past, but a " 'look back to the future,' necessarily dissident and partisan, wedded to constant change."[68] From this standpoint, it is clear that popular memory is the very oil that rekindles the movement toward an alternative future; it is not a romanticized attachment to the past.

I find it informative to recall that a long continuum of Hollywood films bear the unmistakable imprint of such official versions of history. In Francis Ford Coppola's *Apocalypse Now* (United States, 1979), an epic film on the U.S.-Vietnam war, the story decidedly showcases American stakes and issues. Although it appears to present a stinging self-indictment of that infamous U.S. military fiasco, Coppola's film takes its time fetishizing the seductive Western fantasies of invasion without so much as a hint of the interests of the South Vietnamese who are stereotyped as chattering, imbecilic natives devoid of soul and story.[69]

In contrast, Ousmane Sembene's *Xala* makes visible the repressed underside of postcolonial Senegal and the quagmire of its prevailing social, cultural, and political realities. Set at a period shortly after independence, the film uses the symbol of the *xala*, a spell or curse ingrained in the popular memory of folkloric belief, as an indictment of the main character's identification with the "Frenchness"—the ostentatious life of power and privilege—of the neocolonial ruling elite. Here, popular memory renders inert the self-serving devices of the official conjurers of history by targeting their inauthentic hollowness.

Gabriel likens Third Cinema's role as guardian and storyteller of popular memory to a similar function played by Third World literature. Among others, he notes Gabriel Garcia Marquez of Colombia and Carlos Fuentes of Mexico as writers who have relied heavily on the disavowed collective memory. Lifting from Fuentes, Gabriel emphasizes that Third Cinema seeks "liberation through images" as Third World Literature seeks "Liberation through language."

EXPANDING THE VIEW OF THIRD CINEMA

Notwithstanding the undeniable contribution of Teshome Gabriel to the conception of a critical framework for Third Cinema, it was a film theory under threat of calcification given the utter lack of theoretical re-examination and further development in the years that followed. Of late, this gaping lacuna has been propitiously addressed by Mike Wayne in his book *Political Film: The Dialectics of Third Cinema*. Wayne commences his critical inquiry with the consequential argument—"Third Cinema is passionate, angry, often satirical, always complex. Yet at the level of theory, Third Cinema is a concept in need of development in the face of its underdevelopment; a concept in need of clarification in the face of confusion and misunderstanding; a concept in need of defense in the face of contesting and indeed hostile theories and politics."[70]

Wayne enumerates the points for consideration:[71]

• The need to clarify in a more nuanced fashion, the concepts of First and Second Cinema in order to loosen the restriction that Third Cinema necessarily births from the Third World. With this assertion, Wayne emphasizes that Third Cinema may emanate from the First World as much as First and Second Cinema may be a product of the Third World.

• The exploration of points of conversation and interchange between Third, Second, and First Cinema as "all three cinemas take up their own distinctive positionings in relation to a shared referent: i.e. the historical, social world around them."[72] Drawing from Fernando Birri, Wayne notes that Third Cinema does not represent an outright negation of Second and First Cinema but rather, a "dialectical transformation" of them.

• The role of Third Cinema as interlocutor of Second, and First Cinema provides a much-needed "counter-hegemonic" socialist critique to the medium of film, which currently tends to be fortressed in the "ivory-towered paradigms" of postmodernism, postcolonial studies, and Lacanian psychoanalysis.[73] Wayne asserts that the meaning and outlook of ideas are closely linked with the social forces that undergird them.

• Because it draws deeply from the well of "revolutionary conjunctures" and is closely allied to subversive collective memory, the development of Third Cinema Theory may also be counter-hegemonic to the pervading order of neoliberalism.

Wayne pursues his first argument further when he emphasizes that the stunted upgrowth of Third Cinema theory may be traced to the mandatory linear adherence to the demarcated concept of Third Cinema filmmaking as proposed by Solanas and Getino. The second stage of Third Cinema theory spearheaded by the work of Gabriel did propose a more inclusive view of Third Cinema where films of "individual authorship" may be considered provided that they are contexted in the values of collectivity. Additionally, Gabriel underscored the possibility that some films lay in the "interstices" between the three phases of development of Third Cinema thus negating a rigid compartmentalization. However, Gabriel almost always confined his arguments de facto to Third World filmmaking and did not foray into the convergences between Third Cinema and First-Second Cinemas.

It is noteworthy that in 1994, Ella Shohat and Robert Stam envisioned Third World Cinema vis-à-vis Third Cinema in "overlapping circles" that may have mapped the direction for a more inclusive Third Cinema.[74] For instructive purposes and in anticipation of Wayne's project to be subsequently discussed, I include the full text of their classificatory terms:

- a core circle of "Third Worldist" films produced by and for Third World peoples (no matter where those people happen to be) and adhering to the principles of "Third Cinema;"
- a wider circle of the cinematic productions of the Third World peoples (retroactively defined as such), whether or not the films adhere to the principles of Third Cinema and irrespective of the period of their making;
- another circle consisting of films made by First or Second World people in support of Third World peoples and adhering to the principles of Third Cinema; and
- a final circle, somewhat anomalous in status, at once "inside" and "outside," recent diasporic hybrid films, for example those of Mona Hatoum or Hanif Kureishi, which both build on and interrogate the conventions of "Third Cinema."

It can be seen in Shohat and Stam's classification, specifically in the third circle described, that there is an area of convergence between Third Cinema and First/Second World filmmaking. It is precisely from the same premise as this circle that Wayne launches into the crux of his apologia for Third Cinema.

The early Third Cinema theorists saw promise in Second Cinema's sensitivity to sociopolitical issues, notably in the documentary genre.

They envisioned the eventual blossoming of auteur cinema into a cinema truly engaged with mass political struggle.[75] However, Wayne notes that a mutually enriching exploration of the dialectical relationship between Third Cinema on one hand and First and Second Cinemas on the other, has remained largely unexplored and underdeveloped to the detriment of Third Cinema Theory.

Following a brief sketch of what he terms as key "precursors" to Third Cinema, namely, the relevant principles laid out by European cultural thinkers such as Eisenstein, Vertov, Lukacs, Brecht, and Benjamin,[76] Wayne sets out to elaborate on the dialectics of Third Cinema in relation to First and Second Cinema.

Dialectics of First and Third Cinema

Amistad (United States, 1997) is a film set at a time when black Africans were subject to utter commodification by the slave trade of the mid-nineteenth Century. It is also a film produced by a major Hollywood studio and directed by noted commercial filmmaker Steven Spielberg. In an elucidating analysis, Wayne draws the areas of convergence and divergence of Third and First Cinema in the film. Wayne points out that *Amistad*, akin to Third Cinema, pulls no punches in portraying the brutal atrocities inflicted on the captured Africans by the slave traders. Indeed, one poignant scene paints the horror of human rights violations—African captives are thrown overboard as excess luggage when the ship's supplies threaten to run out. Drawing from Marx, however, Wayne notes that while *Amistad's* treatment of the issue of human rights is laudable, it never moves beyond the limited sphere of the liberal idea of human rights. As Marx argues, "None of the so-called rights of man, therefore, go beyond egoistic man . . . that is an individual withdrawn into himself, into the confines of his private interests and private caprice, and separated from community."[77] The structural causes of exploitative wage-slavery then remain unexamined in the film. "Amistad presents history as the outcome of the decisions and actions taken by individuals divorced from any larger context."[78] Wayne contrasts the Spielberg film with Tomas Gutierrez Alea's *The Last Supper* (Cuba, 1976), where the exploited characters become aware of their position of inequality and begin interrogating the status quo perpetuated by the existing social order.

The comparative method Wayne employs is no new contribution to the development of Third Cinema Theory as it carries clear resonances of Teshome Gabriel's earlier work. However, Wayne brings the Third Cinema discussion to more familiar territory as he purposefully makes case studies out of such familiar films as Costa Gravas's *Missing* (United States, 1981) and Regis Wargnier's *Indochine* (France, 1991), comparing and contrasting them with little known examples from Third cinema. Thus, Wayne is able to illustrate the dialectical linkages between Third and First Cinema in an illuminating way before reaching the anticipated conclusion—"there are serious and profound limitations to First Cinema's representations, fully embedded as it is within the social relations of capital."[79]

Favorably, Wayne's project is not just an attempt to further dissect the Third-First Cinema divide but to seek new ways of exploring the dialectical engagement between them. The lack of due attention to this vital link proved obstructive to the development of Third Cinema Theory.

> Third Cinema began to engage with First Cinema (Humberto Solas's 1969 film *Lucia* was groundbreaking in this regard) but the theory did not develop much beyond its initial rejection of First Cinema. This bifurcation between theory and practice has been very costly for a number of reasons. It has meant that Third Cinema films that engage with First Cinema are often not *recognized* as Third Cinema films, which in turn encourages the view that Third Cinema belongs to the past. An engagement with First Cinema is today even more crucial. The cultural and economic hegemony of First Cinema combined with the wider political contraction of revolutionary struggles, demand such an engagement.[80]

In emphasizing the importance of a more perceptive Third-First Cinema engagement, Wayne addresses the shadow cast by the BFI(British Film Institute)-sponsored 1996 Conference on African Cinema where British filmmaker John Akomfrah pronounced Third Cinema as a dead concept.[81] Wayne is convinced of the argument that there are select films from dominant filmmaking that have developed a "latent critical potential in a Third Cinema direction." Though certainly not too common, such exceptional films question unequal power relations across class, race, or gender lines, through an undeniably oppositional utopian perspective. Thus, the closed waters of the Third Cinema discussion begins to open into the wider ocean of mainstream, commercial cinema as Wayne proposes that a film of First World origins may qualify as Third Cinema.

One such Hollywood product that Wayne nominates for inclusion to Third Cinema is the musical *Evita* (United States, 1996). Directed by noted commercial filmmaker Alan Parker and topbilling pop icon Madonna, nothing in the film suggests affinity to Third Cinema proper at first glance. But Wayne gives *Evita*, in a matter of speaking, a "third look" where he sees the film as a flawed but, nonetheless, valid example of Third Cinema. "Evita is a significant musical and a rare example of Third Cinema coming out of Hollywood."[82]

There are two reasons for this proposition:

• First, the screenplay of *Evita* was based on the original 1970s stage musical by Andrew Lloyd Webber and Tim Rice. Wayne argues that this historical context is decisive; *Evita* portrays the political turmoil in Argentina in the late 1930s to the 1940s which represents, in Wayne's intellection, a "coded meditation" on British labor unrest in the 1970s. He adds that the theme of Eva Duarte's rise from the working class woman to Argentinian First Lady broadly mirrors the 1974 election victory of the British Labour Party. Wayne attributes this parallel to the film's "porosity," a term borrowed from Walter Benjamin, which indicates the capacity of film to interfuse with its historical context. Moreover, Wayne notes that the adaptation of the stage musical into film strengthened its social message as filmic conventions bring the material to deeper focus. The crowd scenes, for instance, achieve a more strident foregrounding through thoughtful cinematography, thus, emphasizing the aspect of collective struggle.

• Second, the choral quality of the musical genre works to emphasize the tension between the extremely disparate social classes of Argentina, here, adjunctly dramatized by the strategic use of filmic conventions such as editing and mise-en-scène. The critique of class disparity is further spotlighted by the presence of the character of "Che," an internal narrator who provides vitriolic commentary to Evita's ascension to power and renown.[83] In a manner similar to Third Cinema mode of address, Che is made to speak to us, the audience, so that any uncritical sentimentality over Evita is kept in check.

Thus, Wayne is convinced that a thoughtful consideration of the context and text of the film *Evita* discloses a socially pertinent discourse consistent with the notion of Third Cinema.

At this point, it would be instructive to reiterate Wayne's project which he himself makes abundantly clear:

> The great advantage of Third Cinema is that while it is politically oppositional to dominant cinema(and Second Cinema), it does not seek, at the level of form and cinematic language, to reinvent cinema from scratch (it is too interested in history for that); instead, its relation to First and Second Cinema is dialectical: i.e. it seeks to transform rather

than simply reject these cinemas; it seeks to bring out their stifled potentialities, those aspects of the social world they repress or only obliquely acknowledge; Third Cinema seeks to detach what is positive, life-affirming and critical from Cinemas One and Two and gives them a more expanded, socially connected articulation.[84]

Wayne's efforts to propose a more inclusive Third Cinema Theory is certainly a step towards the continued relevance of the concept; a creative moment that sets the stage for the further development of an alternative textual base for Third Cinema.

CHAPTER 2

Exploring National Dimensions of Third Cinema

This chapter examines the aesthetics of liberation evinced in three films from world cinema. My intention is to spotlight the ways in which Third Cinema finds resonance in varying national contexts. The film titles I chose as case studies represent Third World cultures from three continents—Latin America, Africa, and Asia.

Tomas Gutiérrez Alea's *The Last Supper*, the most historically based of the three titles, revivifies the subject of slavery and religion in eighteenth-century Cuba; Ousmane Sembene's *Xala* scathingly interrogates Senegal's neocolonial elite; and Kidlat Tahimik's *Perfumed Nightmare* problematizes the "American Dream" that haunts Philippine culture. These are obviously films of different hues but they are as similar as they are different. It is informative to underscore some of their commonalities. All three films carry the shared sentence of a colonial history and, as such, birth from a "postcolonial" culture. Both Cuba and the Philippines were Spanish colonies that were ceded to the United States in the 1898 Treaty of Paris (a historical anomaly revisited in *Perfumed Nightmare*), whereas Senegal was under French rule. In view of the ambiguities of the term "postcolonial," I cannot overemphasize that here, it is understood within the frame of a Euro-American colonizing/civilizing enterprise in the modern period, which brought 85 percent of the rest of the world in subjugation by the time of the First World War. I further delimit the use of "postcolonial" to refer to the Third World experience and the sociopolitical, economic, and racial implications that the term evokes. I make this qualification knowing that there is a tendency to collapse spatiotemporal and national/racial distinctions in the current applications of the term "postcolonial."[1] This is worth mentioning because the postcolonial experience factors prominently into the narrative threads of these films, which brings me to the second point of similitude—all three films use satire as a means to expose and denounce their post-colonial demons. In this case, the sardonic humor is not meant to illicit laughter from the audience in the tradition of Hollywood comedies, it is an act of subversion shared between members of the indigenous culture. The onus for social change drives the humor. Finally, although all three filmmakers have moved to exorcise their culture's eurocentric postcolonial demons, they are all indebted to some form of European film training; Gutiérrez Alea in Italy, Sembene in Russia, and Tahimik in Germany. None of them, as such, represent a dogmatic filmmaking practice totally divorced from the contribution of western influences. The filmmakers themselves personify the necessary contradictions of a postcolonial culture.

While cultural synthesis characterizes our globalizing world, there is value in revisiting the national as it is the "primary context" that provides soul and story to many filmmakers.[2] This is particularly true for filmmakers identified with the emancipative Third Cinema vision, as the proceeding explorations attest.

Let me note that in this chapter, I direct the spotlight a little longer on *Perfumed Nightmare*. The positive emphasis is for good reason. I am convinced that *Perfumed Nightmare*'s maximization of filmic grammar—its multilayered symbolic matrix and complex improvisations—may serve as a paradigmatic example of the integration of style and ideology that is a salient attribute of Third Cinema. Furthermore, I believe that it is incumbent upon me, as a Filipino native informant, to redress the near exclusion of the Philippines in the Third Cinema debate. A number of Filipino films that move in the trajectory of Third Cinema have gone unnoticed thus far.[3] *The Last Supper* and *Xala* occupy significant places in the Third Cinema canon; *Perfumed Nightmare* ominously deserves its rightful niche.

Cuba: Tomas Gutiérrez Alea's *The Last Supper*

The circumstantial background that informed the sensibility of Tomas Gutiérrez Alea as a filmmaker was the Cuban Revolution, the propitious event that ended the U.S.-backed dictatorship of Fulgencio Batista and catapulted the communist regime of Fidel Castro. Gutiérrez Alea was a founding member of the *Instituto Cubano de Arte e Industria Cinematográficos* (ICAIC), an organization established by *Nuestro Tiempo* in 1959—three months after the revolution—for the intention of pooling together talent and resources to form a national cinema. *Nuestro Tiempo* was a cultural society that played a key role in the rise of communism.[4] Gutiérrez Alea and his colleagues moved to repudiate the influences of Hollywood in their search for a more socially relevant form of artistic expression. They were drawn toward experimental and anti-commercial tendencies even as they acknowledged their indebtedness to the European avant-garde. They were also fueled by an idealistic vision and were not afraid to dream. The passion and commitment of ICAIC's early members ushered in the development of a vital Cuban national cinema.

Following a Marxist trajectory, Gutiérrez Alea developed a distinct filmmaking style, rooted in his early training in Italian neorealism and the influence of the works of the father of cinematic surrealism Luis Buñuel, but with its own stylistic identity and revolutionary theoretical bed. Unlike his peers, Gutiérrez Alea remained loyal to the ideals of the Revolution but refused to be an obedient servant to them. His filmmaking was not hamstrung by his political affiliations. He successfully drew a balance between his commitment to the Revolution and his critique of its flaws, the ferment of which is sophisticated film making that resists being stigmatized as sheer political propaganda.

Gutiérrez Alea's film philosophy can be derived from the theoretical propositions of his 1988 manifesto *Dialéctica del Espectador* ("The Viewer's Dialectic"), which he wrote twenty years after the Cuban Revolution. Gutiérrez Alea expresses the need to subvert the conventions of documentary filmmaking as Cuban film artists mature politically and aesthetically:

> Cuban Cinema confronts that new and different way of thinking about what social processes are going to hold for us because our film draws its strength from Cuban reality, and endeavours, among other things, to express it. Thus we find it no longer sufficient just to take the camera out to the street and capture fragments of that reality . . . The film-maker is immersed in a complex milieu, the profound meaning of which does not lie on the surface.[5]

For Gutiérrez Alea, Cuban filmmaking is no longer about mouth-agape acceptance of the "spectacular transformations" of the Revolution; it has become a task of interpreting the many layers that make up the complexities of social reality, indeed, a task of critical hermeneutics. As such, cinema lends itself to being an instrument of sociopolitical awareness—"Film not only entertains and informs, it also shapes taste, intellectual judgment, and states of consciousness."[6]

Gutiérrez Alea's work tackles a variety of subjects but the Revolution and its continuing impact on the lives of Cubans is a recurrent theme. His internationally recognized films include *La Muerte de un burócrata* ("Death of a Bureaucrat," 1968), *Memorias del subde-sarollo* ("Memories of Underdevelopment," 1968), *La Ultima Cena* ("The Last Supper," 1976), *Fresa y Chocolate* ("Strawberry and Chocolate," 1994), and his last film *Guantanamera* (1995).

Memories of Underdevelopment, his most significant opus in terms of narrative inventiveness, demonstrates Gutiérrez Alea's Third Cinema perspective, which casts a gimlet-eye on social reality as such. This is personified in the central character of Sergio who is fox-holed in his social class and his neo-European perspective so that he remains apolitical in the midst of the sweeping revolutionary changes in Cuba. Gutiérrez Alea presents his point by negation—Sergio is impotent precisely because he is detached from the collective. Curiously, critics, both "establishment" and "leftist," missed the film's ironic signification.[7] The film had also been noted for its complex narrational strategies that fuses documentary conventions, cinema vérité, extradiegetic inserts, and dynamic editing.

Gutiérrez Alea's other masterpiece is *The Last Supper*. A period piece on slavery in eighteenth-century Cuba, the film is one of only two titles in Gutiérrez Alea's filmography that are historically farthest from the context of the Revolution and are thematically invested on the subject of religion, the other being *Una pelea cubana contra los demonios*.("A Cuban Struggle Against Demons," 1971). Gutiérrez Alea based his story on a historical anecdote about a 1790 slave owner who performs Jesus' foot-washing act on twelve of his African slaves in a pietistic effort at ritualized humility during Maundy Thursday.[8] Kindred with other historical "slavery" films of the decade, *The Last Supper* sees the issue of slavery in the dual categories of master-slave and colonizer-colonized or what is known as the "Calibán" theme. The motif draws from the 1971 essay of Cuban poet Roberto Fernández Retamar entitled *Caliban*, a term etymologically indebted to the name of a merman in Shakespeare's *The Tempest*. The Calibán theme came to symbolize slavery and the colonial project in Latin America.[9]

In *The Last Supper*, Gutiérrez Alea departs from the dissonant stylistic experimentalism of *Memories of Underdevelopment* and employs an uncharacteristic visual style seen nowhere else in his corpus of films. Uniquely, the generation of meaning and sociopolitical comment occurs within the controlled, visually static, arm's length irony of the sustained supper scene. In this tour de force, the film's Third Cinema optic becomes apparent as it fearlessly confronts the role of religion in preserving the subjugated status of slaves and perpetuating the master-slave social hierarchy.

The Last Supper opens with downtrodden African slaves toiling in a Havana sugar mill. The mill is owned by a wealthy count and run by Don Manuel, a brutal overseer. Today, a runaway slave had just been captured. As punishment, Don Manuel cuts off his ear and feeds it to the dogs, after which he has him lashed a hundred times. The count's visit to his mill falls on this ominous day and he is a witness to the scene. Holy Week approaches and to placate his scruples, the count decides to host a meal modeled after Christ's last supper with twelve randomly chosen slaves as his honored guests. But prior to that, he wishes to conduct a foot-washing ceremony. Much to the overseer's chagrin, one of the chosen ones is Sebastian, the runaway slave he had tortured.

The slaves undergo a Bible crash course about the promise of paradise from a priest who plays a pacifist role in the social equation. The priest then takes them to the river and makes sure they are bathed in preparation for the ceremony. In the chapel, the visibly repulsed master washes the disciples feet and flinchingly kisses them.

The slaves take their place at the count's table. As the meal progresses, the count shamelessly brandishes blasphemous Biblical rhetoric with the obvious intention of justifying the master-slave equation as the slaves gorge on the food. But the slaves are more clever than he thought and as they voice their recriminations, he lectures them with nonsensical logic. They in turn tell stories and ask him for favors.

The count, now drunk, falls into a slumber and the slaves share their mutinous thoughts among themselves. When the meal is over and the master awakens, he declares Good Friday a non-working day for the slaves. The next day, the overseer barks back-to-work orders at the slaves, and the count, realizing that this would all redound to more profit for his mill, reneges on his promise. A mutiny ensues. The slaves burn the mill and slay the overseer and his wife. The count is enraged and orders for a manhunt of the twelve slaves. In the aftermath of the maelstrom, eleven bloody heads of African slaves are sticking on wooden stakes; the twelfth is empty. The film closes with a defiant Sebastian running freely uphill.

In *The Last Supper*, Gutiérrez Alea's stylistic option leans more toward vérité camerawork, unobtrusive editing, and, for the sustained segment of the supper, a controlled, chamber-like composition and atmosphere. As I noted earlier, this is a departure from the intentionally discordant fusion of stylistic techniques that had been his signature in *Memories of Underdevelopment*. The Third Cinema resonance of *The Last Supper*'s stylistic strategies lie mainly on the level of mise-en-scène. Visual composition, costuming, symbolic elements, and the characters' actions work together to generate meaning as the film essays the oppressive master-slave dynamic. Some notable camera angling and editing strategies are used in the latter part of the film and I reserve comment on them for later.

A great part of *The Last Supper* takes place at the dinner table and this is where strategic mise-en-scène becomes markedly significant. The section is embedded in a matrix of pious Catholic imagery and allusions. It opens with the dinner setting where the count and his slaves are properly seated and ready to partake of the meal. The symmetrically composed table arrangement is an overt reenactment of the last supper of Jesus Christ with his apostles. The assignment of roles is clear. The count, playing host at the center of the table, is Jesus Christ, while the twelve slaves obviously correspond to the twelve apostles. The scene immediately brings to mind the last supper sequence of the Hollywood Jesus-movie *The Greatest Story Ever Told* (George Stevens, 1965), which was mimetically based on Leonardo da Vinci's fresco. In this painterly scene, Gutiérrez Alea gives a striking irony, a visual representation of what the master-slave relationship is not. There is nothing in the character of the count that is remotely Christ-like. In fact, he is an egocentric Pharisee blinded by the trappings of power and privilege. Neither are the twelve gathered around the count beloved disciples pastured in paths of salvation; they are slaves, stripped of dignity, imprisoned in a life of toil and servitude, and made to live like animals. This is definitely a tragi-comic jab at the role of religion in the master-slave asymmetry, a direction that carries on throughout the long supper scene.

An earlier scene symbolically presents the distorted mode of relationality at work in the master-slave equation when it shows the count talking to his caged pet bird:

COUNT: Now that I've fed you, you must sing for your master!

The scene is a key iconic representation of the rationale of the feast. The slaves are made to feel indebted to the master's "benevolence" and are therefore bound to obedience. The analogy is not subtle—the slaves are caged animals completely subject to the caprices of the master. As the count continues his lecture on the many blessings of being a slave, one elderly bond slave who is about to complete payment for his freedom asks the master to set him free. When he obliges, the slave could not leave; he has so internalized his caged existence that every trace memory of freedom has been obliterated. He has known no other life but slavery and has nowhere to go. The count milks the moment for everything its worth and continues his litany on the benefits of slavery. The referent of the iconic symbol of the caged bird is thus confirmed in the feast—"Now that I've fed you, you must sing for your master!"

Additionally, the very costuming demarcates the master-slave equation vividly. The count is pompously dressed in upper class finery, complete with powdered wig. Contrastingly, the slaves are dressed in filthy rags and look weary and weather-beaten. For sure, this is no gathering of equals.

The center of gravity of the film's Third Cinema vision is worked out in the leitmotiv of resistance and emancipation enfleshed in the character of Sebastian, the tortured runaway slave. At the preceding foot-washing ceremony, he kicks the basin of water as the count attempts to wash his foot. In the supper scene, his conspicuous appearance at the table—with an eye beaten-shut and a glazed-over, defiantly knowing expression—already works as an indictment of the feast and a visual foreboding of eventual turn of events. In contrast to the rest of the slaves who seem oblivious to the manipulative overtures of the count, Sebastian looks intelligently perceptive and self-aware. His missing ear is yet another borrowed biblical image of the high priest's slave whose ear was cut-off by a protective Simon Peter, whom Jesus rebuffs for using the sword and resorting to violence.[10] Jesus miraculously restores the ear in the gospel story but in Gutiérrez Alea's version, miracles are hard to come by. An open, bleeding wound lies on the spot where his ear was. But Sebastian's defiance makes it clear that this is a symbol of the masters' shame, not his. At one point, Sebastian, still in a stupor after his ordeal, collapses face down on the table. The count immediately has him sit at his right side and offers him a drink. He then proceeds to interrogate him. It is interesting to note that the count cribs from the gospel of Mark and appropriates Jesus' question to his disciples—"Who do you say that I am?"[11]

> COUNT: Look, Sebastian, who am I? Come on, identify me. Who am I, Sebastian? Well, recognize me . . . I ask you in the name of Christ: Who am I?

In the Markan pericope, Peter declares "You are the Messiah."[12] In *The Last Supper*, Sebastian gives no answer and spits on the face of the count. Unlike his fellow slaves who are vaguely aware of the fraudulence and malice of the meal, Sebastian, despite one eye beaten-shut, is clear-eyed. He is very much aware that they are being fed with lies.

All these signs of protest and resistance segues to Sebastian's strongest and most lucid indictment of slavery. The count retells the story of the fall of the first man and woman as found in the Biblical account of Genesis[13] with the intent of justifying toil and labor as God's established order. When the count dozes off at the table after one drink too many, Sebastian speaks for the first time in the film. He invokes the Afro-Cuban folk religion known as Santeria and appropriates the story of how the supreme being Olofi created both good and evil. Mise-en-scène plays a key role when Sebastian grabs the head of the roast pig on the table and lifts it to his face. In this strikingly bizarre image, he appears like a man who has a pig's head as he relates how the body of Truth walks around with the head of the Lie. The allusion exposes the master's duplicity, names him a liar, and denounces him for his inhumanity—quite literally, for being a pig. Here, Sebastian subversively draws from folk religion and not the institutional Catholic religion, which had itself become enslaved to his master's self-serving schemes. It is notable that the pig's head was in the foreground of the earlier shot when Sebastian spat at the master.

Gutiérrez Alea satiricizes religion, exposing it as an instrument utilized by society's powerholders to sacralize the status quo. Institutional religion functions to cloak the oppressive master-slave structure with the veil of piety and perpetuates a culture of passivity among the enslaved. The priest, who personifies institutional religion, attempts to moralize the situation and pays lip service but he is emasculated by the powers that be and fails to bring about social change. Teshome Gabriel rightly points out that *The Last Supper* configures Christianity as "the dominant ideology from which the oppressed classes must break away, and both examine the profound impact of that ideology and the difficulty involved in making that break."[14]

The Last Supper has an open-ended denouement suggesting an alternative future for Sebastian. In the final scene, we learn that Sebastian is the missing twelfth slave who escapes execution. He is shown running through the dense forest. Dynamic editing plays a role here. The take showing Sebastian running through the forest is intercut with shots of an eagle in flight, a rushing river, rocks on a landslide, and freely running wild horses. Unfettered, he is moving toward his birthright as an agent of his own destiny. We also get a low-angle view of Sebastian as he takes a leap, emphasizing even more the length of his stride. Additionally, the drumbeats and chants of the rousing musical score convey a kinetic movement. The final shot shows Sebastian running uphill to an undisclosed destination. The syntagmatic elements coupled with the open-endedness of this segment allude to a utopic direction. *The Last Supper* does not paint an image of what the utopic reality might look like but its rumblings are present in indexical fashion, the way smoke signifies a fire.

More to the point, Sebastian is enroute to "destination freedom."

SENEGAL: OUSMANE SEMBENE'S *Xala*

Xala was an acclaimed novel by Ousmane Sembene before it became an acclaimed film made by Ousmane Sembene. I find it fitting to start this section with this statement because prior to his career as a filmmaker, Sembene was an accomplished writer. Among other titles, he wrote the novel *Les bouts de bois de Dieu* ("God's Bits of Wood," 1960), which, along with *Xala*, is recognized as one of the most important works of African postcolonial literature.[15]

A fisherman's son, the young Sembene was raised under reduced circumstances. He was unsuccessful in searching for employment in the Senegalese capital of Dakar and this drove him to migrate to Marseilles, France, in 1947. While working as a stevedore on the docks of Marseilles, he found himself getting involved in trade union struggles, became an activist, and joined the communist party. His immersion in issues of social justice became oil for the fueling of his writings and, ultimately, his literary works paved the way for his sojourn into filmmaking. His novel *O Pays, mon beau peuple!* ("Oh country, my beautiful people!," 1957) reaped international acclaim and became a window of opportunity for him to study filmmaking at the Gorki Studios in Moscow.[16]

Upon his return to Dakar in 1960, he realized that in order to make a contribution to social change, it was expedient that he reach the widest possible audience. His novels were written in French and published in Paris, thus, catering exclusively to the cultural elite of Senegal. But it was the Senegalese masses Sembene desired to reach and film was the medium that would lend him wings. Sembene made his first feature film, *La Noire de . . .*, ("Black Girl," 1966), a 60-minute film based on one of his short stories. It became a landmark film for a couple of reasons. First, it was the very first feature film ever released by a filmmaker from "Africa South of the Sahara."[17] Second, it drew international attention to African films and to Sembene himself when it won the coveted Jean Vigo prize, an award given annually in France in recognition of exemplary films with an independent spirit. While *La Noire de . . .* is a French language film, the continuum of films that followed it are mainly in Sembene's first language *wolof.* Among them are notable titles such as *Mandabi*

("Money Order," 1968), *Xala* ("The Spell," 1974), *Ceddo* ("The Outsiders," 1977), *Camp de Thiaroye* ("The Camp at Thiaroye," 1987), *Guelwaar* (1992), and his latest, *Mooladé* (2004), the film he made at age 87. The uniqueness of Sembene's filmmaking practice is his creative control and "omnipresence" over his materials; majority of his films are based on his own novels.

Sembene's filmic work has a sonorous correlation with the Third Cinema schema in that it is geared toward the promotion of social justice and liberation; and the rediscovery of human dignity. His filmmaking practice seeks to integrate indigenous cultural elements drawn from the rich clay of African oral narratives and resists mimesis of the narrative style associated with Hollywood filmmaking. Sembene's films thus become vessels of cultural confirmation and custodians of popular memory. His decision to make films in the native *wolof* tongue forms part of the cultural consciousness that his work exemplifies. Moreover, Sembene appropriates the tools of Marxist analysis as he seeks to tease out the structural evils that beset his culture and to expose the abuses of those who occupy the apex of the sociopolitical pyramid. In this regard, Sembene's alliance with the Third Cinema optic is hard to miss. Sembene, as such, is predisposed to taking up such relevant themes as colonialism, religious hypocrisy, the failings of the ruling class, and gender oppression.

Xala is arguably the quintessential Sembene film and has been lauded for successfully integrating complex plot development, rich characterization, and an engaging narrative that does not sacrifice the film's purposeful social analysis. The film follows the life of El Hadji, an affluent businessman who has advanced into a new black elite by participating in a native revolt against the French colonial authorities and, along with his colleagues, assumed control of Senegal's chamber of commerce. Corruption sets in, however, notwithstanding the board's rhetoric of compassionate socialism and an enigmatic western businessman hands out suitcases of money to the board members. Intoxicated by power and the monetary windfall, the board members are in a jovial mood and El Hadji deems it appropriate to invite them to his wedding reception later in the day. It is his third marriage and his new wife Ngone is much younger than he. Enroute to his reception, El Hadji pays a visit to his reticent first wife Adja and inadvertently bumps into his outspoken, free-spirited daughter Rama who strongly disapproves of his third marriage. "All polygamous men are liars," she asserts. El Hadji slaps his daughter and angrily reminds her of the cultural value of polygamy. Adja agrees to accompany El Hadji, along with his second wife, Oumi, to the wedding reception, where the two women quickly feel like fish-out-of water in the third wife's house, and are anxious to find a convenient exit.

The bride's mother tries to persuade El Hadji to follow a folk virility ritual in anticipation of the wedding night but El Hadji firmly rejects the idea and dismisses it as nonsense. The morning after, the meddling mother-in law discovers that the marriage was unconsummated. It turns out that El Hadji is impotent and he is convinced that he is under the power of a *xala*, a curse of sexual impotence. He agonizes over his affliction and becomes obsessed with finding a cure. He seeks out numerous *marabouts* or folk healers referred to him by trusted friends but none could undo the *xala*.

One day, when El Hadji notices a band of beggars loitering outside his office, he calls the president and asks for his help in deporting the "human rubbish" from the area. Armed men round up the beggars soon after.

As El Hadji obsesses over his sexual impotency, his financial affairs take a nosedive. His business colleagues add salt to his wounds when they vote him out of their group. And because of the numerous debts he had incurred, the government sequesters his business and all his belongings. Moreover, his second and third wives decide to leave him. The forlorn and disempowered Hadji is left with no other option but to seek refuge in the house of Adja. The next morning, the band of beggars El Hadji had deported make their way into Adja's house and pillage it. One of the beggars claims responsibility for El Hadji's *xala*, the motivation being revenge. He identifies himself as a relative whom El Hadji had cheated out of his inheritance years ago. He challenges El Hadji to "reclaim his manhood" and asserts that the only way to break the *xala* is for the band of beggars to spit at his naked body. The police arrive on the scene but Rama tells them that the beggars are invited guests and El Hadji confirms it. As soon as the police leave, El Hadji strips, and the beggars surround him and spit at him.

Reminiscent of the Luis Buñuel classic *Le Charme discret de la bourgeoisie* ("The Discreet Charm of the Bourgeoisie"/ France, 1972), *Xala* critiques the ostentation and narcissism of the postcolonial *noveau riche* and exposes their irrelevance to the present social realities in Senegal. Satire is the language Sembene uses to problematize the interconnected issues of social injustice—neocolonialism, classism, and patriarchy[18]—and this is mainly played out in the film's mise-en-scène.

The hegemony between colonial ideals and the native culture is a pivotal thematic concern in *Xala*. Ingenius costuming symbolizes the hegemonic contention and this is a clear stylistic option employed by

Sembene in the film. In the film's first segment, the members of the chamber of commerce are in traditional African outfits as they assume power, signifying the ascendancy of the native culture over the colonial French. This is further portrayed visually when the Senegalese board members remove busts of Marianne, the national symbol of France, and put them by the doorstep for the outgoing French members to collect. However, as soon as the new members take their places in the boardroom, they are no longer dressed in African outfits but in French business suits. Analogously, a traditionally garbed pickpocket who steals from a beggar uses the stolen money to buy a handsome European suit. At a later turn, he takes El Hadji's place in the Chamber of Commerce. The pendulous movement between the colonial culture and the indigenous culture is clearly depicted here. But in addition to that, the costuming is a critique of the way in which the new elite merely fitted themselves conveniently into the shoes of the colonizers. The Chamber of Commerce, as implied by the mise-en-scène, is a virtual den of thieves.

The costuming of the women characters also contribute significantly to the weave of meaning in *Xala*. The secretary of El Hadji's warehouse wears the traditional African dress outdoors but takes it off to reveal a European style dress underneath. El Hadji's second wife Oumi undergoes a costume change but in reverse. In stark contrast to the consistently traditional first wife Adja, we see Oumi in a form-hugging European dress for the most part of the film but when she decides to leave El Hadji at a later turn, she is wearing a modest, traditional dress. During the wedding reception sequence, one of the bride's kin also wears the traditional dress but upon closer scrutiny, we see that portraits of European royalty conspicuously adorn the dress. Through costuming, Sembene illustrates the sociopolitcal schizophrenia of a Senegal still haunted by its colonial ghosts.

The western style bridal gown is another costume leitmotif that plays a key role in the film's signification. We see it first worn by El Hadji's third wife in the wedding reception scene. The wedding gown is clearly a colonial remnant and the tiered wedding cake topped with a plastic European bride-and-groom figurine, only work to support this. Later in the film, when El Hadji's third wife decides to leave him, the mother-in-law has the complete wedding outfit and other wedding gifts returned. We see the wedding gown and veil eerily draped over a faceless mannequin, revealed as African only by the black afro wig it wears. The white wedding outfit signifies the old French cultural dominance and the faceless mannequin points to the loss of national identity among members of the indigenous culture who have filled-in the positions of privilege as hypocritical "pseudo-Europeans." This is a strong symbolic indictment of the neocolonial elite who continue to adhere to French ideals at the expense of national identity. The wedding outfit on the mannequin reappears at the latter part of the film, prominently standing in a corner of Adja's living room just as the beggars make their way in. Before the spitting ritual begins, one of the beggars approaches the mannequin, grabs its floral headpiece, and mockingly wears it to the bemusement of his companions. He then puts it on the head of the naked El Hadji before they proceed to spit at him. The linkage is clear: the impotent El Hadji is the defaced mannequin clothed in colonial values. Thus, El Hadji loses his authentic identity and "loses face" before his own people. It is his inauthenticity that renders him impotent and that is the deeper meaning of the *xala*.

The symbolic power of mise-en-scène reaches a crescendo during the dramatic ending of the spitting ritual. The beggar whom El Hadji had cheated out of an inheritance and who cast the *xala* provides a lead-in to the scene's deeper meaning.

> BEGGAR: If you want to be a man, undress. Nude in front of every-
> one. We will spit on you.

While this obviously refers to the breaking of El Hadji's *xala*, the connotational meaning cannot be missed. Taken within the film's consistent denunciation of neocolonialism and its purveyors, the spitting ritual connotes a sort of exorcism rite meant to purge El Hadji of neocolonial values. It is also his rite of reintegration into a Senegalese culture that is truly free from the colonial demons. It is notable that the beggars who spit at El Hadji are the same ones he had removed from the premises of his office earlier for being "human rubbish." They may well represent those who have been disenfranchised and "robbed" by the neocolonial powers that be. A clue to this interpretation is the accusation of the beggar responsible for the *xala* that El Hadji stole his inheritance. As such, El Hadji symbolically gives back the "stolen inheritance" of his country.

Because of the dissonance created by the spitting ritual, which may be a bit of a shock for western viewers, *Xala* might be seen as a bleak film devoid of hope. But the film's editing strategy at this precise point proposes that a conversion in El Hadji floats in the realm of possibilities, albeit diegetically unconfirmed. Here, Sembene concludes *Xala* with a 24-second freeze frame just as the spitting ritual progresses, thus, leaving the plot open-ended. Meaning is no longer confined to the mise-en-scène as the open-endedness invites the viewer's participation in the interpretive process.[19]

I also find a touchstone for the possibility of an alternative post-colonial reality in the very metaphor of the *xala*. It is a spell of impotence that is temporary.

Change is possible.

PHILIPPINES: KIDLAT TAHIMIK'S *PERFUMED NIGHTMARE*

Kidlat Tahimik is identified with a group of socially engaged Filipino filmmakers who worked within the repressive political climate of the 1970s. The Philippines was under the regime of Ferdinand E. Marcos, a U.S.-backed dictator who had imposed martial law in 1972 as a reaction to the growing political dissatisfaction over his despotic government. Massive demonstrations denouncing the "politically bankrupt liberal democratic system"[20] reverberated in the streets of Manila, the country's capital, and activists were jailed without due process; many, tortured by the military. Under martial law, the mass media were under the control of the state and the film industry was fettered by strict censorship laws.

Nonetheless, a creative storm issued from the repression and produced some of the country's most notable works of social cinema. Cognizant of the French *Nouvelle Vague*[21] and the art cinemas of India and Japan, filmmakers were unafraid of bridging aesthetics with politics. A number of films made during the turbulent period were veiled barbs against the U.S.-sponsored Marcos dictatorship, among them, Lino Brocka's *Maynila: Sa mga Kuko ng Liwanag* ("Manila: In the Claws of Neon," 1975), a serious examination of the structural evils that thrive in the capital; Eddie Romero's *Ganito Kami Noon, Paano Kayo Ngayon?* ("This is the Way it was, How is it Today," 1976), a peasant's journey toward national identity; and Lupita Concio's *Minsa'y Isang Gamu-Gamo* ("Once there was a Moth," 1976), an indictment of the presence of U.S. military bases in the country. Kidlat Tahimik's *Mababangong Bangungot* ("Perfumed Nightmare," 1976) arises from the same sociopolitical humus but stands apart in that it does not come out of the mainstream film industry and it never had a commercial run in the Philippines. Additionally, *Perfumed Nightmare* was shot in three countries—France, Germany, and the Philippines—during Tahimik's European sojourn.

Tahimik's filmmaking experience began during his encounter with a community of artists in Germany where he serendipitously got acquainted with the Bolex camera and the 16 mm independent camera through a film student. Prior to that, he had acquired an MBA from the University of Pennsylvania's prestigious Wharton School of Finance. Then known by his birth name Eric de Guia, Tahimik literally tore his diploma in 1972 to mark his complete turnabout from the world of business and his entry into the world of film. Ironically, his Wharton training in ESP/LSD (Economies of Scale Profits/Law of Supply and Demand) would fuel his "revolt against artificially inflated filmmaking."[22] Armed with his silent Bolex, he lensed *Mababangong Bangungot* ("Perfumed Nightmare") from expired film stock donated by Kodak. The film introduced an original stylistic signature that made the European film community take notice. *Perfumed Nightmare* won the *Prix de la Critique Internationale* and both the Catholic and Ecumenical Jury prizes at the 1977 Berlin Film Festival.[23]

Tahimik refuses to be party to the excesses engendered by the studio system as demanded by the high-stakes entertainment industry. He insists on direct involvement at every stage of the filmmaking process:

> My main film credit is as "director" of my film, which in Hollywood parlance is just one cog in the supermachine. As a filmmaker, I fit in more with the French cinema term *le realisateur*, the one who "realizes" the film, taking total responsibility for the movie from conceptualization to its final technical realization.[24]

One of the ponderable features of Tahimik's filmmaking style is his notion of a "scriptless" film. In a reversal of the tried-and-tested studio process, the innovative filmmaker derives the filmic narrative organically from the collected footage during the post-production stage of editing thus rendering superfluous the function of the scriptwriter:

> I am also an *auteur* (author) as the contents of my film plots do not rely on borrowed novels or on scripts crafted by scenario writers. My texts grow on the editing table, organically with the images.[25]

Hence, there is no blueprint of how Tahimik's film might take shape prior to the editing process and no timetable to indicate when exactly the final cut might be completed.[26] This is further compounded by the sporadic sourcing of funds associated with Third World independent filmmaking that provides no guarantee of project completion. Tahimik's open-ended style of filmmaking is then unencumbered by the profit-motivated dictates of the studio system and progresses at its own "cosmic" pace. His brand of filmmaking draws mainly from native creativity, intuition, and a filmmaking philosophy appropriate for his sociocultural milieu.[27]

Tahimik metaphorically describes the process as a vehicle that moves with a cup of gas at a time in stark contrast to the mainstream industry's commercial assembly-line. Chilean writer Ariel Dorfman describes Tahimik's filmmaking as "not only Third World in subject, but also Third World in process."[28] But of greater interest is the apparent link between Tahimik's Hollywood counterstyle project and the prognosis of the original 1969 Third Cinema manifesto *Hacia Un Tercer Cine* ("Towards a Third Cinema") by Fernando Solanas and Octavio which views mainstream Western cinema as "one more consumer good":

> It was surplus value cinema . . . destined to satisfy only the ideological and economic interests of the owners of the film industry, the lords of the world film market, the great majority of whom were from the United States.[29]

Tahimik's notion of filmmaking also dovetails with Julio Garcia Espinosa's *Por un Cine Imperfecto* ("For an Imperfect Cinema," 1969) which espouses a resistance to the technical "perfection" requisite of Hollywood movies—"Imperfect cinema is no longer interested in quality or technique. It can be created equally well with a Mitchell or with an 8mm camera, in a studio or in a guerilla camp in the middle of the jungle."[30]

At the core of Kidlat Tahimik's filmmaking is a philosophy rooted in his reappropriation of the interlinked values endemic to Philippine culture—*Bathala Na* and *indio-genius.* In Tahimik's view, the precolonial *Bathala Na* (literally "God's will be done") alludes to hopeful risk-taking, the harnessing of the best of one's abilities while trusting the cosmic forces to cooperate. *Bathala Na* is Tahimik's re-rooting of the more common colonial expression *Bahala Na* ("let come what may"), a fatalistic resignation to the status quo, which is left entirely in the hands of the Divine, and accompanied by a defeatist shirking of responsibility. *Indio-genius* is a wordplay of the English term "indigenous" and the colonial *indio,*[31] a racist pejorative used by the Spaniards to designate their Filipino subjects. *Indio-genius* refers to the innate talent and giftedness of the Filipino who insists on creativity and life though the baggage of centuries of colonization and subjugation warrant otherwise. Tahimik thus reassigns meaning to the racist moniker and uses it as a positive wordplay:

> *Bathala Na* is an ancient pre-Filipino gift. To me, it means we put our
> best energies, our inputs(intelligence, sweat, muscle power), our best

heart, into any endeavor (*todo bigay*). The rest we resign to the Cosmic Will. *Bathala Na*, the ancient Pinoy (Filipino) mindset, allowed the *indio-genius* in everyone to blossom.[32]

These two critical principles undergird Tahimik's work. Whether it be *Perfumed Nightmare* (1976), *Turumba* (1983), or *Why is Yellow the Middle of the Rainbow?* (1993), Tahimik's films are synechdochic representations of the struggle to exorcise the spectre of a complicated colonial past that continues to haunt Philippine culture. The result of Tahimik's unorthodox filmmaking is an original cinematic style epitomized by *Perfumed Nightmare*—"To be sure, he is neither Eisenstein, Godard, nor Kurosawa—Tahimik is inventing his own filmic signature."[33]

Perfumed Nightmare opens with the image of a jeepney, that curious Philippine taxi originally recycled from the wreckage of an American military jeep, moving back and forth across a crude concrete bridge. The protagonist Kidlat,[34] a thinly fictionalized version of the filmmaker himself, narrates how the bridge serves as the crucial link between his quaint Philippine barrio and the rest of the world, "our bridge of life." Kidlat is president of the Werner von Braun Club of Balian, a parodic organization honoring the discoverer of the first space rocket to the moon; its members being a motley crew of giddy village children. Kidlat's idolization of Von Braun is just a drop in the sea of Western utopic cultural images—symbolized in the film by the radio program "Voice of America," the Statue of Liberty, bubble gum machines, and the Miss Universe beauty pageant, among others—of progress and affluence that make up the utopian "American Dream."

Kaya, Kidlat's friend who is the village guru of sorts, enthuses him to draw strength from the subversive memory of his late father, a local war hero who fought in the revolution against the Spaniards and who was later killed by the soldiers of yet another colonizing power, the United States. He describes how Kidlat's father literally blows away 15 American soldiers before he was finally killed. He then draws a pithy reminder—"the sleeping typhoon must learn to blow again."

Kidlat takes on a job with an American businessman who owns a chewing gum business. The foreigner takes him to Paris and along with him, a Philippine jeepney. The French capital would be for Kidlat a springboard to his dream destination, the United States, site of Cape Canaveral. The provincial lad is stunned by the high-tech Charles de Gaulle airport and the countless bridges he sees while being driven through the city. In Paris, Kidlat drives the conspicuous jeepney as he happily goes about his task of refilling gum machines at various points in the city. One day, he meets an elderly pushcart vendor whose small-scale business is threatened by the impending opening of a massive

Supermarket complex. A paroxysm of indignation drives Kidlat to pelt the building with stones. Later, in a short trip to Germany, Kidlat discovers that artisans in that country are also in danger of being displaced by progress and technology. To top it all, bad news from back home reaches Kidlat—his forested village had been flattened to make way for the construction of a highway for tourists and as a result, his mother's hut had been unceremoniously uprooted. Kidlat undergoes a crisis of belief. Anger and protest over the inhumanity of First World style development liberates Kidlat from the spell of the phantom of progress. In a startling series of sequences, Kidlat literally blows away symbolic images of western sociocultural domination during a mock farewell party organized by his boss. He is then seen converting a huge metal chimney from the Supermarket construction into a space ship, propelling it into the sky with the power of his breath. Kidlat's actions evoke the magical exploits of his father during the Philippine-American war—the sleeping typhoon awakens and blows again. Kidlat disappears from the film after this scene, as *Perfumed Nightmare* closes with a silent, open-ended scene of Kidlat's mother slowly closing the window of her hut in the Philippines as a young girl passes by.

In *Perfumed Nightmare* the central rubric of "postcolonial struggle," here taken to mean the ongoing quest for national identity on all fronts—social, cultural, political, economic—is rendered in sharp relief by the "American dream," the ghost of American colonial superiority relentlessly haunting the Filipino psyche. A colonial mentality is enfleshed in the character of the protagonist, Kidlat, who is portrayed as a Filipino bewitched by American popular culture. There is Kidlat's constant absorption of American news through the short wave broadcast of "The Voice of America," his idolization of Miss Universe contestants particularly those from the erstwhile colonizing powers Spain and the United States,[35] and his fascination for First World technology and progress seen in his obsession with space travel and the American moon landing. Nonetheless, when the American businessman asks Kidlat why he loves America so much, the Filipino's naive answer has a bittersweet ring of truth to it:

KIDLAT: In America I can be an astronaut. Here [in the Philippines]
    I am only a jeepney driver.

Closely linked with the theme of "postcolonial struggle" is the concept of "popular memory." *Perfumed Nightmare* questions the colonially fabricated "official versions" of history by offering an alternative historiography akin to oral history. The existence of a revisionist popular canon unearths authentic and self-affirming elements conveniently repressed by disaggregated official history. An illuminating example is the retelling of the historical circumstances that led to the death of Kidlat's father, a guerilla who saw action at the tail end of the Spanish occupation and at the outset of the American takeover of the Philippines. Two "unofficial" versions of the story, that of Kidlat's mother and that of his guru-friend Kaya, serve to nullify the official version which simply states that the guerilla was killed for "trespassing on U.S. property."[36] Both unofficial versions are subversive accounts that weave folkloric elements into the story. Of greater significance is Kaya's version which recasts Kidlat's father as a mythic hero who literally blows away the attacking American sentries by the sheer power of his breath before finally being felled by the bullets of his assailants. This story is of key importance not only because it renders void the indictment of a Filipino national as a trespasser in his own land, but more so because it is a metaphorical rendering of the outrage of the Filipino people against the high-stakes power play between the United States and Spain wherein the Filipinos became the unwitting pawns on the colonial chessboard. Interpreted through the lens of revisionist history, Kaya's story opens a gateway to what had been repressed and forgotten—the collective betrayal of the Filipino nation, here represented by revolutionary leader General Emilio Aguinaldo, by their former and future colonizers (led by American Admiral George Dewey) in a colonial conspiracy sanctioned by the 1898 Treaty of Paris:

> Aguinaldo's men, who had surrounded Manila, were awaiting Dewey's mutually understood signal to enter the city. That signal never came; Dewey had other plans. What happened at Manila Bay was not a battle—it was a transaction. Dewey secured the surrender of Manila from the Spaniards under the terms of a secret treaty between the United States and Spain. It provided for payment of $20 million by the United States; each country agreed to assume the war damage claims of its nationals; and Spain was granted trade rights with the Philippines for ten years on a par with the United States. The attack on Manila was merely a mock assault by which Spain was allowed to offer token resistance to save its honor.[37]

Kaya's story invokes the subversive collective memory to put in check the systematic amnesia of colonial mentality. This is eloquently summarized in Kaya's verdict:

> KAYA: Yes, Kidlat . . . they bought your soul and mind . . . the facts are suppressed to hide our true strength.

As Teshome Gabriel argues, popular memory "considers the past as a political issue. It orders the past not only as a reference point but also as a theme of struggle."[38]

Another significant thematic element is the alienating western-style progress and technological advancement, which finds representation in the trope of the "phantom of progress." Kidlat's home village, site of all the idyllic haunts of his childhood memories, is all but flattened for a highway construction in the name of tourism. Kidlat would learn later that his own elderly mother's bamboo-and-straw hut is not spared by the incursion of progress. On another level, the same damaging impact of progress is seen when Kidlat encounters Lola, the Parisian vendor who is driven out by the ingression of an imposing Supermarket into the urban landscape of Paris. Notwithstanding the fact that *Perfumed Nightmare* assumes the Third World vantage point, it does not confound the issue of First World technological progress with questions of race. The scamper for industrial and technological advancement poses a constant threat to the weakest links of society regardless of racial lines.

Like *The Last Supper* and *Xala*, a good part of *Perfumed Nightmare*'s matrix of meaning is communicated through mise-en-scène. Prior to his departure for Paris, Kidlat prays to the statue of the Virgin Mary, here seen as a handsome Iberian woman, and asks for forgiveness for reneging on his yearly devotion of self-flagellation because of his fear that his wounds would not heal in time for his flight. We hear the statue hilariously "talking back" to Kidlat, connoting the perceived direct involvement of the divine in the day-to-day lives of Filipinos. We also see several bloodied flagellants, masochistically whipping themselves before the statue, among them, Kidlat, shown in flashback flagellating at a very young age. If anything, these images problematize the marriage of colonial Catholicism and folk religiosity in postcolonial Philippines and how it remains a deeply rooted hindrance to the attainment of a liberative consciousness and self-determination.[39]

The central leitmotiv of the bridge symbolizes the movement from the oppressive status quo toward a better, alternative future; a utopic link between the "is" and the "ought." The crude bridge of Kidlat's hometown, for instance, was used by the colonizers for their own purposes. Kidlat, however, would quickly assert:

> KIDLAT: I am Kidlat Tahimik, I choose my vehicle and I can cross this bridge.

The reflexive naming has utopic connotations as "Kidlat Tahimik" means "Silent Lightning," a gathering tempest. On a different level, the symbol of the bridge also works to reinforce the thematic representation of the chasm between First and Third Worlds. Balian's crude bridge is contrasted to the abundance of bridges, doubtlessly engineering wonders, in Paris. As Kidlat would remark to his mother:

> KIDLAT: Bridges, bridges, everywhere bridges! Do you know that Paris has twenty-six bridges? Why can't we have progress like this?

Notable too is the film's use of symbols for an "archaeological" function, that of visually encoding "indio-genius." The wooden horse-figure is a case in point. Carved by Kidlat's mother from the butt of the rifle of Kidlat's father after American sentries indiscriminately kill him, the horse becomes a symbolic link between Kidlat's quest for freedom and his father's before him:

> KIDLAT'S MOTHER: Take this horse on your travels, one day; you might need him to help you find the path to freedom.

She then proceeds to mount the horse-figure on the hood of Kidlat's jeepney, the same one he would use to ply the streets of Paris in his journey toward self-discovery at a later narrative turn. This same horse-figure would reappear in the utopic final scene of the film, this time, perched on the hood of the toy jeepney driven by Kidlat's little sister Alma. In *Perfumed Nightmare*, the horse-figure symbolizes a utopian vision rooted in the past, ongoing in the present, and extending to the future.

Similarly, the jeepney is another symbol of creativity amid the post-colonial ruins. By sheer indio-genius, Filipinos took the U.S. World War II military jeep and re-created it into an indispensable mode of mass transportation. Indeed, in Kidlat's own description, jeepneys are "vehicles of war, which we made into vehicles of life." Conspicuously, the film shows the tag "Liberator" emblazoned on Kidlat's jeepney, an indexical clue to the vehicle's role in the protagonist's liberation later in the film.[40]

I see the horse-figure and the jeepney in *Perfumed Nightmare* as symbols of popular collective memory in a sense correlative to Laura U. Marks's idea of the "recollection-object."[41] Her thesis largely undergirded by Deleuzian propositions, Marks defines the recollection-object as "an irreducibly material object that encodes collective memory."[42] Since Marks argues within the context of postcolonial "Intercultural Cinema" more than that of Third Cinema, she explores the ways in which these recollection-objects function to encode cultural displacement brought about by diasporic translocation. Recollection-objects, in Marks imaginative description, possess "radioactive" power, that is, "they may arouse other memories, causing inert presences on the most recent layers of history themselves to set off chains of associations that had been forgotten."[43] Marks clarifies that unlike metaphors which posit mental association, recollection-objects work on the level of physical contact, their very materiality functioning as a reactivator of revolutionary memories of a given indigenous culture repressed by a transnational milieu. I find Marks's idea of the "radioactivity" of recollection-objects heuristically relevant to the analysis of symbols in *Perfumed Nightmare*. The horse-figure and the jeepney are fossils of original objects, the rifle and the U.S. military jeep. In and of themselves, these original objects symbolize colonial aggression, thus, holding no liberative power per se for the postcolonial culture. However, the re-creation and re-functioning brought about by indio-genius produces renewed objects, indices of the undisclosed history of native resistance to colonialism. Radioactivity is acquired through a process of postcolonial reappropriation and new subversive memories are assigned to the objects. By their very raw material bases, they are always in contact with the original objects but indio-genius had found a way to use the very same objects to subvert what they originally signifiy. Thus, *Perfumed Nightmare* takes the concept of recollection-objects to another level. In their new incarnations, these recollection-objects have become, at one and the same time, dialectical representations, evincing both affirmation and negation. In my estimation, this is a noteworthy Third Cinema adjunct to the concept of recollection-objects. This is also an original Kidlat Tahimik conception.

Strategic cinematography is also frequently employed by Tahimik. Wide-angle shots in the film establish that Kidlat is an individual who cannot be divorced from his communitarian milieu. This is punctuated in the Balian scenes where almost always, Kidlat is seen in constant association with the people of the village. The wide-angle shots in *Perfumed Nightmare* also serve to reinforce the idea that a special bond exists between the Balian community and nature. One sequence, for example, presents a wide-angle view of a green field naturally embellished by hundreds of flittering white butterflies. The butterfly sequence acquires added resonance when it is rendered in conjunction with another cinematographic strategy, the long-take. What is peculiar about this single wide-angle shot is that it is also an uninterrupted long-take lasting some 40 seconds. This may appear slow and illogical, not to mention boring, from the vantage point of western filmmaking.[44] Gabriel proposes that the long-take is an approximation of the unhurried pace of life characteristic of Third World rural communities which is seen concretely in the reflective, deliberate pace of oral folk traditions.

Additionally, the uninterrupted long-take in *Perfumed Nightmare* functions to dramatize the gradual awakening of the Kidlat character from the stupor of his colonial mentality into liberation—"The sleeping typhoon must learn to blow again." We see a strategic application of the uninterrupted long-take in the reappearance of the horse-figure as the film nears its conclusion. In a scene with an unusually extended shot length of 76 seconds, the wooden horse-figure, symbol of resistance and freedom, is shown in the foreground, slowly traversing the conversely static, dystopic backdrop of construction rubble in Kidlat's Paris. This depicts the forward movement of Kidlat's liberative journey amid the stasis created by the phantom of progress. This comes to sharper focus when the scene is annotated by Kidlat's declaration of independence:

> KIDLAT: I, Kidlat Tahimik, out of my own free will, hereby resign as president of the Werner von Braun club and relinquish all rights and duties as president and founder of the club. Furthermore, I totally resign my membership from the club. This resignation is absolute, irrevocable, and is effective now.

Camera angling also factors into Tahimik's ideological use of stylistic options. In *Perfumed Nightmare*, one of the functions of camera-angling is to problematize the issue of colonial mentality. A dramatic example would be the surreal scene featuring the mock farewell party given to Kidlat by his employer as a ceremonial send-off prior to their flight to the United States. In this scene, the masked western guests with their cardboard cutout smiles are shot at a low camera angle as they greet Kidlat at the reception line. This makes the guests appear intimidatingly large and towering. In contrast, when the camera cuts to Kidlat, he is seen from a high camera angle, dwarfing him to

Lilliputian proportions. Kidlat, now keenly aware of his subalternity, would then comment—

> KIDLAT: Why is everybody staring at me . . . I feel I am getting smaller.

When Kidlat blows away the western guests, camera angling is restored to normal straight-on level; the guests and Kidlat now appears on equal footing. The signifying force of the spatial variables achieved by the shifts in camera angling is further dramatized by the timing of their application in the film's plot movement.

While straightforward editing characterizes *The Last Supper* and *Xala*, a dynamic and violative editing strategy is one of the hallmarks of *Perfumed Nightmare*. Akin to Sergei Eisenstein and Jean-Luc Godard, Tahimik employs the "nondiegetic insert," an editing device that breaks the rules of continuity required by classical film narrative.[45] In the nondiegetic insert, the filmmaker cuts abruptly from a given scene to a shot that does not belong to the spatial and temporal world of the narrative, thus, creating metaphorical or symbolic meaning. In his film *Strike* (Russia, 1924), for instance, Eisenstein intercuts the scene of the workers' massacre with a shot of a bull being slaughtered.[46] The nondiegetic inserts function as disorienting devices that provide irony and satirical commentary to the issues in question and prompt the audience to mull over the implicit meanings presented. In *Perfumed Nightmare*, we can see this strategy in the mock farewell party scene where shots of the arrival of the masked western guests at the reception line are juxtaposed with actual news footage of real western leaders arriving in limousines, presumably to attend some important summit. Taken in the context of the events that would later ensue, the message is consistent with *Perfumed Nightmare*'s agenda, that of exposing the structural inequality between the affluent countries of the west vis-à-vis the widescale underdevelopment in the Third World.

The generation of meaning in *Perfumed Nightmare* also lies in its aural strategy. Doubtlessly, the most noticeable aspect of sound in the film is the peculiar out-of-synch or asynchronous dialogue. There are two dialogue tracks—one in English, the other in the native Filipino language—overdubbed simultaneously onto the images. The English dialogue is prioritized over the Filipino, the latter heard as a subversive echo at the beginning of certain lines and then fading out. It is not unusual for Third Cinema to shift between two languages in order to dramatize the hegemony between western colonial culture and the indigenous culture as in the case of Sembene's *Xala*, which has its characters speaking either in the colonial French language or in the native Wolof depending on their sociopolitical affiliations. *Xala*, however, does not use both languages simultaneously. The simultaneous bilingual dialogue is a realistic representation of a cultural given: English is the official language of education, government, and international relations in the Philippines but it fails to supplant the indigenous Filipino language. I interpret this as a pragmatic statement that there are colonial influences in the Philippines that can no longer be undone and must therefore be put to optimal use. As far as *Perfumed Nightmare* is concerned, a return to the paradisial precolonial state is untenable. From the optic of the Filipino value of indio-genius, Tahimik's prioritization of the English dialogue may be understood in functional terms—as an opportunity to attract international reception, thus, making a positive contribution to filmic representations of Third World cultures in global cinema.[47]

Finally, I note the strong undercurrent of utopian sensibility that permeates *Perfumed Nightmare*'s last few sequences. Here, a syntagm formed by composition, lighting, props, and camera angling, first conveys the unfolding of a false utopia. We see an impressionist rendering of the face of Kidlat's American boss on a stained glass window. The backlit window gives the image an ethereal, divinized radiance. Kidlat's face is lit in a more subdued manner and is seen on the foreground. (See figure 2.1.) In a sinister appropriation of one of the last few words of Jesus Christ in the New Testament crucifixion account, the American reassures Kidlat:

> AMERICAN BOSS: Tomorrow, Kidlat, tomorrow . . . you shall be with me in Paradise.

The equation has eerie resonances—if the American businessman is cast in the role of the messiah, then it follows that Kidlat is the condemned thief in need of salvation. This is akin to the pivotal meal sequence of *The Last Supper* where the count cribs on the Bible to justify the master-slave equation. What is presented in the case of *Perfumed Nightmare* is the false utopian promise of Kidlat's American dream. Kidlat would spot the proverbial "tail of the serpent" as he begins to articulate his simmering doubt:

> KIDLAT: Is this the Paradise I prayed for? Is this the Paradise I dreamed of?

The emergence of a genuine utopian vision begins in the sequence when Kidlat boards one of the giant chimneys in Paris and causes it to

Figure 2.1   False utopia in *Perfumed Nightmre: "Tomorrow Kidlat . . . you shall be with me in paradise."*

fly to the heavens by the power of his breath. Recalling the myth surrounding his father's superpowers that enabled him to literally blow away accosting American sentries, Kidlat had himself become an embodiment of Kaya's prophetic-liberating proverb:

> KAYA: When the typhoon blows off its cocoon, the butterfly embraces the sun . . . Where is your true strength, Kidlat? Where is your real strength? The sleeping typhoon must learn to blow again.

Perfumed Nightmare metaphorizes the typhoon as a utopian signifier for social change in a way reminiscent of Vsevold Pudovkin's similar but more literal use of the "storm" as a metaphor for anticolonial revolution in the climactic denouement of *Storm Over Asia* (Russia, 1928).

The closing sequence of *Perfumed Nightmare* features a return to the village of Balian where Alma, Kidlat's little sister, is seen riding her toy jeepney with the familiar horse-figure mounted on its hood. Meantime, Kidlat's mother, peering from the window of her bamboo hut, draws down the window shades.

The last scenes of Tahimik's film stand out for their spatiotemporal ambiguity. As *Perfumed Nightmare* shifts from realism to magic realism and then back, the depiction of space and time breaks the rules of coherence and completeness. Moreover, there is no verbal language from which to frame a preferred meaning or a logical wrap-up. As such, the film's final scenes defy conventional narrative closure; they are, like the conclusions of *The Last Supper* and *Xala*, provocatively open-ended. *Perfumed Nightmare*, however, presents a stronger, more lucid allusion to a utopic vision than the two previous films. The signification of a present rooted in the past and projecting toward the future can be seen in the mise-en-scène, particularly in the iconic characters and their actions. Kidlat's mother stands for the past and its subversive memories of colonial resistance. As she closes the window of her hut, what is conveyed is the impetus to move forward and address the present. Kidlat who contends with the issues pervading the current world order personifies the present. Through his postcolonial contradictions, he undergoes a crisis of belief that reaches a climax when his eyes are fully open to the destructive, alienating impact of western-style progress. This moves Kidlat to protest and break free from his American-dream-turned-nightmare. The scene that shows Kidlat disappearing into the heavens in a magical chimney-spacecraft is expressive of the fact that the Third World postcolonial struggle, with all its social, cultural, and economic ramifications, will have to look toward future possibilities. The future is metaphorized by the child Alma driving her toy jeepney with the subversive symbol of the wooden horse-figure mounted on its hood. Earlier on, the film already drops a hint as to Alma's utopic significance. When Kidlat first gives Alma the toy jeepney, he would advise her:

> KIDLAT: Alma, you are the master of your vehicle. Only you can tell it where to go.

The quest for the alternative future has begun but its completion is an imagined event to be sought after. It will be the next generation that will steer the Philippines into an alternative, liberated future. It is necessary to clarify what I take utopia to mean here. I use the term utopia in a sense akin to Tom Moylan's intellection of "critical utopia," a literary concept characteristic of the oppositional culture of the late 1960s and the 1970s:

> Critical utopias can be read as metaphorical displacements arising out of current contradictions within the political unconscious. The utopian societies imaged in critical utopias ultimately refer to something other than a predictable alternative paradigm, for at their core they identify

self-critical utopian discourse itself as a process that can tear apart the dominant ideological web. Here, then, critical utopian discourse becomes a seditious expression of social change and popular sovereignty carried on in a permanently open process of envisioning what is not yet.[48]

Unlike the metanarratives of progress that characterize positivist utopian visions,[49] critical utopias are grounded in the dissatisfaction over the status quo perpetuated by the current world order. In the case of *Perfumed Nightmare*, the massive global economic divide yields cognitive potential and the power to re-imagine the possibility of a new emancipative order.

CHAPTER 3

Films from a Virtual Geography of Third Cinema

An integrative review of the concept of Third Cinema provides useful heuristic touchstones for this chapter. Third Cinema theory in its present form is not so much a demolition order against the input of the American and European film industries as it is a theoretical framework that seeks to give voice and visibility to socially resonant films that foreground the Third World experience. The sheer explicitness of a film's depiction of Third World misery cannot be confounded with sociopolitical analysis, that is, a causal examination of the oppressive structures at work in the Third World situation. Essentially, this is the linchpin that distinguishes Third Cinema from other political films. The Iranian film *Kandahar* (Mohsen Makhmalbaf, 2001), for instance, essays the grim scenario of mine-infested, Taliban-controlled Afghanistan in riveting documentary realism but the film's sociopolitical commentary is confined to the symptomatic. The more causal, historical issues such as the damaging impact of Cold War geopolitics on the region are left unexplored. The film then, though strongly political and decidedly Third Worldist, does not quite reflect the Third Cinema project.[1] This is not meant to devalue the importance of *Kandahar* or any other Third World film; Third Cinema is a targeted, incisive, and importantly analytical portrayal of the Third World situation but it is by no means the only valid measure of Third World cinematic representation.

Despite the semantic crisis of the term "Third World" in the aftermath of the collapse of the communist bloc Second World in 1989, Third Cinema continues to offer a lucid, alternative view of the sociopolitical realities in an increasingly suprageographical Third World. While a thorough homogenization of the Third World situation is not tenable, underdeveloped countries do share a common disadvantaged situation in the current world order and many of the colonial issues of the past continue to factor into the present situation. The utopic promise of a globalized economy, for instance, has ever more clearly proven to benefit the richest, not the poorest members of the global community. There is, as such, a continuing, relevant task for Third Cinema.[2]

Yet, notwithstanding the corrective voice of the left embodied in the works of Third Cinema, the fact remains that it has always referred to western cinema as its point of departure. It cannot be denied that Third Cinema can only exist in dialectical relationship with the dominant American and European Cinemas. Although earlier positions tended to exclusively delimit Third Cinema to Third World filmmaking, its present evolutionary turn has become less rigid and more inclusive. The original concept of Third Cinema was derived from a wordplay of the term "Third World" but was not intended to be restricted to films of Third World origin. Mike Wayne points out that "First, Second and Third Cinemas do not designate geographical areas, but institutional structures/working practices, associated aesthetic strategies and their attendant cultural practices;"[3] the classification connotes a virtual geography. Some films produced outside of Third World filmmaking have been considered as valid examples of Third Cinema. As I discussed in chapter 1, Wayne argues for the inclusion of the Hollywood musical *Evita* as an example of Third Cinema, albeit a flawed one. I find Wayne's effort commendable as it expands the view of Third Cinema, contributes to its continued relevance, and weaves new threads into the growing Third Cinema canon.

I graft onto Wayne's expanded view of Third Cinema by proposing that certain films normally associated with First or Second Cinema relate dialectically with Third Cinema and thus merit inclusion in the category. For illustrative purposes, I analyze the conjoined thematic and stylistic elements of these films, conscious of the idea that questions of form cannot be divorced from their political contexts. To refer to Teshome Gabriel's apropos argument, "If we accept the notion that artistic choice also connotes ideological choice we must begin to investigate the ideological weight carried by a film's formal elements."[4]

ROMERO: A Prophet on the Silver Screen

Set in the tumultuous 1970s when El Salvador was a national security state, John Duigan's *Romero* (United States, 1989) chronicles the transformation of Roman Catholic Archbishop Oscar Arnulfo Romero from safe and moderate cleric to staunch advocate of the oppressed. The film essays the scenario of a bloody class struggle where the affluent neocolonial class benefits from an abusive civilian-military junta while the underprivileged live in dehumanizing poverty and oppression. Financed by the United States Paulist Fathers and built around the story of a man of the cloth, *Romero* might have been indiscriminately labeled by some critics as just another pietistic excursion in reel hagiography. For sure, it is not. Duigan's opus immediately subverts the cinematic hagiographical portrayals typical of the genre when its main character begins to function as an oppositional voice that questions inauthentic religion from within. The radical Archbishop is seen constantly challenging the harmonizing role played by conservative church members who uncritically acquiesce to the status quo. Third Cinema views religion from a dialectical perspective—a double-edged sword used either as an instrument for social change or wielded as a weapon of oppression, depending on the interests of the class represented.[5] In *Romero*, religion is viewed from the optic of Liberation Theology, a praxically motivated theological paradigm grounded on the critical principle of a preferential option for the poor and downtrodden. Aside from the shared Latin American context, the connection with Third Cinema is a natural, obvious one; that religion expressed in the words and deeds of Archbishop Romero is a religion of justice and sociopolitical change. Audiovisually, the film's central message echoes repeatedly:

> ROMERO: The mission of the Church is to identify itself with the poor and to join with them in their struggle for justice. By doing so, the Church finds its own salvation.

Romero's stark portrayal of the unequal sociopolitical equation in El Salvador gives it an apparent thematic link with Third Cinema. In the film, the Archbishop frequently shares center stage with the marginalized—torture victims, oppressed women, defenseless children, and the elderly—whose stories find thoughtful narrative foregrounding as Romero grows in solidarity with their struggles and becomes their mouthpiece. In one of several scenes depicting Romero as a fiery preacher speaking on behalf of the voiceless populace, the conspiracy of social forces that perpetuates structural injustice is brought to sharper relief and indicted:

> ROMERO: This last week, I wrote a letter to the president of the United States asking him to send no more arms to this country . . . they are only used to kill our people!

Historically, the U.S. government under the Carter administration supplied military equipment worth US$5.7 million for the ruling junta's use.

Romero stakes its claim to authenticity on the historicity of its main character who was, in fact, a heroic modern-day prophet. Yet, it is noteworthy that the film resists unqualified valorization of an individual by depicting Romero frequently immersed in the sociopolitical realities of the collective whose interests he represents. This is comparable to the manner in which Third Cinema makes use of a protagonist:

> Where a central character is used, the viewpoint goes beyond that of the individual to develop a sense of the relationship between the individual and the community, of the collective, and of history.[6]

Notwithstanding their apparent earnestness, First Cinema films with a social slant often foreground the protagonist's courage and charisma at the expense of the much larger social issues, which are relegated to the background or, at best, given a few dramatic moments. Such is the case with Steven Soderbergh's *Erin Brockovich* (United States, 2000) and Steven Zaillian's *A Civil Action* (United States, 1998)—two socially relevant films coming out of Hollywood. Both films are set in seemingly parallel universes where true-to-life cases of industrial waste contamination result in fatal health problems for certain neighborhoods. While these may be pressing communitarian issues pointing to larger socioeconomic roots, they remain largely unexamined because *Erin Brockovich* and *A Civil Action* chose to concentrate on the individual exploits of their protagonists. The deeper structural causes of the problems in question, even if they merit deeper exploration and commentary, take on secondary importance.

Stylistically, the strategic use of filmic conventions such as montage editing also provide *Romero* with ample opportunities to dramatize the power disparity. In a poignant scene, Romero's passionate speeches are intercut with parallel scenes of a high-ranking Salvadoran politican, promising the Salvadoran elite a bright future based on neocolonial ideals:

> POLITICIAN: We developed our country. We penetrated its forests, planted coffee, sugarcane . . . we are like the pioneers of the United States. We do not want what doesn't belong to us. We only want to have what the Northern Americans have—to live as they do.

Romero also employs devices more allied to documentary filmmaking. A couple of scenes, for instance, show disturbing photographs of actual missing people and tortured corpses; victims of the national security state's political witchhunt. Since *Romero* sufficiently essays the Salvadoran collective struggle, this stylistic element only works to punctuate the film's historical context as it infuses a quasi-documentary genuineness to it. It is useful to consider another Hollywood film that employs a similar device but with contrasting results. Oliver Stone's *Salvador* (United States, 1986), a film identically set in the strife-ridden El Salvador of the late 1970s, shows an album of actual photographs of torture victims, perhaps the very same ones used in *Romero*, in addition to gripping, realistic scenes portraying the violence spawned by the abuses of the military junta. But the manner in which the photographs are used for their sheer "shock value," mere accidental spectacles that coincide with the individual issues of the characters—two sleazy American journalists—trivializes the historical, politically charged events unfolding in El Salvador.

On some level, *Romero* also shares the utopic open-endedness seen in *The Last Supper*. The Archbishop's engaged leadership adds fuel to the people's collective protests so that the privileged position of society's powerholders is threatened. For this, he is summarily killed by forces close to the government. But the film does not stop there. In the final scene, the "small people" of El Salvador are shown walking the streets as they go about the business of their daily lives while a voice-over of Romero simultaneously narrates—"I have often been threatened with death. If they kill me, I will arise in the Salvadoran people." The struggle for El Salvador's liberation does not lie on the shoulders of one man, it is a continuing popular struggle fueled by subversive collective memory.

It is worth mentioning that the very same execution scene completely loses its depth and social resonance in *Salvador*. Here, the lead character serendipitously finds himself receiving communion from Romero just moments before the latter's assassination. The event holds no political significance for the character as his only intention in approaching the Archbishop was to win the affections of his Salvadoran girlfriend who happens to be a devout Catholic. From the lens of Oliver Stone, a defining moment in the Salvadoran collective struggle merely serves as a plot device for movie romance. *Romero*, in its strident representation of the Salvadoran struggle for greater justice, keeps self-absorption in check. The characters are not so much motivated by individual psychology and myopic agendas as they are driven by sociopolitical realities. There is a painful national birthing taking place that is fraught with real danger. Surely, a Third Cinema optic sees that the stakes are higher than one man's courtship ritual. Indeed, "All films are political, but films are not all political in the same way."[7]

BREAD AND ROSES: THE SONG OF MIGRANT WORKERS

One title coming out of British filmmaking that has a strong affinity with Third Cinema is *Bread and Roses* (UK/Germany/Spain, 2001) by Ken Loach. Loach is noted for his continuing depiction of significant political issues in his works, which include *Hidden Agenda* (1990), *Land and Freedom* (1995), and *Carla's Song* (1996). In *Bread and Roses*, the British filmmaker details the case of illegal immigrant workers who subsist on poverty wages in the globe's biggest economy, the United States.

Maya, a young girl from Tijuana, attempts to cross the Mexican-US border through dubious means. She is left at the mercy of underground human traffickers who demand money and sex in exchange for the passage. But Maya slips away from the tight situation and successfully locates her sister Rosa, who manages to get her a janitorial job that pays $5.75 per hour without benefits. Through her acquaintance with the other janitors, a diasporic motley crew of earnest, hardworking people, and her close association with the "Justice for Janitors" union organizer named Sam Shapiro, Maya comes to political awareness. She and her co-workers unionize and engage in a series of protest actions against the exploitative labor practices of their employer.

Bread and Roses chooses to explore social reality on a molecular level; the story, after all, has its nerve center in the struggles of one Mexican immigrant and the people who are in the immediate vicinity of her life. Upon closer consideration, however, it becomes clear that the characters are not just individuals in their own right; they are emblems of collective protest and dissent. The personal struggles of these emblematic characters are intricately woven into the larger sociopolitical fabric characterized by the wealth and power imbalance. Against this backdrop, the adjoining issues of ethnicity, class, and gender come into play. A particularly cruel scene shows an elderly janitor being subjected to verbal abuse and then unjustly fired for the lame reason that she reported late for the day's work. As the drama unfolds, the realistic depiction gives an immediate sense of the wider social picture mirrored in the scene. The formula personified by the victim—*woman-elderly-immigrant-janitor*—locates her at the lowest tier of the empowerment and wealth pyramid on every possible count. What is clear and consistent in *Bread and Roses* is that it unequivocally takes the side of the disenfranchised by giving privileged visibility and voice to their marginal status in society's structural imbalance. The resonances with Third Cinema begin to come into clearer focus with this consideration.

In the aspect of style, the film's mise-en-scène further reveals an ethical dimension in ways associated with Third Cinema aesthetics. The casting of a number of multiethnic, nonprofessional actors diffuses the documentary and fiction boundaries and contributes greatly to the sense of historical authenticity pervading the film. The actors, with their nonglamorized appearances, "non-acting" performances, and varied vocal accents, function as close dynamic equivalents of their characters. Moreover, the characters are made to view actual video footage from the 1990 Century City Janitor's strike, the historical event *Bread and Roses* was based on. This contributes further to the documentary quality of the film. Also noteworthy in the film's mise-en-scène is the setting which portrays an unrecognizable, non-touristic view of the city of Los Angeles. The film confines the unfolding story in the characters' site of struggle; the corridors of their deper-sonalized steel and glass work environment, thus, specifying a politicized space rather than the glitz and glamor synonymous with the city.

The evident political use of music is another way in which *Bread and Roses* problematizes the situation of the immigrant workers. In a union gathering, the janitors dance to the rhythm of upbeat Latino music incongruently loaded with indictments on the capitalist order. A live band sings the pointed lyrics:

> I started learning English
> because I had no choice.
> To Fight the Gringo boss,
> I had to have a voice.
> At my job
> they kept giving me anguish
> because I couldn't speak
> the *goddam* English language.
> The gringo boss got angry
> and yelled at me in English—
> "You wetbacks don't understand
> what you are supposed to do."

The band proceeds to sing another song, this time, even more critical of structural injustice and emphasizing the imperativeness of collective action. Before doing so, the lead singer alludes to the key role of the United States in the immigrant-workers' struggle—"Here's one from the people, for the people."

> I'm here to sing to you
> about a sad situation

> Created by the White House
> and US legislation.
> All of us Latinos
> suffer discrimination.
> They steal our rights and harass us
> with laws of immigration.
> But I'm never leaving, I'm staying here forever . . .
> I'm singing this song, so listen to me please.
>
> It's always best to fight.
> Don't stay on your knees.
> We'll carry the struggle
> with famous words like these—
> (Everybody now)
> We can do it!
> We can do it!
> We can do it!

The punctuated use of music illustrates what Gabriel meant when he observes, "In the colonized or neo-colonized countries of the Third World the people have always expressed their joy or despair in music. Musical themes and songs taken from the folk tradition figure in significant ways in the films of the Third Cinema." In *Bread and Roses*, the ethnically flavored music becomes an expression of the immigrants' keen awareness of the structural reasons for their difficult circumstances. It is also a powerful call to social action. There is something distinctly utopian about the incongruent mix of dancing and merrymaking on one hand, and the stridently critical, revolutionary tone of the song lyrics on the other hand. An alternative vision of greater equality is affirmed and celebrated even when it has yet to come to fruition. The tension between present and future is a "creative tension" and is infused with hope.

It might be argued that *Bread and Roses* is not a suitable example of Third Cinema for the reason that it is set mainly in a major cosmopolitan center of the United States and therefore not sufficiently immersed in a Third World country and culture. On the contrary, I propose that the unique setting of *Bread and Roses* contributes greatly to the film's Third Cinema qualities. There are a couple of reasons why I put forward this argument. First, the idea of presenting the pains and struggles of marginalized people of color and illegal immigrants working for poverty wages as cleaners in the world's biggest economy works as a powerful analogy of the inequality spawned by the widening global socioeconomic divide.[8] The film adds salt to the wound by highlighting the Mexican experience where the disparity between First and Third Worlds are drawn by a border; prosperity is a mere step away, so near and yet so far. That the film views social reality from the Third World lens is certain. A First World perspective would most likely moralize about the illegal status of the immigrants, which denies them the right to decent wages or even the right to work at all. *Bread and Roses*, as it adopts the view from the ground up, poses a key question: What drives people to illegal migration in the first place? The film plumbs the pains and struggles of illegal migrants and suggests that there are structural reasons behind illegal migration. The film favors the view that illegal migration is, first and foremost, a consequence of structural inequality before it can be seen as an issue of individuals out to transgress the law. But *Bread and Roses* does not give simple answers. The janitors win their case, indeed, but in the open-ended final scene, Maya is deported for stealing money to help fund a co-worker's education. The struggle has not ended.

The second reason why *Bread and Roses* may be considered an example of Third Cinema despite its First World setting is linked with the previous argument of migration. The rise of diasporic communities due to global transmigration relocates many Third World cultures from their geographically determined boundaries to a new collective social space. This sociocultural reality inevitably skews Third Cinema toward a new, more intercultural context. I see this emerging intercultural quality in the sense in which Laura U. Marks explains her notion of an "Intercultural Cinema":

> "Intercultural" indicates a context that cannot be confined to a single culture. It also suggests movement between one culture and another, thus implying diachrony and the possibility of transformation. "Intercultural" means that a work is not the property of any single culture, but mediates in at least two directions. It accounts for the encounter between different cultural organizations of knowledge, which is one of the sources of intercultural cinema's synthesis of new forms of expression and new kinds of knowledge.[9]

Interestingly, Marks's conception of an Intercultural Cinema dovetails with Shohat and Stam's 4th circle, "a final circle, somewhat anomalous in status, at once 'inside' and 'outside,' comprising recent diasporic hybrid films . . . which both build on and interrogate the conventions of 'Third Cinema.' "[10] However, Marks herself points out the inescapability of addressing the matter of "neutrality," a potential issue that may present itself precisely in the sociocultural "liquidity" of an Intercultural Cinema. This problem is addressed when a film, while being characterized as Intercultural Cinema, aligns itself, first and foremost, to the critical principles of Third Cinema. As a case in point, *Bread and Roses*, with its multiethnic Los Angeles community, may be seen as an example of Intercultural Cinema. But it is primarily allied to Third Cinema in that it infuses its critical Third World vantage point in its intercultural context. Thus, cultural synthesis, is not the bone of contention; the question of how that synthesis becomes a consideration in the quest for structural equality and authentic identity is. *Bread and Roses* has created an "internal Third World" within a First World country; here, the dialectical tension between the two worlds finds emblematic representation. For instance, the American union leader Sam plays a catalyzing role in the janitor's unionizing but is kept in check by Rosa's sharp interrogation; she makes clear whose interests are at stake:

> ROSA: We? When was the last time that you got a cleaning job? You and your union . . . your fat union white boys . . . college kids . . . what the hell do you know?! Don't ever say "we!"

In another scene, Maya questions Sam's intentions:

> MAYA: Have you any idea what it's like to have this life? Can I ask you something? What do you risk? How much do you get paid?

Reverberating a Third Cinema trajectory, *Bread and Roses* negotiates the intercultural terrain on a dialectical level.

The move towards a more intercultural Third Cinema was, in fact, obliquely broached by Gabriel in his 1988 essay "Thoughts on Nomadic Aesthetics and the Black Independent Cinema: Traces of a Journey"[11] where he adopts an Afrocentric perspective while being open to an intercultural synthesis of Latin American, Asian, and European points of reference. Michael Chanan emphasizes the importance of extending Third Cinema into a more "nomadic" cinema considering that the original conception of Third Cinema was predicated on radical political movements that were bound by their socio-historical contexts.[12] This new panorama for Third Cinema, however, is yet to be fully developed by Gabriel or by other Third Cinema theorists with the exception of the tangentially related "Intercultural Cinema" project of Laura U. Marks. It is informative to recall Gabriel's assertion that "The principal characteristic of Third Cinema is really not so much where it is made, or even who makes it, but rather, the ideology it espouses and the consciousness it displays."[13] Though Gabriel himself theorized under the pretext that Third

Cinema emanates from Third World filmmaking, there is a new ring of relevancy in reappropriating his proposition for the expanded view of Third Cinema.

DIVINE INTERVENTION: A DESERT EXPERIENCE

Elia Suleiman's *Divine Intervention* ("*Yaddon Ilaheyya*," Palestine, 2002) essays the Palestinian struggle for national identity and cultural independence; themes worked out in *Xala* and *Perfumed Nightmare*, but its context differs in that there is still an ongoing Israeli occupation that needs to be ended. Relying more on a tableaux of vignettes rather than on a linear narrative, the film is an exposé of the collective humiliation and punishment suffered by Palestinians in Israel. What finds tragi-comic representation is the day-to-day experience of a group of people imprisoned in their own homeland. Akin to *Perfumed Nightmare*, *Divine Intervention* has for its central figure a semi-autobiographical character named E.S. or Elia Suleiman, played by the filmmaker himself. As can be expected, military checkpoints, the crucible of Israeli repression for many Palestinians, serve as a leitmotiv in the film. In one vignette, Israeli soldiers force Palestinians out of their vehicles, harass them and confiscate their possessions, and play a game of mix and match with their vehicles. In another sequence, a tourist asks for the way to the Holy Sepulcher and an Israeli policeman drags a blindfolded, handcuffed Palestinian from the back of a van to give directions. Freedom in the film remains an elusive utopian wish and this is eloquently highlighted in one poignant scene when E.S. releases a balloon imprinted with the smiling face of Yassir Arafat. Cumulatively, the vignettes in *Divine Intervention* allow us to see the Palestinian situation from Palestinian eyes—an overextended desert experience with no oasis in sight.

Divine Intervention carries a second title—*A Chronicle of Love and Pain*. This aptly describes the film's tenor of essaying the experience of the Palestinian people living under Israeli occupation. Palestinian-Christian Naim Stifan Ateek who proposes a "Palestinian Theology of Liberation," paints a vivid picture of the collective trauma and humiliation of all Palestinians:

> Since 1948 and the creation of the state of Israel, Palestinians everywhere have been talking about the injustice done to them—to young and old, educated and uneducated, rich and poor, male and female, religious and secular, Muslim and Christian—all talk about the problem of justice. All of them remember what happened in 1948 and 1967, and they

relate both the story of the loss of Palestine and their own stories of personal loss.[14]

It is thus effortless to conceive that for the Palestinian perspective, "occupation" is the central issue in any discussion of the Palestine-Israel conflict. Notwithstanding the day-to-day reality of living in the "pressure cooker" of a hostile, occupying power,[15] the Palestinian characters in *Divine Intervention* are represented as anything but resigned to their fate.

What is noteworthy in *Divine Intervention* is the way in which it renders the Palestinian resistance, not so much in terms of a bloody uprising, but on the level of protest and liberating anger. Although there appear to be allusions to a kind of *jihad* in the film, they are rendered symbolically so that the violence is underplayed; there is instead a tacit invitation to go beyond a literal, first-degree reading and unpack a more symbolic meaning in the text. A case in point is the film's irreverently humorous opening sequence where a man in a Santa Claus costume, toting a bag brimming-over with presents, runs for his life as stone-throwing Palestinian youths pursue him. At the end of the sequence, we see a knife embedded in his back. If taken at face value, the scene could be interpreted as a grotesque act of violence inordinately committed by misguided, barbaric young Palestinians. But the film obviously means something more than that. The very costuming of the man as a gift-bearing Santa Claus triggers the hermeneutic impulse to interpret the character as an emblematic representation of the United States, bearing gifts of military and moral support for the Israeli occupation. The Palestinian youths indicate that U.S. unilateral intervention will continue to bedevil future generations of Palestinians who seek the restoration of the state of Palestine. The knife on Santa's back is rendered bloodlessly in the scene, suggesting indignation and protest rather than homicide. In an interview, Suleiman himself rebuffs a literal interpretation of the scene and explains the idea behind it:

> I absolutely wanted that scene . . . I hope that my hatred for Santa Claus will spread all over the world. I associate Santa with nauseating sweetness. I enjoy the fact that people are a little shocked by this. Every year, Santa Claus comes with his jingle bells and the world is going to its doom. It's a good idea to rupture the sweetness associated with Santa.

We can see a similar use of the symbolic in one scene when E.S. drives along placidly while eating a peach. He tosses the pit out of the car window and when it hits an Israeli tank parked by the road, the tank explodes. Rendered in magic realism, the scene obviously uses the language of symbol. There are no telltale signs of violence, neither bloodshed, nor charred bodies. The imagery works as an imaginative statement against the Israeli military occupation and the Palestinian indignation over it.

Another scene laden with symbolic meaning is that of E.S. releasing the red Arafat balloon. The balloon floats past an Israeli checkpoint and causes alarm among the soldiers, who do not know whether to shoot it down or not. The balloon is an iconic symbol of subversion, and serves again to represent the Palestinian collective protest against Israeli occupation. The Israeli soldiers themselves validate the symbolic power of the balloon. Armed with high-powered ammunition, they are gripped with irrational fear and threatened, as though the balloon were Arafat himself. The Arafat balloon then hovers over the city where Palestinians live but cannot as yet call their own again. It then travels across the city landscape and finally lands atop the AlAksa mosque on the temple mount, suggesting that allah is imbricated in the Palestinian liberation struggle and commiserates with their plight.

Divine Intervention ends with E.S. and his mother in the kitchen, staring motionlessly at a whistling pressure cooker on a stove. E.S.'s mother then utters a double entendre: "that's enough. Stop it now." It is, in fact, the moral of the story. With that ending, all the seemingly random vignettes of *Divine Intervention* snap into place.

HOTEL RWANDA: THE HUMAN FACE OF SUFFERING

It is easy for Western media to "depersonalize" Third World peoples. When a tragedy happens in the United States or in Europe, we see news coverage of families—fathers, mothers, children—people with soul and story that easily win the world's sympathy and empathy. But more often than not, the coverage accorded to a Third World tragedy is an impersonal affair, a sea of nameless weeping people facing myriad sufferings the affluent citizens of the First World watch on TV while they eat their dinners in peace and comfort. At best, such news reporting produces dramatic charity cases that appeal to guilty consciences.

It's been ten years since a million Rwandans were murdered in what is considered the worst genocide in recent history. True enough, the affluent world ignored the slaughter and allowed it to happen even as TV news cameras covered the unfortunate events. It was as though Rwandans were mere statistics, not members of a shared humanity.

What Terry George's true-to-life film *Hotel Rwanda* (UK/Italy/South Africa, 2004) does is to put a human face to the tragedy. Paul Rusesabagina, manager of the 4-star *Hotel des Milles Collines* in Rwanda, is a good man who has adopted all things European and who is thoroughly infused with a colonial mentality. He is the consummate professional—loyal to his Belgian boss and almost wired to cater to every need of the establishment's wealthy clientele. But he soon finds himself caught in the crossfire of a civil war rooted in the former Belgian colonizers' handling of Rwanda's two opposing tribes, the Tutsis and the Hutus. As bloodshed becomes the order of the day, Paul finds it difficult to refuse the Tutsis refuge in the European Hotel. Paul is a Hutu married to a Tutsi woman. In the aftermath of a cowardly exit by a Euro-American UN contingent, Paul realizes that he has to search for an authentic identity from within, as a Rwandan, not as a pseudo-European. At the heart of his inner journey is his family. Empowered by a deep desire to help his fellow Rwandans, Paul courageously and slyly uses his impeccable hotel management skills to save the lives of the innocent as he provides sanctuary to 1200 Tutsis.

For a film that retells the story of one the bloodiest massacres in recent memory, *Hotel Rwanda* handles the bloodshed with uncharacteristic restraint. The film separates itself from the typical political thriller—*The Killing Fields* (Roland Joffe/UK, 1984), *Schindler's List* (Steven Spielberg/United States, 1993), *Last Man Standing* (Walter Hill/United States, 1996), *Black Hawk Down* (Ridley Scott, 2001) to name a few—when it resists the temptation to aestheticize violence. It is perceptible in *Hotel Rwanda* that George did not want to do a heavy-handed exposition—"The whole gore factor didn't interest me in the slightest."[16] *Hotel Rwanda*'s depiction of the horrific event is mainly atmospheric. The film has a feverish sense of impending violence that constantly stalks the characters. George opts to capture dead bodies strewn on the streets using long shots and when the character of Paul encounters them during an early drive, the scene is bathed in a spectral fog. It is the reaction of the characters that communicate the unfolding horror, not lingering shots of rotting corpses and dismembered bodies.

Because *Hotel Rwanda* avoids making a spectacle out of violence, the social analysis is not drowned out in the narrative. One of the issues problematized in the film is the role of colonialism in the deepening ethnic division between the Tutsis and the Hutus. When the Belgians took over Rwanda in 1918, they heavily favored the dominant Tutsis to their advantage. Supposedly, the favoritism was also racially motivated: the Tutsis' taller frame, finer features, and lighter skin were closer to a European body image.[17] In the film, we encounter this in a dialogue between the American cameraman and a Rwandan journalist:

CAMERAMAN: What's the difference between a Hutu and a Tutsi?
JOURNALIST: According to the Belgian colonists, Tutsis were taller and more elegant. They picked people—with thinner noses, lighter skin, they use to measure the width of their noses—to run the country for them.

The Tutsis thus enjoyed a position of privilege under the Belgians while the Hutus were increasingly relegated to the margins. This gravely worsened the already existing tribal rift. When the Belgians made their exit in 1962 and the Hutus rose into power following the gunning down of the Tutsi president's plane, they exacted vengeance against their former feudal lords and the mass slaughter of Tutsis ensued.

The impairment wrought by colonialism is clearly seen in the post-colonial contradictions of the character of Paul. We see that he has the veneer of a European gentleman—well mannered, neatly groomed, and deliberate in speech. He also works in a Belgian-owned hotel, the *Hotel des Mille Collines*, which is a hub for foreign diplomats and the country's elite. As the violent events unfold around him, Paul puts his trust in the UN Assistance Mission in Rwanda (UNAMIR), believing that a concerted foreign intervention will abate the unrest and Rwanda will normalize. As it turns out, however, the UNAMIR, along with the governments of Belgium, France, the United States, and the rest of the international community, did not have the resolve to act decisively and the dilatory response proved grievously deficient. In the impending abandonment, Paul realizes the futility of his Eurocentric delusions. We discover that Paul begins to find his own voice when he gets into an unfeigned dialogue with his wife Tatiana:

PAUL: They told me I was one of them and I . . . the wine, chocolates, cigars, style. I swallowed it. I swallowed it, I swallowed all of it. And they handed me their shit. I have no, no history—I have no memory. I, I'm a fool, Tatsi.
TATIANA: You are no fool. I know who you are.

Paul's transformation plays out further during the exodus scene when only the western guests are evacuated by a UN contingent. In the frenzy to get into the UN vans, Paul tries to urge the Rwandans to let go and get back into the hotel where they will be taken care of. Framing group action through wide-angle shots, the scene symbolizes Rwanda's need to separate from the colonial *weltanschauung* and to start to find answers within themselves. In a sense, Paul shares with them his newfound inner sense of liberation. His transformation is dramatically confirmed through mise-en-scène during the scene following his encounter with hundreds of corpses littered on the street on a drive out for supplies. When he gets back to the hotel, he locks himself in his quarters to change. He towels off some blood on his cuff, proceeds to change his shirt, and struggles to fasten his tie. Pent-up emotions take over and Paul rips off his shirt. The pivotal scene connotes that his colonial ways, as represented by his European costuming, are now irrelevant to the horrific realities of his country. His failure to fasten his tie and the ripping of his shirt signifies the peeling away of his inauthentic layers. Salvation must come mainly from self-agency, not from European intervention.

Hotel Rwanda also presents a critique of the detached arrogance and indecision of western powers even as they receive confirmed reports of the eruption of violence. In one scene, a western radio broadcast blares out the west's preoccupation over the semantics of the term "genocide" and whether the Rwandan situation can be classified as such. As the radio continues to play, we see a montage of Rwandan faces, both young and old. The film insists that Rwandan lives hang in the balance and putting off action will mean death to countless people. As history tells us, that is exactly what happened.

Today, we are left with a film that functions as Third Cinema, a repository of the dangerous memory of the Rwandan genocide lest the global powers forget and history repeats itself. As the impassioned voice of *Hotel Rwanda*'s true-to-life protagonist defiantly exhorts:

PAUL: Let them know that if they let go of that hand . . . you will die. We must shame them into sending help.

THE MOTORCYCLE DIARIES: CROSSING THE RIVER OF INEQUALITY

The conversion to political engagement is not so much a singular event as a protracted process. For Argentinian revolutionary martyr Ernesto Guevara de la Serna, the process took off with a journey of eight thousand miles—from Buenos Aires up the spine of Chile, across the Andes, and into the Peruvian Amazon—mostly by motorcycle. Walter Salles' *The Motorcycle Diaries* (*"Diarios de*

Motorcicleta," 2004) retraces this audacious Latin American journey using source material drawn from Guevara's actual memoirs and those of his co-traveler Alberto Granado, who, at eighty years old, was able to give a firsthand reconstruction based on personal memory.

The year is 1952 and in an act of inspired madness, 23-year old Ernesto and his good friend Alberto, a biochemist, leave Buenos Aires and set out to discover the real Latin America in a dilapidated 1939 Norton 500. The motorbike, not surprisingly, breaks down in the course of their eight-month journey, but they hold out, traveling on foot and hitching rides along the way. In their travels, they encounter homeless miners exploited by multinational companies and indigenous farmers evicted from their own ancestral land. They also have a quasi-religious experience when they behold the sublime ruins of Machu Picchu, even as they contrast it with the churlish urban sprawls that have supplanted the Incan heritage. Toward the last leg of the journey, they do volunteer medical work at a leper colony in the Peruvian Amazon. Here, the two men are confronted by a sobering reality: much of the pain and suffering that the poor have to endure is caused by the structural asymmetry brought about by the prevailing economic system that prizes progress above all.

The geographical, cultural, and historical richness of their cumulative experiences makes them see Latin America through different eyes; a vision of greater ethical responsibility and political engagement looms in the horizon.

In *The Motorcycle Diaries,* Ernesto's encounters with people from the grassroots are the key moments that signal his gradual social awakening. Camerawork italicizes these encounters through a shift in framing and angling whenever indigenous people—evidently nonactors who are close equivalents, if not true-to-life portrayals of their characters—are presented onscreen. Salles uses a semi-documentary "testimonial" motif in the cinematography of such scenes. We see the indigenous people from Ernesto's over-the-shoulder vantage point as they recount the harsh realities of their struggles as a marginalized group. This angling strategy suggests that Ernesto is giving the indigenous people privileged space and paying attention to their stories. As the journey moves forward, formalistic options that establish a bridge between the indigenous people and Ernesto develop more as intrusions into the narrative. Midway through the film, when the two men take a ferry trip to the leper colony, a narrow dingy boat catches Ernesto's attention. Compared to his comfortable ferry, the boat is obviously decrepit and cramped. At this point, a medium shot of the boat, rendered in contrasting black-and-white, is edited into the scene. The shot stands out not only because it is rendered in black-and-white but because the passengers, who are all indigenous people, keep themselves as motionless as they can, in what appears to be a mimetic approximation of still photography. They are also shot frontally so that it looks like they are establishing eye contact with the camera. It is notable too that their expressions are pensive; their stares, piercing. There is a reprisal of this device in the penultimate sequence of the film. The indigenous people Ernesto encountered in the course of his journey—miners, farmers, peasants, beggars, poor workers—make a reappearance in a montage of shots rendered in the same black-and-white tableaux style. The primary suggestion of this motif is worked out on an ideological level and the use of black-and-white instead of full color cues us to this deeper connotational layer. There is a praxical imperative that haunts the memory of Ernesto, and, in a blurring of diegetical-extradiegetical boundaries, the normally uninvolved audience. The images thus serve as representations of the call for social change. A similar device is employed in *Perfumed Nightmare*. When a burning indignation over social injustice brims over in the protagonist Kidlat, he is shot in close-up as he looks straight to the camera and breaks out into mocking laughter. In the Third Cinema perspective, social comment is prioritized over personal psychology and the use of such cinematographic strategies in both films bears this out.

Ernesto's clearer view of the displacement of the indigenous peoples by the ingression of progress and development becomes apparent in their Peruvian stopover. While enthralled by the wonders of Machu Picchu, Ernesto's brewing internal conflict rises to the surface. Salles employs cut-to-cut editing of an aerial shot of the Incan ruins as against that of the urban sprawl of Lima while we hear the protagonist commenting:

> ERNESTO'S VOICE-OVER: How is it possible to feel nostalgia for a world I never knew? How can a civilization that built this [Machu Picchu] . . . be destroyed to build this [Lima urban sprawl].

Again, a useful comparative example would be the way that *Perfumed Nightmare* shifts between the contrasting location settings of an idyllic Philippine *barrio* and cosmopolitan Paris abuzz with development.

One of the most consequential symbols in *The Motorcycle Diaries* is the Amazon River that separates the leper colony on the south bank, and the doctors, nurses, nuns, and medical personnel on the north bank. On a denotational level, the two sides of the river clearly

represent the polarity between the healthy subculture and the objectified "other" subculture of the unhealthy. In the middle of his birthday
celebration on the north side, Ernesto decides to leave the party,
heads for the riverbank, and exclaims:

ERNESTO: I'm going to celebrate my birthday on the other side.

In yet another act of inspired madness, he braves the dark waters and
ignores the imperilment of a possible asthma attack, and swims to the
south bank. This would seem like a setup for a hagiographical representation and indeed, Ernesto is the hero who dares to bridge the
North-South divide, and his courage is celebrated when he makes it to
the other side. A connotational reading, however, proposes a meaning
beyond the virtual canonizing of Ernesto. The North-South
dichotomy has deeper resonances for the continent. The North represents the European colonizing powers, the *conquistadores* who laid
claim to the south. Ernesto's successful swim to the south suggests an
equalizing of the structural inequality rooted in the continent's colonial past and ongoing in the present. It is a visionary sequence and
Ernesto's swim plays out as a symbolic critical utopia, a "seditious
expression of social change."[18] It is also worth mentioning that Salles
himself downplays the hagiographical dimension, pointing out
Ernesto's character flaws and the subtle portrayal of lead actor Gael
Garcia Bernal:

> This is about Che before he became history. It's about finding the
> young man before the myth and humanizing the icon. The way I react
> to that observation is that well, here you have a young man at the
> beginning of the story who is introspective, asthmatic, not successful
> with women, can't dance—that information goes completely against
> the image of a heroic figure. The beauty of what Gael offers is that he
> doesn't "hero-ify;" he plays in a very economical manner, offers a
> young Ernesto full of doubts.[19]

The Motorcycle Diaires is not just about Ernesto, the medical
student, who crosses the river to magically emerge as "El Che," the
political icon. The film offers a poetic synthesis of the Third World
condition. As long as the partying continues in the self-absorbed
North and the powers that be refuse to swim to the other side, the
South continues to suffer the weight of social injustice.

The imagery, poignant and subversive, may very well be a poetic
synthesis of the continued relevance of Third Cinema in its virtual

Third World incarnations, not to mention a fitting conclusion to this chapter. The power of Third Cinema is the power to cut deep into the reality of a virtual Third World, which, despite the current tendency among the players of globalization to homogenize the world, continues to exist. Third Cinema raises our consciousness about the many inequalities that continue to separate the Third World from the First, the impoverished from the affluent, the weak from the powerful.

The river is yet to be crossed.

PART II

Theological Principle

CHAPTER 4

Political Holiness: The Eschatological Perspective of Schillebeeckx

In the foreword of *The Schillebeeckx Reader*, an anthology of Schillebeeckx's works from a wide selection of sources, he likens the process of putting together a reader with that of making a film.

> From all the originally photographed footage, which had been worked on for years, a film of only a few hours is created. Choices are made, focusing is done, editing takes place. Something similar happens in the compiling of a Reader. It differs from a film, however, in that it is ultimately not the product of the author about whom it is really concerned. Someone else makes his own film out of the original footage, albeit with complete and integral preservation of the original material.[1]

I begin the chapter with this imaginative description by Schillebeeckx not just because I find it interesting that one of the world's most important modern theologians would even so much as allude to film in his work. I do so because writing a chapter on "political holiness," the general rubric of Schillebeeckx's eschatological understanding of salvation and liberation, entails a certain process of selection, focusing, and editing, indeed, quite akin to post-production work in filmmaking. This is not the easiest of tasks considering that Schillebeeckx never really expounds on eschatology in a neat, systematic way; his ideas on the subject are worked out in the other cogent topics of systematic theology such as anthropology, christology, soteriology, and ethics, among others. Moreover, there are numerous theological research works assembled from Schillebeeckx's "reels of original footage," so much so that there is always the hazard of investing time and effort on something that had been done many times before. Akin to a dutiful film editor then, I aim for specific principles of Schillebeeckx's thought insofar as they contribute to my critical interest of retracing the distinct lines of his eschatological perspective. I provide some useful, direction-setting information on the development of Schillebeeckx's thought at the outset with the intention of using it as a springboard to the discussion proper. And then, through a selective, deductive layering of the pivotal lines of Schillebeeckx's arguments, I move into sharper focus as I present a detailed discussion of his eschatological conception of political holiness. The chapter unfolds as follows:

The first part serves as a basic orientation to the development of Schillebeeckx's thought with emphasis on the liberative currents sparked at the beginning of his theological turnabout, a marked intellectual shift quickened by the spirit of the Second Vatican Council starting in the mid-1960s. This historical turnabout is an important point of departure because it laid the groundwork for the emerging reconfiguration of Schillebeeckx's thomistic frame of reference into a praxical-critical theology angled toward a more liberationist trajectory. In this introductory portion, I am necessarily indebted to the various available sources that deal with this topic extensively.[2]

The brief prologue then segues to the discussion proper, an exploration of the praxical dimension of Schillebeeckx's eschatological view of salvation and liberation.

I begin the discussion with a consideration of the concept of the *humanum* or potential, authentic humanity. Schillebeeckx speaks of the *humanum* as the vision of a full humanity that is not antecedently given by God but remains as a goal to be sought after and struggled for in a world that often obviates it. Here, the anthropological emphasis of Schillebeeckx's eschatology becomes apparent.

What follows is Schillebeeckx's proposal of "The System of Coordinates of Man and His Salvation," where he puts forward the idea that there is no normative definition of what constitutes "livable humanity" as it is a future, eschatological concept. Instead, Schillebeeckx proposes seven anthropological constants that provide a descriptive framework for an understanding of the *humanum*.

The discussion moves on to Schillebeeckx's arguments about the problem of "an ecumene of suffering," the continuing scarlet thread of suffering in human history. Schillebeeckx has a keen grasp of the reality of suffering in the world, most especially the plight of people from the Third World who are marginalized by structural inequality and injustice. Theologian Robert J. Schreiter notes, "Schillebeeckx is at his most eloquent on this when he speaks of human suffering."[3] For him, suffering is inconsistent with the very character of a God who is "mindful of humanity." Nonetheless, he sees an epistemological value in suffering, which evades theological comprehension.

In the next portion, I foreground Schillebeeckx's acknowledgment of the need to bridge Christian salvation and sociopolitical liberation. Taking into serious account the scandal that is human suffering, Schillebeeckx considers this dialectical relationship as a necessary focal point in soteriology. He emphasizes the relevance of theologies of liberation in the universal quest for the *humanum*.

At this juncture, the eschatological perspective of Schillebeeckx naturally gravitates to the centrality of the gospel metaphor of the "Reign of God," the dynamic, praxical imperative interlinked with the eschatological symbol of "final good," the coming "Kingdom of God." This portion presents Schillebeeckx's understanding of the concept of God's Reign based on his exploration of the proclamation and saving activities of Jesus, the eschatological prophet. What is clearly established here is that the inbreaking Reign of God has the poor and oppressed as its first beneficiaries.

I devote attention to the topic of "eschatological salvation" in the next portion. Schillebeeckx maintains that sociopolitical initiatives are, at best, fragmentary signs of the Reign of God. He proposes an "eschatological proviso" from which all praxical initiatives are relativized, but at the same time, emphasizes a dialectical "eschatological superabundance" of God's transcendence; a relativizing surplus that safeguards against the devaluing of liberative movements.

I explore the pivotal concept of "negative experiences of contrast" in the succeeding discussion. Schillebeeckx argues that it is the very experience of injustice that yields cognitive power when it brings about indignation and protest; the refusal to acquiesce to situations of suffering and disordered relations. The experience of a positive moment within the crucible of critical negativity becomes a critical force that quickens human hope and catalyzes the movement toward possible praxis. While it may also be correct to introduce negative experiences of contrast in the earlier section on the *humanum*, I find it more resonant to situate the topic in a more liberative, eschatological frame; in the way Schillebeeckx works it out in closer proximity to the historical praxis of mysticism and politics. This option will be appreciable as the chapter unfolds.

I then discuss Schillebeeckx's proposal that the liberationist spirituality of "political holiness," and its social expression in "political love," have become the appropriate and relevant expressions of mysticism today. Schillebeeckx expounds on this ethical imperative in the light of the cruel context of Third World sociopolitical realities.

Finally, I include a rare face-to-face interview with Edward Schillebeeckx as an addendum to this chapter. Here, Schillebeeckx himself clarifies and confirms "human liberation" as the epistemological project of his theology.

I am convinced that in my attempt to read the undeniable praxical emphasis of Schillebeeckx's eschatological perspective by way of my own optic, that is, through the eyes of one who indeed comes from the Third World, there will still be, as the Dutch theologian puts it, "a complete and integral preservation of the original material."

THE THEOLOGICAL TURNABOUT IN THE THEOLOGY OF EDWARD SCHILLEBEECKX: A BRIEF ORIENTATION

In the years that preceded the Second Vatican Council, Professor Edward Schillebeeckx, then occupant of the Chair of Dogmatics and the History of Theology at the *Katholieke Universiteit Nijmegen*, was called upon to be an adviser to the Dutch Bishops. Schillebeeckx became the main voice of influence behind a joint pastoral letter issued by the bishops in 1961. The document is of key importance because it provided a liberal agenda meant to orient and prepare Dutch Catholics at the dawning of the Council, and because it is a foreboding of the key conclusions that were later taken up by the Council, such as, liturgical renewal and the collegiality of bishops.[4] During the deliberations of the Council, Schillebeeckx continued his advisory role to the Dutch bishops over and above his role as a sought-after lecturer to many other bishops of various constituencies.[5] Consequently, his work made a significant impact on Conciliar documents, specifically, on the development of the Constitutions on the Church and the Church in the Modern World.[6] Important turn of events that influenced the development of Schillebeeckx's thought came in the mid-1960s when he became one of the founding editors of *Concilium*, a progressive international journal of theology fueled by the Conciliar spirit. In 1967, Schillebeeckx embarked on his first visiting lecture to the United States. This period was annotated by Schillebeeckx's encounter with the phenomenon of secularization and the radical "God is Dead" theology, as well as by his meetings with Latin American liberation theologians[7] during a trip to the Americas later that year.

The "Council Years" in Schillebeeckx's intellectual life is relevant to this research because it was around this period that his theological thought underwent a radical turnabout. A Dominican cleric, Schillebeeckx's epistemological project had originally been couched on an explicit Thomistic frame of reference. His later theological thought, however, shifts to a new key, reflecting liberative currents that were previously uncharted in his earlier works. It is not within the scope of this research to retrace Schillebeeckx's earlier intellectual history in any great detail but I find it informative to make mention of two influences that made a deep impression on his earlier thought—Dominicus De Petter and M.D. Chenu.[8]

Schillebeeckx trained under D. De Petter during his early years of philosophical studies in Ghent.[9] While metaphysics and epistemology were De Petter's central philosophical interests, he oriented Schillebeeckx to a novel approach to Thomas Aquinas that eschewed the traditional scholasticism popular at the time—he fused a Thomist theory of knowing with the phenomenological concern for the "ultimate inadequacy of human conceptuality to grasp experience."[10] De Petter was an important influence on Schillebeeckx because he endeavored to hurdle conceptualism and dualism in philosophy.

The single greatest influence on the early Schillebeeckx, however, was M.D. Chenu, one of his mentors during his post–World War II years as a student at *Le Saulchoir*, the Dominican theological school located at the outskirts of Paris. Chenu emphasized the importance of solid historical research for theology. The concern for "historical context" is reflected in his work *Une Ecole de Theologie: Le Saulchoir* ("A School of Theology: The Saulchoir"), a modest work that nonetheless left a deep impression on Schillebeeckx. Moreover, Chenu bridged his academic expertise in Medieval History with his direct engagement with the French worker-priest movement. His grounding on history and commitment to justice coupled with his concern for the contemporary issues confronting the church resonated in Schillebeeckx's works for many years.[11] Kennedy aptly summarizes the influence of De Petter and Chenu on Schillebeeckx:

> Through Chenu and De Petter, therefore, Schillebeeckx was stimulated to relativize theology conceived as a conceptual system, and to place theological reflection in a historical (Chenu) and human-experiential context. (De Petter)[12]

Schillebeeckx's Nijmegen experience and his exposure to conflicting theological and philosophical views during his North American sojourns contributed greatly to the turnabout in his theology. While basic areas of concern remained, Schillebeeckx's interpretive framework underwent a momentous change.

Schreiter maps the turnabout in two evident shifts:[13] First, Schillebeeckx distances himself from the Thomistic epistemological project; he set aside the single, unitary metaphysical framework characteristic of his earlier theology, which was rooted in the philosophy of De Petter. He opted instead to appropriate a wider range of interpretive frameworks. Schillebeeckx wanted to assert that as "scientific investigators," theologians must be open to have their "thesis of faith" validated, in one way or another, in human historical experience, or face the charge of reasoning in a closed, vicious cycle. This signaled a turnabout from the "implicit intuition" of meaning-totality espoused by De Petter and classical philosophy.[14]

Schillebeeckx's encounter with the critical theory of the Frankfurt School of social criticism angled his thought toward the question of meaning of faith in the light of sociopolitical questions. The works of Jurgen Habermas, specifically his three early books *Theorie und Praxis* (1963), *Erkenntnis und Interesse* (1968) and *Zur Logik der Sozialwissenschaften* (1969), proved to be a great influence on Schillebeeckx. Habermas' western Marxist sociology addresses the view from the oppressed underside of society and keenly examines how social structures are kept calcified by society's powerholders in order to perpetuate the status quo.[15] The work of Habermas resonates with the basic hermeneutical focus of neo-Marxist social theories, expressions of which can be found in "contextual theologies" such as Latin American Liberation Theology and Feminist Theology:

Critical theory attempts to exploit one of the fundamental insights of the Marxist tradition—now a commonplace in a variety of forms of social thought—that the interpretation of any tradition likely involves systematic distortions of communication in the interests of those who have power and privilege.[16]

Another significant influence among the Frankurt School thinkers was Theodor Adorno, whose notion of "negative dialectics" deals with the phenomenon of human suffering and its role in the concept of the *humanum,* or full authentic humanity, construed here as a tacit future concept. Schillebeeckx would later replace "negative dialectics" with the term "Critical negativity." Additionally, Anglo-American analytic philosophy and the "new hermeneutics" of the neo-Heideggerians factor into the cacophony of interpretive frameworks appropriated by Schillebeeckx.[17]

Second, Schillebeeckx underwent a significant shift in perspective. The fecund environment surrounding the years of the Council counterpointed by the wave of secular thinking proliferating around that period enjoined theological renewal. This necessitated a shift in tone in Schillebeeckx's theology—from a language that bespeaks of churchly, institutionally infused presuppositions and argumentations, to a more current and accessible language geared toward reaching a wider audience; whether church or non-Church, Catholic or non-Catholic. The intention was to try to make theology speak again to western peoples in the context of a rapidly secularizing world and in a changing sociopolitical global landscape.

Additionally, Schreiter points out that the theological turnabout was also indexical of Schillebeeckx's intense struggle to make sense of his own personal search, thus, highlighting the close link between the theologian's biographical history and the evolution of his theological thought.[18]

Basic Motifs of Schillebeeckx's Thought

It is useful to clarify the main insights that provide coherence to the intersecting themes of Schillebeeckx's work. Schreiter is the first to note that it is no easy task to give an overall characterization of the ideas of a theologian as prolific as Schillebeeckx with more than 40 years of active theologizing and 400 written works published in 14 languages. He nonetheless paints a clear delineation of Schillebeeckx's thought in three unobscured brush strokes:[19]

Divine revelation is situated within and mediated through human experience. A lasting imprint of D. De Petter, Schillebeeckx's starting point is human experience, that is, the full range of human perceptions, activities, and events, rather than its interpretive frameworks, such as language and concepts. Human experience is the locus in which revelation, offering a critique of our experience in dialectical fashion, is mediated—"the crossing of a boundary within the dimensions of human experience."[20] By situating revelation within the compass of human experience, Schillebeeckx expands the comprehension of revelation beyond linguistic categories. This is apparent in the book *Christ: The Experience of Jesus as Lord*, where Schillebeeckx argues that the genesis of Christianity is rooted in the disciples' experience of Jesus, which assumed specific forms. It did not, as classical theology would proffer, begin with absolutizing doctrines.[21]

In concurrence with the centrality of the concept of experience in his theology, Schillebeeckx gives due importance to the concreteness of history. The word "concrete" figures repeatedly in Schillebeeckx's later work and points to his concern for bridging theorizing with action, or the foregrounding of "orthopraxis" as a pivotal concept in doing theology.

A commitment to the concreteness of human history means that one must come face to face with the reality of human suffering, sin, and injustice. The subject of suffering occupies a central place in Schillebeeckx's theology. While he does not accept the theory that suffering and evil originate from God, Schillebeeckx sees a critical positive moment in the human experience of suffering. It is the very experience of suffering and injustice that yields cognitive power when it brings about indignation and protest; the refusal to acquiesce to situations of meaningless suffering and disordered relations. Schillebeeckx proposes the term "negative experiences of contrast" or "negative contrast experiences," to describe the dialectical tension between the committed quest for the *humanum,* or full authentic humanity, despite a world that chronically subverts it.

Schillebeeckx's notion of negative experiences of contrast is a key concept of this research, as such, I will give appropriate attention to the topic in a subsequent section of this chapter.

The mysterious, sovereign God is a "God mindful of humanity." Although Schillebeeckx's later theology had decidedly become more anthropological in focus as compared to his earlier thought, he is careful not to advocate a theology that is anthropocentric. Schillebeeckx is unequivocal in emphasizing the significance of the mystery of the God of graciousness in human history. The abiding concern of the sovereign God is the deepest well being of humanity; "God has made humanity's cause a Divine cause."[22] Schillebeeckx has stressed the life-giving presence of God in history in Jesus Christ, who is the parable of God's closeness to, and solidarity with, struggling humanity. The universal significance of Jesus lies in his liberating praxis on behalf of the poor, the oppressed, and the defenseless. This represents an assertion of the emancipative vision of the Reign of God as the pathway to the *humanum* and an affirmation of the utter graciousness and love of God.

I wish to point out that the motifs outlining Schillebeeckx's thought are to be taken as coherent, interdependent concepts:

Experience is grounded in a God who wishes to communicate, the contrast experiences draw us closer to that God, and the experience of God "mindful of humanity" affirms that act of intuition and faith by making a mediation of the paradoxical experience of the immediate. In doing this, Schillebeeckx achieves a great deal in his hope of making the Christian message of God and the experience of salvation offered in Jesus Christ more available to a secularized society.[23]

Having recapitulated the basic heuristic lines of his thought, it is informative, at this juncture, for me to give an account of the salient points of Schillebeeckn's theological method.

Distinguishing Features of the Theological Method of Schillebeeckx's Later Theology

I begin the summation of Schillebeeckx's method with a useful, albeit amusing description of his approach in carrying out the task of theology according to William L. Portier:

> He is rather like a master chef who doesn't cook from recipes but simply has a sense for the right ingredient. To speak of "method" in Schillebeeckx's theology, then, is not to speak in the usual terms of the discussion of theological method in the academy.[24]

Schillebeeckx, in fact, scarcely preoccupies himself with the methodological question as could otherwise be expected of one who has made a major academic contribution to contemporary theology. This option could very well be related to Schillebeeckx's primary public. To be sure, he is set apart from Karl Rahner, Bernard Lonergan, and David Tracy, theologians whose main foci lie within the religious and academic sectors, by insisting that his main intended public is the ordinary Christian. He expressly articulates this in the foreword of the book *Jesus: An Experiment in Christology*

Although I regard this book as a Christian interpretation of Jesus—a Christology—however unconventional it may be, it has not been written to resolve the sometimes very subtle problems that interest the academic theologian. Not that these are unimportant. But the fact is that believers are raising questions about Christ, which are not the ones that normally preoccupy academics. I have tried to bridge the gap between academic theology and the concrete needs of the ordinary Christian or, to speak more modestly, I have tried here to shed some light on the nexus of problems presaging that gap and giving rise to the questions that seem most urgent to the ordinary Christian.[25]

Portier views the trajectory of Schillebeeckx's theological approach as accordant with the Anselmian *fides quaerens intellectum* or "faith seeking understanding." Schillebeeckx, first and foremost, is "a believer who reflects."[26] As such, he becomes a mouthpiece for the ordinary Christian whose concerns resonate with his own. Taking into account Schillebeeckx's chosen primary public, it is clear that his main concern is laying a bridge between the more abstract concerns of academic circles and the legitimate questions posed by contemporary Christians in the context of their real sites of struggle. Quite apropos, the central concern for bridging these oftentimes polar milieux provides a clue to understanding Schillebeeckx's theological method.

Tradition and Situation

For Schillebeeckx, Christian theology needs to address the hermeneutical issue of the polarity that exists between the Christian tradition of faith and the life-context of believers who live in the here and now. As in all great religious traditions, Christianity is primarily a tradition characterized by a disclosure of meaning[27] passed on and accumulated transgenerationally by the living faith community—"What was experience for others yesterday is tradition for us today, and what is experience for us today will in turn be tradition for others tomorrow."[28] It is this cumulative disclosure of meaning that offers a potential bridge to the experiential context of people in the present. In the Christian tradition, the meaning that is disclosed is drawn mainly from a narrative culture. Yielding both critical and practical effect, these stories filtered through the tradition of faith bear liberative power, the confession of healing and wholeness for a wounded humanity. The Gospel story of the tax collector Zaccheus as retold by Schillebeeckx is a case in point:

> When Jesus saw tiny Zaccheus, so small that he had to climb into a tree to watch Jesus pass by, he did not say to him "God loves you" (like the modern fundamentalist posters in our crowded streets). Something rather different happened. Jesus went to his house and by eating and talking with him actually showed Zaccheus that God loved him. By doing this he disclosed something, which transcends our humanity. Zaccheus abandoned his corrupt life and gave half of his possessions to the poor.[29]

The liberative force of these stories generated by tradition come not so much in telling them but in being "caught up"[30] with them; the bearers are bound by the praxical imperative of the message. As to the matter of "situation," Schillebeeckx advances that it is more than just the medium through which faith is communicated—"The situation, the context of faith, is itself theologically relevant."[31] He is keenly aware of the complexity of the present world with its divergent social, economic, and political specificities. Hence, the work of theological hermeneutics must consider the wider collective, that is, the local Church communities that represent a heterogeneity of cultures, and not just the propositions of any single theologian.

Interrelationship between Cultures and Traditions of Faith

Situating revelation within the bounds of human experience exacts a mutually critical correlation between tradition and situation. While Schillebeeckx adopts the term "correlation" in his works,[32] he shows a preference for the term "interrelationship":

> I have chosen the term 'interrelationship' deliberately: it is vague enough to cover the broad spread between clear identity on the one hand (it clicks) and unmistakable non-identity on the other (it clashes): from correlation to conflict and confrontation, from complete identification to partial recognition and finally non-recognition.[33]

With his option for the term "interrelationship," Schillebeeckx avoids the inevitable identification with Paul Tillich's original conception of "correlation,"[34] which considers the Christian tradition as the normative source for theology while bypassing the contemporary situation as a determinative element in an understanding of revelation. Schillebeeckx counters that "the question of meaning logically precedes that of the truth, and a statement only has meaning if in one way or another it expresses lived experience."[35] Thus, he avoids two theological extremes—one that leaves believers beholden to church authority, which binds them to particular faith expressions while God consigns them to freedom, and another which accedes to the interpretations set by the believers and theologians that may represent distortions of the authenticity of the gospel.

Schillebeeckx views the Christian message as "trans-cultural," not so much in the sense that it does not belong to any one culture nor in the affirmation that there is a timeless substance of faith but rather in a "constant dialectic" between the universality of the gospel and in its concrete appearance in particular cultures:

> [T]his universal message, open to all cultures and a challenge to all men and women, can be found concretely only in the forms of particular cultures (Jewish, Jewish-Hellenistic, Hellenistic; later the culture of late antiquity, Carolingian culture, Celtic, Romanesque, contemporary African, Asian and Latin American culture, and so on), never neat, above or outside any culture, and therefore never in an "abstract substance of faith," stripped down and free of any culture . . . only in concrete particularity can the gospel be the revelation of the universality

of salvation from God, because men and women are cultural beings with their own particular cultures and can only be reached as human beings in them.[36]

Schillebeeckx thus speaks of the continued meaningfulness and relevance of the "offer of revelation," which is "constantly young" but always "acclimatized in a particular culture." It is necessary then to forge a "mutually critical encounter between faith cultures" to be able to see the offer of revelation in the Christian gospel. The term "correlation," Schillebeeckx explains, may prove misleading in this case as a clear-cut correlation does not exist between the poles of tradition (as source) and situation (as medium):

> The contingent situation of the past is already present in the Christian tradition, twisting it, and in our contemporary situation God is as creative in liberation as he was before: he has not ceased to be "the biblical God" in the meantime.[37]

The question then does not lie in the interpretation of the gospel in the light of the contemporary situation but the interrelationship or encounter of various cultural forms predicated on one understanding of faith. Two critical principles that form a dialectical whole come to play here. First, any theological proposition must be capable of being expressed with reference to the Christian faith tradition. Theology, after all, is a hermeneutical enterprise that maintains connections with the past while using modern critical methods. Second, any theological proposition must be validated by reference to an analysis and interpretation of the contemporary situation. Schillebeeckx argues that a failure to consider these two critical principles results in a short-circuiting of the connections between the categories of thought and experience, as such; no bridge is built between the past and the present.[38]

A Constantly New Inculturation of the Gospel

Schillebeeckx explains that revelation is passed on to successive generations through a continuing process of "experiencing and understanding" of revelation. The earliest followers of Jesus described their collective experience in faith by way of a semiotic system,[39] their socially shared system of meaning-making. This served as the cultural network through which their collective experience was communicated to their contemporaries and to later generations. The appropriation of the gospel message then is culture-specific—"living contact between the gospel and the changing, culturally-shaped understanding of reality by believers in a particular cultural period."[40] Schillebeeckx thus insists that "the identity in the meaning of the gospel" can neither be based in the fundamentalist predilection for a mere material repetition of the past tradition nor at the level of the past or present situation as such. Rather, the identity of meaning is situated in a non-static level Schillebeeckx refers to as the "middle-field":

> This identity of meaning can only be found in the fluctuating "middle field," in a swinging to and fro between tradition and situation, and thus at the level of the corresponding relationship between the original message (tradition, which also includes the situation of time) and the situation, then and now, which is different each time.[41]

In Schillebeeckx's illustration, tradition and the ever-changing situation are interrelated kinetically as like a pendulum, rhythmically swinging back and forth. Identity of meaning is not predicated on a direct parallelism between the Bible and the contemporary situation but on the "correspondence of relationships" between the message and situation, then and now.[42] Schillebeeckx insists that there can never be an indelible, direct view of Christian identity of meaning. Particular historical mediations produce discordant voices that prevent Christian identity from being harmonized on one and the same level, so it is never a complete identity but a "proportional identity." Thus, Schillebeeckx calls for a "constantly new inculturation":[43]

> For although the offer of revelation with its non-objectifiable meaning and content is indeed present from the beginning, this meaning as assignable and expressed is to be found only in the believing interpretations of men and women in a particular social and cultural context. The periodical twists in the cultural understanding of reality rule out a purely explicative process. Something else is involved. What we have is, rather, the process of a constantly new inculturation of a gospel which is not bound to one culture, but which is not given in the Bible, either, apart from a limited, particular cultural form.[44]

Christian identity of meaning is passed on in a living tradition, in a continuous, open-ended weaving of new meaning from the tapestry of the Bible tradition and the praxis of the believing community, constantly re-read within new situations in "creative trust." Nonetheless, Schillebeeckx asserts that the Christian perception of the meaning of revelation is united in depth, that is, it still maintains one fundamental perspective of the mutual relationship that exists between God and humanity though it has been mediated through sociocultural worlds of divergent hues.

Ideology-Critical Hermeneutics

Schillebeeckx argues that a purely theoretical hermeneutics in theology runs the risk of erroneous actualization and may present problems of contextual credibility. Such an approach ignores "ideological moments" present in both the Christian tradition and the contemporary situation. Schillebeeckx thus proposes a theological critique of ideology.[45] In prologue to this proposal, however, Schillebeeckx first clarifies the definition of the term "ideology." He insists that the term can be understood in a positive sense prior to the ascription of negative "pathological traits" or unfavorable meaning onto it as per the work of Karl Marx, Sigmund Freud, and Friedrich Nietzsche:

> "Ideology" I understand in the first instance as something positive, which, however, can come to manifest pathological traits. The negative or unfavorable meaning of ideology I see therefore as derivative, that is, as a pathology of something good. In a positive sense, I define "ideology" as an ensemble of images, ideas, and symbols which a society creates to give an account of' its own identity. Ideology is the reproduction and confirmation of one's own identity by means of "foundational symbols" (symbolic universe of meaning) . . . the function of ideology becomes pathological, especially insofar as that legitimation is distorted, manipulated, and monopolized by dominating groups in society. In this way ideology becomes a means for maintaining dominant interests, and is as such the mirroring of a false group consciousness.[46]

Schillebeeckx emphasizes that the negative meaning of ideology is derivative considering that communities cannot give false views of themselves without first being constituted on the level of their symbolic structures. The entry of the negative pathological traits is traced to the "dominating groups" whose self-serving interests are perpetuated at the expense of the communities in question.[47] For Schillebeeckx, the "de-ideologization" then entails the "unmasking" of the naive assumption that being and language are coextensive notwithstanding the conceptual inadequacy already previously recognized. Language as construed in terms of speech and thought is characterized by a dependence on all sorts of interests, both collective and private, and often serves to legitimize and support the status quo of power structures and distorted relations. The continuum of power-holders who worked to marginalize potential, alternative evangelical currents in the history of theology attests to this. If theologians then are committed to the essence of an authentic evangelical vision based on the teachings of the church and of Scripture, they will acknowledge the expediency of ideologically-critical hermeneutics in theology. This, according to Schillebeeckx, is grounded precisely on fidelity to the Word of God.

Bypassing the process of de-ideologization in theological hermeneutics may mean either of two tendencies—on one hand, a "false *aggiornamento*" where the Christian tradition is accommodated to the modern, technocratic, particularly Western, belief in progress; and on the other hand, an uncritical estimation of the faith tradition in purely evangelical terms, as such, the postulation of inadequate, outdated concepts as normative for Christians. Either way signifies the diminishing of the liberative power of the Christian faith.[48]

For Schillebeeckx, an ideological-critical hermeneutics in theology is primarily a critique of the false consciousness perpetuated within the church and society in general by the dominant ideology. The recognition of the indispensible place of this hermeneutical option in theological thought has significant implications for the church's quest for genuine self-transcendence into an eschatological future that is already given embodiment and expression in praxis.

THE ESCHATOLOGICAL PERSPECTIVE OF EDWARD SCHILLEBEECKX

The eschatological perspective of Schillebeeckx evolved during the radical shift in his theology in the years following the Second Vatican Council. As earlier mentioned, the period was characterized by new liberative trends borne out of the rising phenomena of secularization, the "God is Dead" theology, and other questions about God and history. Jurgen Moltmann's 1967 landmark book *The Theology of Hope* set the drift in eschatology and was said to have recouped the impact of secularizing thought.[49] In gist, Moltmann emphasized that the God of revelation (in contrast to the God of epiphanies), is the God of promise and demand. The promise alludes to a world of complete healing and reconciliation that is yet to exist. Revelation then, does not impart a harmonizing message but a critique of the present order, which is seen as incongruous with the new order to come. The demand refers to the human responsibility to militate against the status quo and move toward the promised land. Creative tension thus exists between history and eschatology.[50] Two of Moltmann's main sources for the theology of hope were philosopher-scientist Teilhard de Chardin and Marxist philosopher Ernst Bloch. Teilhard combines nineteeth-century doctrines of progress and scientific evolution into a unified cosmic drama of salvation spanning from creation to the Kingdom of Heaven. A similar eschatological vision of God and humankind is implicit in Moltmann. Bloch's work represents an attempt to forges a humanistic Christian-Marxist dialogue. Rosemary Radford Ruether notes that the assimilation of Bloch's thought into Moltmann's theology of hope results in "a Christian-Marxist synthesis on the basis of which a new Christianity questions the adequacy of its recent theological heritage, and tries to recover anew the literal faith in the biblical Kingdom to come."[51]

Schillebeeckx eschatological perspective coincides with the essential trend of the theology of hope in that it rejects a flight from historical responsibility and advocates a dialectical involvement in the human struggle for justice. "It is a struggle for the redeeming of the world, not a redeeming of the soul from the world."[52] This tendency becomes more apparent as the discussion of Schillebeeckx's eschatological perspective unfolds.

As I suggested earlier, Schillebeeckx presents eschatology as the perspective from which the cogent categories of theology are played out rather than as a neat, systematic component of his theological thought. In order to achieve a clearer grasp of his eschatological perspective, I attempt to tease-out relevant thematic lines from the various topics in which they had been interwoven.

The Quest for the Elusive Humanum

Indeed, for Schillebeeckx, it is the human that is the royal road to God.

Schreiter, The Schillebeeckx Reader[53]

In the statement above, Schreiter rightly identifies Schillebeeckx's thought as human-centered, thus, the human is understood metaphorically as the paradoxical, glorified "road" or pathway to the divine. From the lens of Schillebeeckx, the eschatological question is first and foremost an anthropological question. That question, however, is premised on the hard truth that in the reality of the present, the human is not on a clear journey toward the divine; something is out-of-joint in human existence. If, indeed, the human is the royal road to God, then what is missing in the equation is a royal road map toward that direction. This prompts Schillebeeckx to query:

> What is it to be a true and good, happy and free man, in the light of the awareness of the problem which mankind has so far developed while it looks for a better future, the problem with which man had been confronted since his origins? What is livable humanity?[54]

The quest for full, authentic humanity or what is construed by Schillebeeckx as the *humanum* has always been an elusive endeavor. Because the *humanum* is constantly threatened, the journey toward "salvation" has always merited universal attention and has become the great overriding incentive of world religions and of modern history. In response to his self-query, Schillebeeckx asserts that a definitive disclosure of what constitutes the *humanum* does not exist; it is, in fact, an eschatological concept. Drawing from utopian Marxist philosopher Ernst Bloch[55] who proposes that humanity can only be defined in negative terms, Schillebeeckx asserts—"We do not have a pre-existing definition of humanity—indeed for Christians, it is not only a future, but an eschatological reality."[56] Thus, Schillebeeckx casts a suspicious eye on people, Christians included, who claim to possess a decisive road map to the *humanum*. He points out the danger of "totalitarian" claims which may be used as a power principle that falsely-names non-adherents as "enemies of true humanity":

> However, there are people who give the impression that they have a blueprint for humanity. They have a fully drawn picture of man and a specific image of coming society, an "entire doctrine of salvation," a dogmatic system which, paradoxically enough, seems to be more important than the people with whom it is really concerned. This total-itarian conception intrinsically issues in totalitarian action, which is simply a question of application, of technology and strategy. Moreover, in that case those who neither accept nor apply this concept of true humanity are obviously regarded as the enemies of true humanity. Even Christians sometimes think in this way.[57]

Schillebeeckx insists that neither can a definitive disclosure of the way to the *humanum* be found in "ordinances of creation" nor the theory of evolution. He also discounts the idea of a "universal human nature" prescribed by the principle of "natural law," a humanity that is governed by a naturally predestined goal as in the case of plant and animal life. He further rejects propositions that any kind of self-reflection can result in a crystallized general substratum of rationality for the human, independent of time and space.[58]

Moreover, Schillebeeckx criticizes historicist views of humanity which overlook the metaphysical aspect of human existence. He does not consider structuralism's analysis of constant deep structures in society as any more helpful in suggesting a template for the *humanum* than the aforementioned approaches. "These structures do not relate directly to reality, but to the *model* which man has made of it . . . Structuralism in fact excludes the human subject and therefore does not provide any criteria for human society."[59] Existentialism, on the other hand, works on the level of the symptomatic when it deals with the basic features that determine human life, for example, despair and hope, finitude and guilt, but Schillebeeckx points out that it fails to provide answers to such. Additionally, a positivistic empirical approach, while presenting some clarificatory value, proves inadequate in raising "the factical" or the operative norms derived from statistical methods, to a universal norm for moral and meaningful action.

In view of his objections to the possibility of prescribing a normative definition for full humanity, Schillebeeckx concludes that the *humanum* is not antecedently given but remains as a noble goal to be sought after and struggled for in history:

> Man's critical awareness must therefore put us on the right road . . . Man is a being caught up in history. His *nature* is itself a history, a historical event, and is not simply *given*. So something of this nature can only be seen in the course of his historical history; in the history of humanity.[60]

Anthropological Constants

As there is no predetermined, normative definition of the *humanum*, Schillebeeckx proposes a more fluid conception based on presupposed "constitutive conditions" in which humans may creatively develop. He refers to these coordinates as "anthropological constants" in a sense akin to the concept proposed by sociologists Peter Berger and Thomas Luckmann.[61] These anthropological constants are primarily derived from a critical analysis and interpretation of the contemporary human situation; they are interpreted in manifold ways depending on differing historical contexts. As such, they are "analogical" in meaning.[62] Anthropological constants provide heuristic touchstones for human values but their specific norms need to be worked out through human creative collaboration as the process of history unfolds.[63]

Schillebeeckx outlines and describes seven of these anthropological constants:

The Relationship of Human Corporeality, Nature, and the Ecological Environment. Livable humanity requires respect for certain boundaries that exist in the relationship between human beings and their own bodies—the human being, to be begin with, "is a body but also has one"[64]—and to nature. There is first the need to acknowledge that there are "limits of the mutability, conditioning, and capability" in the human in both physical and psychological aspects although empirical methods have yielded little in defining those limits. Framed by the awareness of such limits, the corporeal needs of the human "cannot be manipulated without the realization that there is an attack on human goodness, happiness and true humanity."[65] Human history has proven that the abusive overstepping of such boundaries may fuel militant collective protests. In the same vein, the limitations imposed by the natural ecological environment demands respect as it stands against the abusive human domination spawned by a technocratic value system. The same constants, Schillebeeckx qualifies, do not require advocacy for an anti-technological or anti-industrial culture, as a "rational alteration in nature" is a requisite to the creation of an appropriate human environment or a "metacosmos" in contrast to a "natural cosmos" as such. In this case, science and technology becomes a service in the quest for livable humanity.

Schillebeeckx thus concludes that Christian salvation must take into account this first anthropological constant if it is to be a truly human project. Otherwise, the concept of salvation becomes vacuous and irrelevant, and thus, Schillebeeckx muses, comparable to dreaming of "a salvation for angels, but not for men."[66]

Being Human Involves Fellow-Humans. The structure of personal identity mandates a relationship of "co-humanity" or mutuality between people. In this context, a human being, distortions to his or her identity notwithstanding, is allowed to live and share with others in a community of responsibility. Schillebeeckx uses the example of the human body, which is designed in such a way as to preclude the capability of seeing one's own face, as an analogy for the human need to be in constant relation to others. Because the human is a social being destined to encounter fellow-humans, it is incumbent upon him or her to build an inclusive society that takes responsible account for "the other":

> This lays on him the task of accepting, in intersubjectivity, the other in
> his otherness and in his freedom. It is precisely through this mutual

relationship to others that the limitation of man's own individuality is transcended in free, loving affirmation of the other, and the person himself arrives at personal identity.[67]

Schillebeeckx adds that human encounter goes beyond the "I-Thou"[68] model; a complete humanity ought to consider a third dimension, the "he" (or for that matter, the "she"). Drawing from Emmanuel Levinas, Schillebeeckx emphasizes the universality of human relationships that is posited on the "Law of the Other."[69]

The Connection with Social and Institutional Structures. The third anthropological constant underscores that the social dimension is not a mere addendum to personal identity but is constitutive of it. Although social and institutional structures are human constructs, these structures take on a life of their own and appear as natural givens so pervasive that they seem resistant to change. Schillebeeckx counters that precisely because they are created by humans, social and institutional structures are contingent; they can be changed by humans. Empirical sciences, Schillebeeckx argues, tend to overlook the contingency of such structures:

> The empirical sciences often do not take into account that this appearance of regularity depends on the hypothesis of our given (changeable) objective form of society: given the hypothesis, they rightly discover these sociological or socio-psychological regularities, but sometimes treat them as though they were a natural law or a metaphysical datum.[70]

While on one hand, social and institutional structures provide social consensus and foster values; they do not, on the other hand, possess an encompassing "general validity" because they are subject to change.

The Conditioning of People and Culture by Time and Space. Schillebeeckx asserts that humanity cannot dissociate itself from the anthropological constant of time and space, that is, the historical and geographical situation of peoples and cultures. Humanity is then confronted with the dialectical tension between nature and history within particular cultures. Schillebeeckx explains that some forms of suffering and threats to human life lie within the human sphere of control. There are, however, forms of suffering that can neither be addressed by social action nor science and technology. The creative tension gives rise to the "question of meaning" for the human:

> The historicity and thus the finality of man, which he does not know how to escape so that he can adopt a standpoint outside time, makes

him understand his humanity also as a *hermeneutical* undertaking, i.e., as a task of understanding his own situation and unmasking critically the meaningless- ness that man brings about in history.[71]

However, certain problems arise from the human hermeneutical enterprise, for instance, the emergence of historical and geographically conditioned norms that purport to be universal a priori presuppositions. Schillebeeckx singles out the problem resulting in the formation of values that command a set of norms applicable only to the affluent, highly industrialized Western cultures while marginalizing other cultures. This lopsided equation resonates with the observation of Gustavo Gutierrez when he notes how underdeveloped countries are relegated to the margins of the global socioeconomic value system— "The predominant characteristics of this complex and widespread world of the poor . . . its unimportance in the eyes of the great powers that rule today's wider world . . ."[72] Schillebeeckx thus insists that "Western men have a duty to international solidarity, above all towards poor countries (regardless of the historical question of how far they themselves are the historical cause of the poverty of these poor countries)."[73] Additionally, Schillebeeckx emphasizes the importance of a "critical remembrance of the great traditions of mankind" in the quest for norms for action toward the flourishing of full humanity.

Mutual Relationship of Theory and Practice. Human culture, as the center of gravity of the hermeneutical endeavor and the effort to introduce change in the world, requires constancy and permanence. That permanence, according to Schillebeeckx, can only be achieved in the bridging of theory and practice or human action. Unlike the animal world where permanence is based on the evolutionary law of survival of the fittest, the humanly responsible assurance of a permanent culture is predicated on respect for the dialectical relationship between theory and practice.[74]

The Religious and "Para-Religious" Consciousness of the Human. Schillebeeckx considers the "utopian" element in human consciousness as an anthropological constant. He understands the term "utopian" to mean:

> [T]he way in which a particular society has given specific form to the hermeneutical process in everyday life . . . or looks for another social system and another future in protest against the existing attribution of "meaning." These are totalitarian approaches which teach us to experience human life and society, now or in the future, as a good, meaningful, and happy totality of man—a vision and a way of life which seek to give

meaning and context to human existence in this world (even if only in the distant future).[75]

Whether of a religious or non-religious nature, these totalitarian views, or what Schillebeeckx terms as "cognitive models of reality," are expressive of what inspires human beings to live meaningful lives in the light of a promising future of wholeness yet to be realized. Schillebeeckx observes that not a few of these utopian concepts envision humans as active subjects, who, at one and the same time, contribute to the flourishing of humanity and yet are exempted from direct personal responsibility for history and its ultimate outcome. While nonreligious views may consider the utopian principle as synonymous to fate, evolution, or nature, a religious understanding attributes it to "the living God, the Lord of history." Schillebeeckx insists that regardless of the form the concept may take (barring a nihilistic perspective), it is always a form of faith, that is, in the sense that utopia cannot be demonstrated empirically or rationalized. Faith, the "ground for hope," has been proven in history as an anthropological constant and, as such, is an essential part of the authenticity and wholeness of humanity. That said, Schillebeeckx makes a clear and convincing argument for the fundamental value of religion to humanity:

> For those who believe in God, this implies that *religion* is an anthropological constant without which human salvation, redemption, and true liberation are impossible. In other words, that any liberation which by-passes a *religious redemption* is only a partial liberation, and furthermore, if it claims to be the *total* liberation of man by nature, destroys a real dimension of humanity and in the last resort uproots man instead of liberating him.[76]

Schillebeeckx describes the ultimate impact of a denial of religion in the human's total liberation as an "uprooting," a metaphorical allusion to a forcible pulling away of a plant from the very soil that provides it sustenance and life. Thus, he reemphasizes that the human religious or para-religious consciousness is not just an anthropological constant, but "a fundamental one" at that.

Irreducible Synthesis of these Six Dimensions. For Schillebeeckx, the irreducible synthesis of the six aforementioned dimensions in itself constitutes an anthropological constant because human wholeness and salvation lies in this synthesis:

> Thus *Christian salvation*, in the centuries-old biblical tradition called redemption, and meant as salvation from God *for men*, is concerned

with the whole system of co-ordinates in which man can truly be man. This salvation—the wholeness of man—cannot just be sought in one or another of these constants, say exclusively in "ecological appeals," in an exclusive "be nice to one another," in the exclusive overthrow of an economic system (whether Marxist or capitalist), or in exclusively mystical experiences: "Alleluia, he is risen!"[77]

To speak then of the primacy of "spiritual values," while this may seem valid, represents an undervaluing of the material conditions of such values thus eventually backfiring on the "spiritual." Schillebeeckx is careful to point out, however, that these anthropological constants do not present specific norms applicable as such in the here and now. As they are precisely coordinates for an anthropology, these dimensions set the course for the quest for human norms, a process that necessitates negotiation through particular cultures.

Schillebeeckx concludes that in view of the existential dialectic between the "is" and the "ought," there are bound to be human misjudgments and failures along the way that may represent an assault on these anthropological constants. Thus, the efforts to prevail over the shortcomings of humanity form part of the quest for liberation and, Schillebeeckx adds, may well be its most important form—"In that case that might then be the all-embracing 'anthropological constant' in which Jesus the Christ wanted to go before us."[78]

An Ecumene of Suffering

If a reasoned understanding of the *humanum* involves having to define it in negative terms, then there is no escaping the question of human suffering. That human history is tainted by such an excess of horrific, meaningless suffering—Auschwitz, Cambodia, Rwanda, to name a few—has always been an incomprehensible scandal that escapes adequate hermeneutical, ontological and ethical analysis. According to Schillebeeckx, human suffering cannot be objectified because in the final analysis, it is also "my suffering, my evil, and my death." Ineluctably, human history is an "ecumene of suffering":

> [T]his suffering is the alpha and omega of the whole history of mankind; it is the scarlet thread by which this historical fragment is recognizable as human history: history is "an ecumene of suffering." Because of their historical extent and their historical density, evil and suffering are the dark fleck in our history, a fleck which no one can remove by an explanation or interpretation which is able to give it an understandable place in a rational and meaningful whole.[79]

While human efforts to explain suffering and evil in theory have proven inadequate, Schillebeeckx explains that human critical rationality does allow for the remembrance of specific experiences of suffering in particular historical contexts. These "critical remembrances" rekindle practical reason and offer the potential for liberative action. Hence, various cultures in human history proffer different perspectives and theodicies that attempt to make sense out of suffering in their resolve to cope with it and eliminate its causes; none has ever been successful in giving a rational theory for suffering. Nonetheless, Schillebeeckx finds it informative to survey these critical remembrances, as the problem of suffering is "too vast for a single fragment in our history to be able to express the one liberating word about it."[80]

While it would be disproportionate to present Schillebeeckx's thorough historical survey of human suffering in any great detail, I find it relevant and informative to present some of the salient points of his discussion.

Critical Remembrance of Suffering Humanity
The ancient Greeks made sense out of human suffering from an anthropological perspective by proposing an ethical spiritual aristocracy that relativizes suffering.[81] The Romans had a more humanistic, sociopolitical explanation—suffering is one of the sacrifices that insures good harvests, paves the path to bravery, and contributes to the upbuilding of Rome. Schillebeeckx observes that in both the Greek and Roman notions of suffering, it is the voice of the aristocrats and elite philosophers that is heard, those who are actually yoked by suffering are voiceless. "The voice of the suffering slave Spartacus, who rebelled against dehumanizing forced labour, is silent."[82]

Contrastingly, Israel accords to the poor and oppressed the privileged position of interlocutor as attested by not a few references found in the Hebrew Bible. Israel accepts human suffering when it represents a redemptive suffering for others or a consequence of human sinfulness and folly, in which case, suffering is part of God's will in the sense that it opens a window to forgiveness and conversion. However, when suffering is a result of injustice and oppression and is thus unmerited and devoid of redemptive significance, the typical Jewish sensibility would protest and militate against it. In fact, Israel would not hesitate to furiously question its own God when he seems reclusive in the face of his own people's unjust suffering. This can be seen clearly in the lament of the Psalmist:

> Rouse yourself! Why do you sleep, O Lord?
> Awake, do not cast us off forever!

Why do you hide your face?
Why do you forget our own affliction and oppression?
For we sink down to the dust;
our bodies cling to the ground.
Rise up, come to our help.
Redeem us for the sake of your steadfast love.
                    Psalm 44:23–26 (NRSV)

Moreover, on the basis of the concept of a just and merciful God, the prophetic-liberating tradition of Israel offers numerous references where oppressors who cause unjust suffering are rebuked and judged severely. The book of the prophet Isaiah is a case in point:

Ah, you who make iniquitous decrees,
who write oppressive statutes,
to turn aside the needy from justice
and to rob the poor of my people of their right,
that widows may be your spoil,
and that you may make the orphans your prey!
What will you do on the day of punishment,
in the calmity that will come from far away?
To whom will you flee for help,
and where will you leave your wealth,
so as not to crouch among the prisoners
or fall among the slain?
For all this his anger has not turned away;
his hand is stretched out still.
                    Isaiah 10:1–4 (NRSV)

While noting the differences between the Greek/Roman perspectives on suffering as against that of Israel, Schillebeeckx points out that they do converge in one aspect—"good, rather than evil and suffering, has the last word."[83]

For early Christianity, the concern for suffering hinges on the collective trauma of persecution. Because the focus was on the suffering Christian, the New Testament does not preoccupy itself with the search for a solution to suffering. It does, however, offer several angles to the problem. One key principle is that the Gospel message is for the poor. This is seen clearly in the Lukan pericope where Jesus, quoting from the prophet Isaiah, delivers a programmatic discourse inaugurating his ministry:

The Spirit of the Lord is upon me,
because the Lord has anointed me;

> to bring good news to the poor,
> He has sent me to proclaim release to the captives,
> and recovery of sight to the blind,
> to let the oppressed go free,
> to proclaim the year of the Lord's favor.
>
> Luke 4:18 (NRSV)

Schillebeeckx notes that Jesus' understanding of suffering springs from his devoted, personal relationship with God, who is the God of life—"God and suffering are diametrically opposed; where God appears, evil and suffering have to yield."[84] Thus the Kingdom that Jesus proclaimed has the poor and oppressed as its first beneficiaries. In Schillebeeckx's description, the Kingdom represents "a deep community experience which has the power to heal."[85] The messianic Kingdom, therefore, is not about a breakthrough in power that will demolish the forces of evil; it is a Kingdom that works through *metanoia*. I present a more in-depth discussion of Schillebeeckx's understanding of the Kingdom or Reign of God later in this chapter. Suffice it to say that the liberation, which Jesus proclaimed, involves suffering for the cause of righteousness and justice. This constitutes the birthpangs of the new order of righteousness and peace (as found in Mark 13:8, Matthew 24:8, and Romans 8). The post-apostolic Christians understood the reality of suffering, many, following the path of persecution and martyrdom for the sake of the Gospel.

Among the early church fathers, Augustine presents a theodicy based on the theory of original sin. Man was originally created perfect but brought suffering upon himself because of his fall from grace. On the other hand, Ireneaeus likens the fall of humanity to the sin of a child insofar as it represents the realization of the mixture of good and evil as humanity moves toward salvation. Human suffering, as it were, does not mean punishment for sin. Schillebeeckx proposes that the opposing views of Augustine and Ireneaus are unified by the fundamental conviction that "it is better to have known human existence than not—this is a basic anti-dualism and a kind of delight in 'being a man,' despite everything."[86]

Schillebeeckx also investigates how Enlightenment and Marxist philosophies address the question of human suffering.

According to Schillebeeckx, the Enlightenment thinkers such as G.W. von Leibnitz, Christian Wolff, Shaftesbury, and Alexander Pope, downplayed suffering as a form of intellectual deception brought about by the human senses. The universal view of the Enlightenment considers evil the result of a contingent, superficial view of things; in the larger panoramic context of history, suffering is, in fact, good. Pope thus writes, "All partial evil, universal good . . . One truth is clear: whatever *is*, is *right*."[87] Reconciliation is already antecedently given in the *harmonia praestabilita* and *metanoia* therefore consists of a turning away from myopic thinking and the liberating realization of this divine offer. Schillebeeckx argues that "The men of the Enlightenment in fact wanted to justify God by means of human reason, which now itself called God to answer for his apparently bad direction of the world and history."[88]

The philosophy of Marx views the problem of human suffering from the vantage point of an economic theory. This approach presents the argument that social suffering is the result of an economic system that thrives on the laws of profit and competition. The conditions of production relegate workers to the position of mere wage-earners who have no claim to capital. The ground principle at work here results in the alienation of the workers—"alienated from their work and themselves, purely reified ingredients in an economic process which, moreover, does not belong to them and lies outside their control."[89] Competition between humans in a seeming reprise of the law of the jungle, is then presented as the viable option for survival. Marx was convinced that the structural causes of suffering could be dealt with and removed. Through a dialectical, historical process of becoming, nothing less than a revolution can bring about a fundamental change in the oppressive socioeconomic order. Marx believed that this is the necessary pathway toward the alleviation of human suffering. Because, ultimately, the revolutionary utopian future can only emerge through class struggle, it involves a form of suffering for a good cause. As for religion, Marx sees it as a protest against human misery albeit insufficiently understood. It represents a passive reflection of society's economic conflicts. To the degree that religion is ignorant of its own nature, it also remains ignorant of the human suffering that serves as the base of its own existence. Thus, Marx considers religion as the opium of the people. Schillebeeckx makes clear, however, that in contrast to other Marxists, Marx himself does not blame religion for all alienation but sees it as a victim of social and economic alienation "which precisely in being a victim then keeps this economic alienation firmly in the saddle."[90] As such, Marx only speaks about human liberation and self-realization through labor.

From the critical optic provided by the synthesis of Schillebeeckx's proposed anthropological constants, this perspective does not paint an acceptable, holistic understanding of the human whose identity is here reduced to nothing more than labor and the means of production.

God Does Not Will Human Suffering

That the history of humanity is a scandal-provoking ecumene of suffering is an undeniable reality. Schillebeeckx insists, however, that human suffering cannot be viewed as a problem for theoretical comprehension—it is a mystery. The question then of why there is an atrocious overspill of human suffering is an unanswerable question. Moreover, the unavoidable problem of a God who is seemingly impassive amid the flood of human suffering is unjustifiable. If the critical and creative force of religion can be accepted—that God is pure positivity and infinitely good—then suffering and annihilation cannot be attributed to the divine will. Schillebeeckx argues that the primitive idea of a God who metes out life and death at will is an anthropocentric conception in which God's freedom is defined as "a finite freedom to decide between good and evil."[91] Human suffering does not square with a God who is mindful of humanity. That said, Schillebeeckx recognizes an ensuing problem—the search for a non-dualistic ground for suffering and evil. The Christian message offers a way to protect vulnerable humanity as it were, from accusation and indictment:

> It is well worth remembering that faith does not disqualify human reason and its liberating practice in order to claim honour of being able to offer a correct solution once reason has conceded defeat. For religious belief does not blame man for his ultimate theoretical impotence and his practical failure in the face of evil and suffering. This bitter insight, this "accusation," stems from our own human experience and critical reason. By contrast, religious belief seeks to rescue us from this fatal experience and give[s] our action new meaning by breaking its impotence in the light of a new possibility *from* God: Thanks to the proclamatory reminiscence of Jesus as the story of the crucified man who is now alive, through whom a future is given to those who have come to grief in history, even those who (for the moment) are victors at the expense of the defeated.[92]

While the mystery of human suffering remains unanswered, the Christian message does present the subversive memory of Jesus as the hopeful promise that neither suffering nor evil is the last word. Schillebeeckx, however, rejects two tendencies that attempt to explain the Jesus story. First is the argument that God himself decreed the death of Jesus as a mandatory propitiation for the sinful history of humankind. Describing this explanation as blasphemous, Schillebeeckx notes that none of the authentic branches of the Christian tradition deem this "sadistic mysticism of suffering" acceptable. The other objectionable tendency is the "eternalizing" of suffering in God; the argument that ultimately, God accords glory and splendour to suffering. Epitomized by the soteriology of Jurgen Moltmann, this view proposes that God ostracized Jesus as a sacrifice for the sins of humanity. Schillebeeckx recognizes the schizophrenic confusion this argument presents despite its correct insight of a God who suffers with humanity. "The difficulty in this conception is that it ascribes to God what has in fact been done to Jesus by the history of injustice."[93]

Schillebeeckx turns to Thomas Aquinas for a reasonable perspective that does not force an explanation for the incomprehensible. Schillebeeckx notes Aquinas's two-pronged approach to theodicy:

On the one hand as a theologian he dares to write: "The first cause of the lack of grace lies in us;" and on the other, as a philosopher: "Although God is the creative cause of our (human) will—i.e. the one who calls up out of nothing—this will has this 'being from nothing' from no other than itself; and precisely for that reason the defects of the will which follow from a creaturely deficiency may be carried back to a higher cause." As soon as there are *creatures*, there is the *possibility* (not the necessity) of a negative and original *initiative of finitude*, if I can put it that way.[94]

Thus, Schillebeeckx uses the concept of "first causality" in Aquinas's *Summa Theologiae* to posit the center of gravity of evil and suffering in creaturely finitude. Aquinas, however, stops short of naming human finitude as such as the ground of evil emphasizing instead the "possibility" of sin and human disobedience. Since humans were created *ex nihilo*, our flawed will cannot be ascribed to the Creator. God is the "creative cause" not of evil and suffering but of the finite human will. To confront arguments that impute God for the problem of evil and suffering, Schillebeeckx proposes the idea of the "defenceless superior power of God":

To be created is, on the one hand, to be taken up as a creature into God's absolute free and saving nearness, but on the other hand, seen from God's side, it is a sort of "divine yielding," giving room to the other.[95]

Schillebeeckx puts forward the paradoxical notion that "God wills to be our God in our finitude."[96] The divine will does not assign suffering upon humans. On the contrary, God resists evil and suffering via his immanence, that is, his active presence from within creation. God's opposition to suffering is expressed through human agents who actively work for human emancipation in history.

Thus, the ground of existence for human suffering cannot be identified; what is clear in Schillebeeckx's view is that the God who is mindful of humanity stands opposed to it.

Christian Salvation and Sociopolitical Liberation

In the light of the horrific reality of an ecumene of suffering, the dialectical relationship between the Christian concept of salvation and sociopolitical liberation becomes pivotal for the expression of God's abiding concern for wounded humanity. Schillebeeckx consistently maintains that Christian salvation, as communicated by Jesus the Christ and by his praxis of God's eschatological Reign, has serious and far-reaching sociopolitical implications.

As such, a privatized notion of salvation characterized by a personal "flight to inwardness" confines the liberative currents of God's reign to the level of the personal. Soteriologies that follow this trend of thought are "vertical soteriologies,"[97] that is, they propose a fideistic view of salvation as a "disembodied and dislocated interiority"[98] resulting in a shirking of historical responsibilities. The world is under the power of demonic powers so salvation can only be viewed as a metaphysical, antisocial journey; an ascent of the soul toward a realm of purity beyond the system, hence, the social impulse of detachment and removal from the present system.[99] Schillebeeckx astutely calls this tendency a "flight into the social status quo"[100] in which case social structures remain unexamined, unquestioned, and are perceived as belonging to the natural order of things. Through passivity and acquiescence, vertical soteriologies ultimately contribute to the perpetuation of disordered sociopolitical relations and oppression. Schillebeeckx, however, rejects the argument that interpersonal and sociopolitical forms of love necessarily have to stand in polarity with each other:

> For Christians, affirmation of another's personhood, readiness to identify oneself with another and affirm his own subjectivity, is from the start a readiness to make the economic, political and social world habitable for humanity.[101]

Schillebeeckx thus bridges interpersonal liberation as potential openness to sociopolitical liberation.

On the other hand, there are "horizontal and futurist soteriologies" that swing to the opposite extreme. Strongly social and outwardly directed, such soteriologies understand salvation completely in terms of sociopolitical change. Salvation is realized when the present corrupt system is overthrown and a new order representing its polar opposite stands in its stead. Horizontal and futurist soteriologies are characterized as "instrumental" insofar as they absolutize a contingent sociopolitical movement as the definitive way to historical salvation.[102] This tendency represents "a social religion of oppressed people"[103] borne out of the cruel context of injustice and a sense of powerlessness under the present situation. The potential danger here lies in the legitimation and sacralization of various forms of systematic violence as a way toward normative ideals that work only to benefit dominant interests.[104]

A third type, "religious and political soteriologies" emphasize the progressive and political meaning of the religious. These soteriologies avoid both the fideistic withdrawal into the personal and the instrumental totalization of the political. This third way is thus characterized as "interactive" between religious and political; its project being to transform the political.[105] This has been the consistent focus and concern of the soteriology of Schillebeeckx as it is developed in his major body of work, the trilogy consisting of *Jesus: An Experiment in Christology, Christ: The Experience of Jesus as Lord*, and *Church: The Human Story of God*. The original Dutch title of the second volume clearly evinces his interactive soteriology—*Gerechtigheid en Liefde: Genade en bevrijding*, which translates as "Justice and Love: Grace and Liberation."[106] This is substantiated in Part Four of the book where Schillebeeckx sets the experience and interpretation of Christian salvation against the contemporary backdrop of human suffering.[107]

The interactive character of Schillebeeckx's thought is also evidenced in his acknowledgment of the need to develop a Western form of liberation theology that could serve as a dialogue partner to its seminal Third World counterpart.[108] His efforts to actualize a decisively liberationist soteriology is a movement toward that direction. Akin to the liberation theologians, Schillebeeckx seeks to locate historically the content of faith including the content that had otherwise been deemed transcendental; a historicization of salvation.[109]

Schillebeeckx's keen sensitivity over the plight of Third World suffering is lucidly expressed in the book *Church*. For Schillebeeckx, the continuing existence and proliferation of "non-persons," most ironically, in countries with a Christian colonial history, is an inconceivable scandal:

There is good reason for the statements in the EATWOT conferences of Third World theologians that "the believing but exploited people" in the Third World contrast with "the secularized and exploitative West."

> The two problems are interconnected and cannot be separated. The existence of the "non-person," the poor and oppressed, in a subcontinent like Latin America or a country like South Africa, lands which have been dominated by Christians for centuries, is a scandal for any belief in God. For many people it makes belief in God look incredible. Therefore in the West we can no longer talk of God without relating our thought about God to the massive suffering of men and women elsewhere and anonymously among us.[110]

Thus, in a self-reflexive query, Schillebeeckx wrestles with the hard, dialectical reality of an egocentric, affluent Western world afloat in a sea of massive global inequality and poverty:

> Therefore, for example in Latin America and Asia, liberation theology, despite or more precisely in its geographical contextuality, is a question of universal significance. Can there be authentic meaning in my history if the history of more than half the human race is meaningless and absurd? Is that not a threadbare regional, cynical egoism? That is where the "crisis of meaning" lies today. It is not just a problem for the poor but also for the rich: a universal problem. The Christian option for the poor, taking their side, is therefore a contextual expression of universal love for men and women.[111]

Here, Schillebeeckx emphasizes the significance of theologies of liberation in the universal search for the *humanum*. This is made even more clear by his use of the phrase "Christian option for the poor," which is derived from the concept of a "preferential option for the poor," a programme of engagement in the struggle for social justice rooted in the 1968 Medellin General Conference of Latin American Bishops and coined ten years after in the documents of the 1978 Puebla General Conference.[112] The concept springs from the eschatological principle of the Kingdom of God, which has the poor and oppressed as its first beneficiaries. A more detailed discussion on this partisan concern for the oppressed and marginalized as it relates to the concept of the Kingdom of God follows this section. Suffice it to say that the preferential option for the poor is a succinct rendering of the uncompromising concern and care of Jesus for the downtrodden as worked out in the context of Latin American Liberation Theology.[113] A preferential option for the poor is definitely not an option adopted by the rich and powerful, otherwise, there would be no poor in the world. That said, the concept also takes on a prescriptive, and not just a descriptive sense. Schillebeeckx's point is straightforward in this— the Christian option for the poor is a forceful moral imperative meant primarily for the ears of the rich and powerful in the West. He argues that the only meaningful salvation for the contemporary human situation is one that considers the "existential context of oppression and liberation."[114] For Schillebeeckx, soteriologies that conveniently overlook the ecumene of suffering are, quite plainly, implausible and irrelevant.

At this juncture, the discussion necessarily angles to the centrality of the concept of the Reign of God in Schillebeeckx's eschatological perspective. This has profound soteriological implications for the peoples of the Third World who bear the cross of abject poverty and cultural marginalization on a daily basis. As Jon Sobrino asserts, "The Third World continues to stand in urgent need of liberation, and the best theological way to deal with liberation continues to be to do so in terms of the Reign of God."[115]

The Praxis of the Reign of God

At the heart of Jesus' message is *Basileia tou Theou*, the inbreaking of a new order based on God's love, graciousness, and justice, close at hand but not yet consummated:

> And for Jesus this means the proximity of God's unconditional will to salvation, of reconciling clemency and sufficing graciousness, and along with them opposition to all forms of evil: suffering and sin . . . It does not denote some area of sovereignty above and beyond this world, where God is supposed to reside and to reign. What Jesus intends by it is a process, a course of events, whereby God begins to govern or to act as king or Lord, an action, therefore, by which God manifests his being-God in the world of men.[116]

Schillebeeckx notes that references to this dynamic symbol can be found in no less than five complexes of tradition—the communities represented by the three synoptic gospels Mark, Matthew, and Luke; the Q community; and the epistles of the New Testament.[117] Two aspects—the Kingdom of God and the Reign of God—converge in the unifying concept of *Basileia tou Theou*. The Kingdom of God alludes more to the eschatological "final good," the vision of a definitive eco—human salvation and liberation to which God's saving activity is directed—"Your Kingdom come. Your will be done on earth as it is in heaven." (Matthew 6:10 NRSV) "That this kingdom comes," Schillebeeckx explains, "means that God looks to us men and women to make his ruling 'operational' in our world."[118] The Reign of God as referred to in the Marcan and Lucan gospels represents "the dynamic, here-and-now character of God's exercise of control" and is invoked by historical signs of justice, solidarity, freedom, and a preferential option for the poor and defenseless. As such, the Reign of God affirms and strengthens the idea that *Basileia tou Theou* is "a theological and yet also anthropological reality grounded in human experience."[119] While Jesus declares that the Reign of God is close at hand, he does not define exactly what it is. Nonetheless, Schillebeeckx maintains that the key to understanding the Reign of God lies in the life praxis of Jesus:

> God's lordship, as Jesus understands it, expresses the relation between God and man, in the sense that "we are each other's happiness." Ultimately, it is the ancient covenant of love, fellowship with God, in which God nevertheless remains the sovereign partner. Thus anyone having anything to do with Jesus is confronted by the God of Jesus. The one thing that Jesus is getting at is that this God is a "God of human kind". . . His very life is given decisive shape by his expectation of the kingdom of God in surrender to God's lordship. Jesus is gripped by that lordship, is compelled by it, so that his whole life is on the one hand a "celebration" of that lordship and on the other it gives a lead in orthopraxis, the right conduct of the kingdom of God. It is what he lived for and what he died for: God's concern as man's concern.[120]

It is clear that "Jesus is about God's business," that is, the universal salvation of humanity. At the very core, the message of the Reign of God in Jesus' life praxis is this—without reservation, the sovereign love and graciousness of God insists on the flourishing of life even though the empirical experience warrants suffering and death. Hence, the critical locus of his ministry naturally gravitates to the liberation of marginalized and oppressed humanity. Jesus comes to help the sick and needy, not the healthy and affluent. In Luke 14:1–5, Jesus insists on healing an epileptic even on a sabbath day and poses a moral question to the disapproving pharisees who are more concerned about the legality of the act rather than the alleviation of the suffering of a fellow human being, "If one of you has a child or an ox that has fallen into a well, will you not pull it out on a sabbath day?"

Schillebeeckx, however, issues a caveat that while the emphasis of Jesus' message is an *evangelion*, or "heartening news"(in contrast to John the Baptist's one-sided proclamation of God's approaching judgment) he also preaches that God will stand in judgment of history—of humanity, culture, and society. Schillebeeckx insightfully warns that the God of Jesus is "not a kindly granddad, disposed to be not so very critical."[121] To be sure, Jesus' message is positively orientated. The "anti-" applies only to everything that negates the message of God's Reign. Still, Jesus does not condemn anyone, "his concern is with the potential for the future, in the 'now' of the *metanoia*."[122] Sobrino echoes the same understanding when he writes about Jesus' denunciation of forces in society that serve to perpetuate the "anti-Reign"—"The purpose was to expose the causes of the anti-Reign and transform it into the Reign, although on this point Jesus offers no technical means but only calls for conversion."[123] The Reign of God is neither a confirmation of the present reality nor its history; it represents a judgment of that reality with the positive vision of re-creating it.[124]

Thus, Jesus bridges the eschatological inbreaking of the Kingdom of God and the *metanoia* brought about by the praxis of the Reign of God.

To further appreciate the content of the Reign of God, it is necessary to discuss Schillebeeckx's proposal that Jesus' actual conduct and ministry at the service of God's lordship sheds light on what the Reign concretely means. I do not propose to offer here a thorough exploration of Christology as found in Schillebeeckx's monumental *Jesus: An Experiment in Christology*. Instead, I use the heuristic guideposts set by Schillebeeckx's eschatological perspective to clarify the identity of Jesus in relation to the eschatological concept of the Kingdom of God and to explore how his activities contribute to the clarification of the nature of the Reign.

What Jesus Proclaimed

Jesus lived in a storytelling culture where the communication of what is truly meaningful in life is funneled through stories and parables. According to Schillebeeckx, it is difficult for people who live in the present—in a culture that is largely shaped by historical sciences—to negotiate through an ancient narrative culture. Amazed at some disastrously absurd notion derived from the indiscriminate reading of the bible stories solely through modern-day glasses, he exclaims— "Obviously we have lost all our 'narrative innocence'!" For Schillebeeckx, the hermeneutical challenge in the struggle to understand the New Testament lies in a systematic balancing out of a narrative innocence with historical disciplines. Drawing from the hermeneutics of Paul Ricoeur, Schillebeeckx sees the exigency of a second primitive stage, a "second narrative innocence."[125] It is illuminating to quote Ricoeur at this point:

> Does that mean that we could go back to a primitive naïveté? Not at all. In every way, something has been lost, irremediably lost: immediacy of belief. But if we can no longer live the great symbolisms of the sacred in accordance with the original belief in them, we can, we modern men, aim at a second naïveté in and through criticism. In short, it is by interpreting that we can hear again . . . This second naïveté aims to be the postcritical equivalent of the precritical hierophany.[126]

Thus, in attempting to grasp the message of the gospel text, Schillebeeckx stresses the need to be conscious of the ancient narrative culture as the well from which to draw the first basis of understanding. The historical mediation follows as part of the constituent whole.

As much as they are constitutive of an understanding of the praxis of the Reign of God, the parables and beatitudes of Jesus discussed from the optic of Schillebeeckx are given focus in the next section.

Jesus' Parables

Schillebeeckx begins his discussion on Jesus' parables by first establishing one point—"Jesus is a parable." Quite naturally, the explanation for this statement comes from the descriptive footprint of the very term "parable". Schillebeeckx offers some operational definitions:[127]

- A parable is a story that turns around a "scandalizing" center, at any rate a core paradox or novelty.
- A parable often stands things on their head; it is meant to break through our conditional thinking and being.
- A parable is meant to start the listener thinking by means of a built-in element of the "surprising" and the "alienating" in a common everyday event.

The "existential earnestness" of the storytelling enshrined in the parable works in quickening a person to take inventory of his or her own life and view it from a different angle, a different perspective, for once. Because they challenge conventional ways of thinking and behaving, parables offer the possibility of renewal in a person's life and in the life of society. Schillebeeckx points out that save for three parables, namely, The Rich Fool, Lazarus, and, The Pharisee and the Publican, all of Jesus' parables are down-to-earth; as it were, God does not necessarily affix his explicit "signature" to the story. Nonetheless, the message undeniably proclaims the salvific vision of God's Kingdom:

> God does not come into it, directly; and yet anyone who attends to them knows that through these stories he is confronted with God's saving activity in Jesus; this is how God acts, and it is to be seen in the actions of Jesus himself, if, at any rate, you see with a heart ready to be transformed.[128]

The message of the parables, however, is open-ended as it can only find completion if and when the hearers issue a positive response to it and thus, become open to *metanoia*:

> The parable remains "suspended," therefore, so long as the listener has not decided for or against the new possibilities for living opened up in it—and eventually decides for or against Jesus of Nazareth.[129]

The explanation as to why Schillebeeckx asserts that Jesus is a parable becomes clear. Parables mirror Jesus' person and what his life, ministry, and conduct stand for; his witness offers the best explanation for parables. Ultimately, the central issue of parables is Jesus himself:

> Jesus and his world in the end become the issue in the parables, which open up a new world, in which only grace and love can dwell, and which places under judgement and seeks to change this history of ours, the course of human suffering that is the outcome of our shortsighted actions.[130]

In Schillebeeckx's survey of the authentic eschatological parables of Jesus, he notes that all of them center on the theme of the Kingdom of God and its conjoined praxical expression in the Reign. To wit:

- In Jesus, the Kingdom of God is at hand (Mark 1:15) and already at work in the present (Luke 11:20)
- Yet its coming is still anticipated (Matthew 6:10, Luke 11:3), the timing unknown (Mark 13:32) and cannot be calculated beforehand (Luke 17:20–21)
- Salvation will come to the watchful, including repentant sinners (Luke 18:9–14) and those who consider themselves unworthy (Matthew 8:8–9)
- Judgement is reserved for those who take no heed and and refuse to take action (Matthew 7:24–27).

The inextricable link between the Reign of God and orthopraxis is brought to sharper focus in the Parable of the Talents (Matthew 25:14–30, Luke 19:12–27). Here, the emphasis is on the here-and-now character of the praxis of the Reign, which demands a radical and immediate reordering of the accustomed way of living. The servant who merely buries the talent given to him is reproached not so much because he is no risk-taker as the other two are but because "he never seized even the one opportunity that was altogether free of risk, and had therefore been really careless with what had been entrusted to him." Schillebeeckx reiterates, "God's lordship demands a corresponding resort to action."[131]

It is plain and unmistakable that Jesus cannot just be counted among the anonymous sages of his time who go about telling popular folklore. Although elements reflecting folk-wisdom may have factored into Jesus' parables, Schillebeeckx explains that they assume a new focus, a new appropriated sense that only serve to express the central message of God's lordship.

Insofar as Jesus' parables consistently function within the framework of the Reign of God, they can only be correctly understood in consideration of this context.

Jesus' Beatitudes

Schillebeeckx traces the idea of blessing for the poor to the days of the Jewish settlement in the land of Canaan when various forms of inequalities were borne out of the efforts of the farming population to amass property. Social laws were set in place to keep this trend in check, among them, the promulgation of the sabbatical year, a law requiring the cancellation of all debts and the liberation of slaves every seventh year. Through this radical law, it was hoped that the equality originally attributed to God's covenant with Israel could be restored in some measure (Exodus 21:2–6, 23:10–11; Leviticus 25:1–7, 18–22; Deuteronomy 15). The advent of the monarchy, however, ushered-in the return of social disparities and this fueled the strident prophetic critique of society's powerholders which was premised on the kingship of the God of justice. The rampant corruption and misuse of power among the ranks of the aristocracy at the expense of the common people who were enslaved by debt was an affront to God. Against the powers that be, Israel's poor were those who had no clear future because justice was beyond their reach. Their only hope rested in the God who is the Righteous One. The poor during Jesus' time were the offshoots of generations of injustice in Israel.

The beatitudes follow the Old Testament genre of a prophetic eschatological proclamation. "This central core of the complex of beatitudes is set in the perspective of the eschatological coming of God's rule and the kingdom of God."[132] There are two versions presented in the New Testament, the Lucan "Sermon on the Plain" (Luke 6:20–26) and the Matthean "Sermon on the Mount" (Matthew 5:3–5). Organized in a pattern of "blessings," the beatitudes ostensibly earmark them for the edge of humanity, not the center. It will be the underside of society—the poor, the hungry, the sorrowful outcast—who will be blessed in the eschatological Kingdom. Collectively, they are the very people who have no position in society; the non-persons who are nameless, faceless, and voiceless. They will be blessed not because suffering had made them more virtuous, but because the realization of the Reign of God will change their situation of oppression:

> Blessed are you who are poor,
> for yours is the kingdom of God.
> Blessed are you who are hungry now,
> for you will be filled.
> Blessed are you weep now,
> for you will laugh.
> > Luke 6:20–21 (NRSV)

Schillebeeckx points out that the first blessing is in the present tense—"the kingdom of God is yours"—while the two that follow are in the future tense. The inbreaking Kingdom exists in dialectical tension; it is already here but the harvesting of its fruits—the joy and satisfaction—only finds completion in the future.

Conspicuously, antithetical "woes" immediately follow the blessings in the Lucan version, a feature absent in Matthew.

> Woe to you who are rich,
> for you have received your consolation.
> Woe to you who are full now,
> for you will be hungry.
> Woe to you who are laughing now,
> for you will mourn and weep.
> > Luke 20: 24–25 (NRSV)

According to Schillebeeckx, what resonates here is the earlier Jewish "apocalyptic principle of a reversal of values." He downplays these apocalyptic curses as secondary texts:

> Without having before one the Jewish and late Jewish background to this noble utterance of benediction, these are indeed disconcerting texts which we moderns feel to have even a reactionary ring about

them: the poor are having a bad time of it now but—just wait a bit—in the hereafter they are to be the privileged ones. Apocalyptic circles even added: and then they will have a good laugh at the deposed and impoverished rich. Is this the Jesus of Nazareth? Absolutely not.[133]

The emphasis of Jesus' message is profoundly positive, it is about the sovereignty of the God of love and utter graciousness, not about the prospects of the poor to get even. In Schillebeeckx's view, the Reign of God does not represent a direct overturning of existing societal structures but an eschatological one:

> Indeed Jesus did not preach social revolution, although his eschatological message brings the whole pain-ridden history of mankind radically under God's critical judgement and so calls for an about-turn . . . What they quite unmistakably enshrine is a spiritual affirmation of the ultimate power of powerlessness—of a belief that however much improving the world by our human resources is necessary (that is to make God's explicit "no" to suffering in history), at the deepest level there is a suffering, an impotence which no human being can remove and from which we can be liberated only by virtue of the fact that "God will rule" for the final good of all men.[134]

Thus, God's Reign is not about a social revolution, but an eschatological revolution.[135]

> From Jesus' eschatological message we hear only God's radical 'no' to all forms of evil, all forms of poverty and hunger that leads to tears. That is Jesus' message; and it has enormous consequences. That in it God is also refusing to acknowledge the strength of evil and so with his own being as God is standing surety for the defeat of evil in all its forms can in no way be turned to reactionary or conservative ends. Jesus gives us on God's behalf only the message that God stands surety for us. And therefore the poor, the suffering and the deprived do indeed have grounds for positive hope.[136]

Popular Jewish tradition expected the coming of the "eschatological prophet" who would bring glad tidings to the poor. Schillebeeckx emphasizes that Jesus enters the scene not as a kingly Davidic prophet but as the eschatological prophet who is present here and now. In the beatitudes, Jesus restores hope to the disinherited by making them aware that God is on their side and disapproves of their situation of suffering. Jesus, the eschatological prophet, assures them that the lasting joy and fulfillment of the inbreaking Kingdom is primarily reserved for them and that the Reign of God begins now. Because the poor now have a future, the good news is indeed, "blessed are you who are poor."

Jesus' Saving Activities
Jesus did not passively await for the inbreaking of the Kingdom of God, his proclamation was essentially accompanied by activities in the service of the Reign. Bringing liberation to people and making them glad, Jesus' saving activities represent God's offer of salvation, an invitation in faith into companionship with God. The active ministry of Jesus contributes to a determination of the nature of the Reign by making its formulation more concrete and visible.

Jesus' Miracles
Schillebeeckx explains that the miracle stories have their origins in the collective memory of ordinary country folk of Galilee who were marginalized in more ways than one:

> In the miracle tradition, we are confronted with a memory of Jesus of Nazareth as he comes across more especially to the ordinary country folk of Galilee, neglected as they were by all religious movements and sectional interests . . . In that kind of setting the veneration felt for one who has done so much good naturally expands into a certain legend-making process in which, since power is put to the service of being and doing good, as with Jesus, it is the power that in particular affects the popular imagination.[137]

Thus, miracles had a special resonance to those who were in most need of salvation in their daily lives.

Only two miracles are admitted by the reserved Q tradition—the exorcism found in Luke 11:14–23 and the healing found in Luke 7:1–10—and these serve as the points for analysis in Schillebeeckx's discussion. Schillebeeckx observes that the distinctive feature of the Q accounts is that they do not emphasize the miracles themselves but the great power behind them. The central focus then is on God's saving activity in Jesus. In the miracle of exorcism, Jesus expels a demon of muteness from an afflicted man and he begins to speak again. Late Jewish demonology attributes sickness to demon possession so it was not particularly phenomenal that Jesus performed this miracle; exorcism was a normal part of the cultural and religious landscape. The Q tradition gives the miracle a different focus—Jesus is the eschatological prophet and the miracle is a sign that the Reign of God is dawning. The second miracle story speaks of the healing of a centurion's servant. Schillebeeckx notes that the miracle is set at a low key because Jesus has no contact with the sick. In Jesus' cultural context, Jews do not enter the homes of pagans (Luke 7:6) so the healing occurs at a distance; it is a "remote" healing. Here, the Q source is not aiming at sensationalizing the miracle itself. The crux of the story is that Jesus' word has complete authority and is likened to the commanding jurisdiction of the centurion over his troops. In turn, the centurion acts by his faith on the power of Jesus' word. The emphasis of the Q source is soteriological—God saves through Jesus.

Jesus performs the miracles of the eshchatological prophet. Thus, his miracles serve as signs of the Reign of God. Sobrino puts it lucidly, "As signs of the Reign, the miracles are before all else salvation—beneficent realities, liberative realities in the presence of oppression."[138]

Moreover, Schillebeeckx maintains that where Jesus is asked to perform a circus-type spectacle to prove that his prophetic ministry indeed has heaven's endorsement and thus elicit the belief of the people, he plainly refuses to do so. "Jesus does not seek to legitimize his mission and ministry, in whatever he does, including his miracles, he is simply himself."[139] Jesus and his ministry must be accepted on the basis of trust:

> Here salvation is given to people who in their sense of its opposite, of misery and evil, fulfill the only proper condition for eventually being able to receive the gospel as glad tidings. Jesus' being thronged by the people is like the helpless cry of mankind's ongoing calamity. At the same time it represents the hope which, thanks to Jesus, now enters into that sad history; someone who goes about doing nothing but good; a man in whom there is no evil.[140]

The Marcan gospel is replete with references that Jesus' miracles are consistently motivated by his passionate concern for the liberation of the needy (Mark 1:41, 5:19, 6:34, 8:2, 9:22, 10:47–48). In Jesus, the eschatological prophet, God draws near to society's weakest links who are in pain and suffering.

Jesus' Fellowship-Meals

Aside from performing mighty acts attributed to the ministry of the eschatological prophet, Jesus also shared meals with people in his desire to free them and give them a new lease at making a joyful commitment to the living God. Jesus expands his table fellowship with the disciples so as to include outcasts, corrupt tax-collectors, and various "sinners." This facet of Jesus' life, Schillebeeckx suggests, can be understood by taking a closer look at the pericope in the Marcan gospel concerning the dispute over the disciples' non-fasting in the presence of the living Jesus (Mark 2:18–22).

In the Matthean gospel, Jesus and his disciples had been accused of being drunkards and gluttons, and of being transgressors of the law by socializing with tax collectors and sinners (Matthew 11:16–18). In response to these charges, Jesus assails the way in which the law of God had been turned into a heavy, punitive yoke on the shoulders of ordinary people, rather than used as a window to God's mercy in the face of life's difficulties. Schillebeeckx maintains, "It is evident from this that Jesus never takes abstractions or general norms as a basis for living: always he sees a man in his most concrete situation."[141]

Against this backdrop, God's compassionate dealing with humanity is brought to focus in Mark. Here, Jesus' presence in festive celebration and fellowship precludes fasting and mourning. Schillebeeckx notes the double-edged impact of this non-fasting: it is a scandal to those who refuse to see Jesus as a parable of God's love toward humanity; it means joy and freedom to those who see God's salvation in Jesus' living presence:

> Indeed, by way of a minor, as it were, marginal incident in the life of Jesus—the fact that his disciples did not fast—Mark manages to portray the new thing that has been manifested in Jesus, in masterly fashion at once true to Jesus and yet extremely personal. Mark's message is that with Jesus a radically new change has entered our history, a stumbling block to the man scandalized by him, but the salvation of anyone who commits himself to trust in the mystery of this person, Jesus.[142]

Jesus' fellowship-meals with sinners is a manifestation of his role as the eschatological messenger, the one who proclaims the inbreaking Kingdom and invites outcasts and sinners to share in the great eschatological feast with God. The table fellowship Jesus offers is inclusive, it extends beyond class boundaries set by the official, iron-handed interpretations of the Jewish law:

> The *sadikim* or righteous are by no means excluded from the divine invitation brought by the eschatological messenger; what Jesus means is to include those who are excluded by the Pharisees because of the (ritual) cleanness-regulations (no intercourse with sinners). From the viewpoint of official Judaic piety Jesus has "de-classed" himself by eating with tax-collectors. His self-defense is that it is precisely to sinners, to those beyond the pale, that the invitation to communication must be carried

out: the sinners must be invited to God's table and his fellowship with human beings, in order to bring them out of their isolation.[143]

Additionally, Schillebeeckx notes that references to Jesus' power to forgive sins (Luke 7:36–50, Mark 2:10) are translations into faith language of actual occurrences when Jesus attended gatherings thrown by people who were socially isolated because they were ritually unclean sinners.

Another eschatologically significant aspect of Jesus' fellowship-meals is made apparent during the instances when he serves as host in the meal gatherings. While Jesus was an itinerant preacher who didn't even have a stone on which to lay his head (Matthew 8:20, Luke 9:58) and who could only play host under an open sky, there was always more than enough to eat in the fellowship meals he hosted. The message of abundance can be seen evidently in the gospel accounts of the "multiplication of the loaves" (Mark 6:34–44, 8:1–9; Matthew 14:14–21, 15:32–38, 16:5–12; Luke 9:11b–17, John 6:1–5). From an eschatological standpoint, these miracle stories point to the here-and-now affirmation of the wonderful abundance the inbreaking Reign of God promises to bring.

Furthermore, the post-easter meal accounts (Luke 24:28–31, John 21:12–13) reveal the eschatological meaning of Jesus' fellowship-meals. Here, Jesus restores in the present the communion he had with his disciples prior to his death. Schillebeeckx postulates that as a fundamental trait of the historical Jesus, the fellowship-meal represents "enacted prophecy." In the fellowship-meal, Jesus, the eschatological prophet, offers a foretaste of "final good" or eschatological salvation here and now.[144]

Eschatological Salvation

It is clear that the critical principle of the Reign of God links salvation with liberation. To recall, Schillebeeckx's emphasizes that the only meaningful salvation for the contemporary human situation is one that considers the "existential context of oppression and liberation."[145] Sociopolitical liberations and emancipative struggles, however, remain incomplete and transitory given the reality of a constantly shifting landscape of suffering related to human finitude. Schillebeeckx argues that within the realm of human existence, there is a type of suffering that stays below the radar of sociopolitical movements:

> [A]lienation in human life cannot be completely overcome either personally or socially; liberated freedom or salvation transcends person or

society. There is human suffering which does not allow itself to be stilled with social and political measures; people can still perish from loneliness in the best social structures; even optimal structures do not automatically make men good, mature human beings; nature has to be humanized, but to a large extent and inescapably it remains alien to man (one has to think of death); and finally, there is our inalienable finitude, which can be the origin of anxiety as well as trust in God.[146]

Here, Schillebeeckx clarifies that notwithstanding the fact that the active pursuit of liberation and justice from the perspective of eschatological salvation carries universal significance, it does not precipitate a complete and definitive salvation for humanity. Eschatological salvation, the consummated search for "final good," is not forthcoming in history through the sheer accumulative total of liberative praxis:

> In contemporary situations, the impossibility of a total, universal and final liberation through emancipation is the context in which the question of the ultimate meaning of human life can be put. Thus a fundamental question mark is set against the project of emancipation, a question mark which goes with the dynamics of any historical process of emancipation . . . Therefore the history of emancipation cannot be identified with the history of redemption from God, nor the latter be detached from human liberation . . . Christian redemption is something more than emancipatory liberation, though it shows critical solidarity towards that.[147]

Praxical initiatives on behalf of sociopolitical change work together as manifestations of the inbreaking Reign of God albeit provisional and fragmentary. The menacing dark clouds of aggression and violence looming in the background whenever there are inroads in liberating praxis evinces the fragility and incompleteness of a purely sociopolitical liberation. Jesus enters this very finitude in the radical, transforming lifestyle of God's Reign but was promptly crucified on the cross of society's powerholders. A reorientation of his death in the promise of definitive salvation, symbolized and embodied in his resurrection, reveals a more profound scheme that exceeds the fragile human initiatives toward liberation. Jesus "refused to accord evil the same rights as good"[148] as he trusted in the eternal God who holds the last word.

Schillebeeckx asserts that religion sees the holy manifested in humanity's search for justice and good in the world. "For the believer, man in the world is the fundamental symbol of the holy, of God as champion of all good and judgment."[149] Any claim to definitive salvation proffered by a sociopolitical liberative movement, no matter how comprehensive, is a misrepresentation of human life, an anthropological oversight. Schillebeeckx had already established this guidepost clearly as one of the proposed anthropological constants where the "religious and 'para-religious' consciousness of man" is accounted for.

Thus, Schillebeeckx proposes that an "eschatological proviso" curbs the tendency to totalize liberative movements:

> In other words, religions, even Christian faith, is politically relevant, in that it opposes a *complete identification* of human salvation with politics. God's proviso, which for men takes the form of an eschatological proviso, makes it impossible for the believer to absolutize politics. Christianity *desacralizes* politics . . . This criticism based on religion is in fact religion's contribution to the world, but it is a contribution in and through *service to God*.[150]

The eschatological proviso designates that no utopian movement of emancipation can be seen as the harbinger and agent of universal salvation.[151] Regardless of their authenticity, all sociopolitical initiatives are relativized by the eschatological proviso. Eschatological salvation simply cannot be reduced to politics.

Schillebeeckx, however, is careful to point out that the eschatological proviso cannot not be taken to an uncritical extreme where efforts at kindling social change are de-emphasized and undervalued. In such case, the eschatological proviso not only relativizes sociopolitical movements for justice, it also, detrimentally, neutralizes them. Ironically, the first victims in such an equation will be the very people Christian solidarity claims to exercise a preference for—the world's poor and oppressed. Schillebeeckx debunks this option as unjustifiable:

> A merely formal use of the eschatological proviso would simply throttle the humanitarian impulse which is present in liberation movements, whereas at the same time by keeping silent one obviously cannot use God's proviso against the status quo . . . At all events, it emerges that religion always has political relevance.[152]

The eschatological proviso cannot be used to support an escapist view that Christian salvation carries no sociopolitical implications. If anything, the eschatological proviso radicalizes liberative initiatives by strengthening the link between faith in a God who promotes good and opposes evil, and the praxis such a faith entails. Schillebeeckx reiterates that the orientation toward sociopolitical action had been clarified by the synthesis of all the anthropological constants. Based on the heuristic framework of the anthropological constants, Schillebeeckx clarifies and steers the course for Christian sociopolitical action[153] (here, enumerated for emphasis):

To fight energetically against everything which,

- vitiates a human being's physical life
- burdens his/her psychological life
- humiliates him/her as a person
- enslaves him/her through social structures
- compels and drives him/her into an irresponsible adventure through irrationality
- makes the free exercise of his/her religious feeling impossible
- infringes human rights and reifies human beings as a result of their working conditions and the bureaucracy which shapes them.

Far from neutralizing sociopolitical action, the eschatological proviso offers a productive and critical impulse to intensify praxis. Despite all the disappointments and insufficiencies of their efforts, humankind can still, in the furthest expediency, entrust their failures to God who is "the sole subject of universal providence."[154]

Creative tension exists then between God's transcendence and immanence within history. This is made apparent in the later emphasis Schillebeeckx accords to an "eschatological surplus" of God's transcendent love in his abiding concern and preference for the downtrodden:

> As a Christian I do not insist so much on a "proviso" (unless the outlines, limits, and possible misunderstandings thereof are clearly circumscribed beforehand in an accessible language). As I now see it, I insist much more on an "eschatological superabundance," a surplus, that for God's activity an inner, positive connection exists between, on one hand, what humans here on earth realize in terms of true justice for everyone and of authentic love for other humans, and, on the other hand, the ultimate figure that God will give to what the Christian originary tradition calls the Reign of God.[155]

The eschatological surplus or superabundance of God's transcendent love surpasses all human efforts in achieving liberation and reorients them in the light of the all-encompassing breadth of the eschatological salvation of God's Kingdom. The promised eschatological salvation, Schillebeeckx maintains, "must take on a recognizable content within our history in forms which will nevertheless be transcended."[156] From the vantage point of this relativizing surplus, praxical movements are fragmentary but essential constituents of definitive salvation.

The question thus beckons- what is the exact definition of eschatological salvation? In view of the creative tension at work between the eschatological proviso and the eschatological surplus, Schillebeeckx opines that no matter how persistently human beings conjure a salvation based on valid dreams and desires, there is no fixed concept of "final good." The actual shape of eschatological salvation is as open-ended as God's absolute and surprising freedom. Schillebeeckx returns to Jesus' praxis as a point of reference:

> Jesus did not act from a well-defined concept of eschatological or final salvation. Rather, he saw a distant vision of final, perfect and universal salvation—the kingdom of God—*in and through* his own *fragmentary actions*, which were historical and thus limited or finite, "going around doing good" through healing, liberating from demonic powers, and reconciliation. Understood in this way, Jesus did not live by a utopian, distant vision or by a consummation of all things in God which had already been brought about "ideally," but he recognized in his specific action of doing good a practical anticipation of salvation to come. This confirms the *permanent validity* of any practice of doing good which is incomplete because it is historically limited.[157]

Thus, whatever glimpses of full salvation human beings derive from "historically broken situations of experiences," they amount to a "negative awareness."[158] However, far from taking negative awareness to mean stasis and passivity, Schillebeeckx insists that it can be a dynamic critical force toward achieving meaning in our history:

> What then is salvation in Jesus from God? I would want to say: being at the disposal of others, losing oneself for others (each in his own limited situation) and within this "conversion" (which is also made possible by structural changes) also working through anonymous structures for the happiness, the goodness, the truth of mankind.[159]

Eschatological salvation is shaped by the genuine commitment and initiatives of people to bring about salvation for their fellow human beings in the spirit of mutual love.

Negative Experiences of Contrast

For Schillebeeckx, living in the crucible of the meantime where human suffering is a constant human reality, offers a special epistemological value and power. The key to this potential liberative force within the experience of suffering is the indignation and protest that this experience evokes. Schillebeeckx proposes the idea of "negative experiences of contrast," a dialectical concept which hinges on the premise that although the eschatological salvation as represented by the *humanum* remains elusive and constantly threatened, liberative currents that contribute to the flourishing of the *humanum* are made manifest in the refusal to acquiesce to situations of suffering and injustice. Because suffering is a negation of the divine will, God becomes present in the human resistance to suffering. As Mary Catherine Hilkert puts it, "God is the source of a creative dissatisfaction with all that is less than God's vision of humanity."[160] Schillebeeckx thus argues that the very experience of suffering yields cognitive power when it inflames protest and resistance.[161] While on one hand, suffering is plainly a "negative mis-experience," it offers on the other hand, the possibility of laying "a bridge toward a possible praxis"[162] which seeks for the removal of suffering and its causes. Regardless of the open-ended character of their outcome, negative contrast experiences represent a practical-critical power that quickens a new praxis which opens up alternative future possibilities:

> As a *contrast* experience, the experience of suffering presumes, after all, an implicit impulse toward happiness. And as an experience of injustice, it presumes at least a dim consciousness of the positive prospects of human integrity. As a contrast experience, it implies indirectly a conscious- ness of an appeal of and to the *humanum*. In this sense, activity which overcomes suffering is only possible on the basis of at least an implicit or inchoate anticipation of a possible, *coming* universal meaning.[163]

Negative experiences of contrast possess a paradoxical revelatory character where the indignation and protest over the "is" presumes a given consciousness of the "ought." Such experiences, Schillebeeckx maintains, can be described in the tripartite attribute of protest, promise, and praxical challenge. "The prophetic voice that rises from the contrast-experience is therefore protest, hope-inspiring promise and historical initiative."[164]

Schillebeeckx refers back to the praxis of Jesus in illustrating the prophetic voice arising from the paradox of negative contrast experiences. Consistently, what he brings to an understanding of contrast experiences is the eschatological factor—the dialectical link between the contemplative and the practical experience of meaning within the context of human suffering in the light of the inbreaking Reign of God:

> Out of this experience of contrast between the contemplative and also the practical experience of meaning and the human history of evil and

suffering, Jesus makes demands on us which humanly speaking are obviously impossible. One example of the way in which the gospels understood Jesus may be enough: "When you prepare a meal, then invite the poor and the lame, the cripples and the blind." (Luke 14:13); in a vision, in a very fragmentary and historically limited event—a drop of water on a hot stone—Jesus anticipates the real possibility of perfect eschatological salvation, in the same way as Micah and Isaiah saw the wolf and the lamb grazing together in peace and the child playing happily over the snake's hole, in universal meaningful reconciliation. Such a prophetic promise is a permanent force, critical of society, which still discovers subtle forms and causes of suffering and evil on the basis of mystical experience of God, where they are not encountered without mystical experience. Mysticism is therefore itself a liberating force.[165]

From a Christian perspective, the anticipation of the *eschaton* symbolized in the Kingdom of God is the ground principle at work in the positive moment of negative experiences of contrast. The vision of full eco-human salvation militates against the bleak picture of the prevailing order stained by the history of woundedness and alienation. The experience of this positive moment found within "critical negativity"[166] is the very oil for the rekindling of human hope and for the possibiliy of praxis.

Schillebeeckx, however, insists that the notion of negative experiences of contrast is not confined to religious terms; it is, in fact, a fundamental, "pre-religious" human experience. There is a blurring of religious-secular boundaries, a universal consensus in the human "no" to suffering which discloses a "yes" to the possibility of a more humane alternative reality. Schillebeeckx refers to this convergence as a "consensus of the unknown," as the ideal, utopian world is nowhere to be found; it is yet to exist:

> The fundamental human "no" to evil therefore discloses an unfulfilled and thus "open yes" which is as intractable as the human "no," indeed even stronger, because the "open yes" is the basis of that opposition and makes it possible. Moreover, from time to time, there are fragmentary but real experiences of meaning and happiness on both a smaller and a larger scale, which constantly keep nurturing, establishing and sustaining the "open yes." Both believers and agnostics come together in this experience. That is also a rational basis for solidarity between all people and for common commitment to a better world with a human face.[167]

Sensitive to his European secular milieu, Schillebeeckx underscores that in an "autonomous ethic," there exists a form of utopia which, at the very least, represents a dissociation from injustice. The key to an understanding of negative contrast experiences need not be premised on the explicit belief in God's active involvement in the history of human liberation; the language spoken here is the common, inclusive language of solidarity. The bone of contention then is, "Which side do you choose in the struggle between good and evil, between oppressors and the oppressed?"[168]

The Ethical Challenge of Political Holiness

We see clearly that there is no dichotomy between the experience of God and the human arena of struggle in Schillebeeckx's eschatological perspective. Fragmentary experiences of salvation come about through Christian discipleship which consists of both interpersonal relationships and the commitment to sociopolitical change. This is the ineluctable, essential character of spreading the gospel amid the present global reality of massive structural injustice. Gustavo Gutierrez gives a poignant litany of the kind of lives multitudes of people in the Third World are forced to live:

> A thousand little things: lacks of every type, abuses and contempt suffered, tortured lives in search of work, incredible ways of making a living or more exactly a crumb of bread, petty quarrels, family separations, illness no longer existent at other social levels, malnutrition and infant mortality, substandard payment for their work or merchandise, total disorientation as to what is most necessary for them and their families, delinquency by abandonment or despair, loss of their own cultural values.[169]

Schillebeeckx emphasizes that the cruel context of injustice and misery that involves more than half of the world's population calls for not just "caritative diaconia" (as epitomized by the exemplary ministry of Mother Teresa of Calcutta) but, more so, "political diaconia," the committed effort to address the structural causes of injustice and everything that diminishes human dignity and the integrity of creation. As such, Schillebeeckx proposes that the form of Christian spirituality appropriate for these times is the liberationist concept of "political holiness;"[170] the meeting point between "mysticism," an intense personal relationship with God, and "politics," an intense form of social engagement. The social expression of political holiness is "political love," which Schillebeeckx considers an expedient form of love of neighbor. As holiness in Schillebeeckx's conception is always contextual, political love becomes an urgent call to action on behalf of the oppressed and defenseless:

> Given the current situation of suffering humanity which has now become conscious universally, political love can well become the historically urgent form of contemporary holiness, the historical imperative of the moment, or in Christian terms, the contemporary *kairos* or moment of grace as appeal to believers.[171]

Let us allow Jon Sobrino to describe in some detail what constitutes political love, as there are specific nuances that differentiate it from other forms of love. He points to four characteristics:[172]

- It requires *metanoia* to see the truth of the world as it is, in the manifestations of death, which are visible, and its structural causes (Romans 1:18).
- *Pity* for the unhealed—but not unhealable—suffering of the oppressed majority
- Awareness of *responsibility* when asked the question, "What have you done with your brother?" (Genesis 4:10) and co-responsibility for his condition and destiny.[173]
- Political love tries to be *effective*—it must be expressed in a fitting manner in consideration for the oppressed who are not objects, but enactors of their own destiny.

Schillebeeckx reiterates the unmistakable liberationist angle of his conception of the universal validity of ethical praxis in the world, "I am inspired to say this above all by Latin American, Asian, and African forms of liberation theology, and for a long time this has also been a theme of my own theological quest."[174] I wish to note, however, that while his appropriation of the twin concepts of political holiness and political love validates his kinship with the liberation theologians, Schillebeeckx brings these concepts within his own distinct frame of reference. Schillebeeckx returns to his key proposition of negative experiences of contrast and recasts political holiness as a "new experience of Transcendence."

He speaks of the two facets of such an experience:[175]

- On one hand, a person, especially someone poor and oppressed, and someone who has declared him—or herself in solidarity with these, experiences that God is absent in many human relationships of property and power in this world. Thus they experience alienation, the distance between God, the reign of God, and our society.

- On the other hand, the believer experiences precisely in political love and resistance against injustice an intense contact with God, the presence of the liberating God of Jesus. In modern times, authentic faith by preference seems to be able to be nourished in and by a praxis of liberation.

For Schillebeeckx, political holiness arises from a Christian conception of negative contrast experiences where the positive, liberative moment is attributed to God himself who is the "the heart and source of all truly human liberation." That said, it becomes clear that though the concept of political holiness is an appropriation of liberation spirituality, the unique understanding of it in the framework of negative experiences of contrast is vintage Schillebeeckx.

Schillebeeckx sees political holiness and love as sociopolitical implications of the witness of the inbreaking Reign of God. The creative tension effected by the eschatological proviso indicates that the quest for salvation is at one and the same time, a gracious gift and a formidable task. Political love as a present-day prophetic task entails the interpretation of the "signs of the times" in the light of God's Reign. Schillebeeckx puts it beautifully—"For 'signs of the times' do not speak; we must cause them to do so."[176]

The prophetic-critical task of making the signs of the times "speak" is exemplified by Schillebeeckx's own criticism of dehumanizing forces in contemporary society, a running theme in his later theology. In Schillebeeckx's clear-eyed view, these dehumanizing forces have undeniable structural roots. The world's affluent powerholders perpetuate a situation of injustice as they work to preserve self-serving structural relations that relegate a large base of lower-ranked societies and cultures to subalternity:

> While two-thirds of the world population is crying out for justice and love, a powerful block made up of the remaining third, in East and West, is concentrating all its knowledge and its science, its power, its diplomacy and its tactics and means of subjugation, on keeping what it has.[177]

Schillebeeckx is strident in his denunciation of such power blocks, whatever name they go by—capitalism, multinational corporations, "Americanism," or communist state capitalism—and their inauthentic, ideologically determined utopian promises of well being and progress that, in their seeming absolute character, work only to sacralize the status quo of inequality:

> [N]othing alters the fact that the great majority of those who may call themselves human beings here and elsewhere are kept down and oppressed, made slaves in practice, despite the all-too-similar slogans of all these power blocks. They promise freedom and happiness and true democracy, and at the same time themselves decide what is good for others.[178]

History has thus taught that the "unbridled Western concern for self-realization" did not bring about salvation to humanity on any level, be that personal, political or social. Moreover, Schillebeeckx argues that the inordinate desire for economic expansion emanating from the Enlightenment mantra of "unlimited progress" has all but endangered both humanity and the environment. The crux of the problem, he asserts, lies in the extreme idea of a positivistic "total liberation of man by man."[179] Using haunting imagery that recalls, quite aptly, imagery from a horror film, Schillebeeckx denounces this dehumanizing project as demonic:

> The programme of a total liberation of man by man at present seems to be a greatest threat to all humanity. The "modern western world" is in particular need of salvation today, for liberation and redemption precisely from those dark powers which modern man has himself called to life. The demonic in our culture and society has taken on a different name and content from the demons of the Medieval Ages, but it is no less real and just as threatening.[180]

Schillebeeckx clarifies that his criticism is not directed at science and technology per se but against those who enjoy a monopoly of control and use over them. For Schillebeeckx then, it boils down to the question of power:

> Science and technology work miracles when they are used to bring about the freedom of others, solidarity among men and women. But in fact the sciences function as an instrument of power: power over nature, power over society and also power over men and women, even extending to power over masculinity and femininity. Science is the key to the military power of nations; it is the secret of their economic and social prosperity—at the expense of others.[181]

Appropriating the words of Luke 22:25–26a, Schillebeeckx prophetically appraises these "signs of the times" in the light of the gospel message—"The kings (rulers, or power blocks) of the Gentiles exercise lordship over them, and those in authority over them are called benefactors. But not so with you."[182] Additionally, he asserts that identifying a lopsided and exploitative utopian system with the divine will is tantamount to using God's name in vain, a manipulation of God in support of dominant ideological interests:

> The guideline here is that it is right to associate the name of God with a utopia in the light of Jesus' proclamation of the kingdom of God as a kingdom of justice and love among men and among women, and this name may not therefore be used to justify our existing economic system which exploits men and women structurally. Christians need to use the name of God only where it belongs: in solidarity with the victims of our economic situation, in the struggle for the furtherance and redistribution of work, income, and spiritual goods, and so on.[183]

The hard reality, however, attests that political love is often a precarious endeavor. There are sacrifices demanded of those who commit to the praxical imperative. Political holiness has had a long list of "political saints"[184] who paid the price for the work of justice in various missions. Having been accomplices in the colonial enterprise, the Christian churches have historically found themselves on the side of the rich, not on the side of the defenseless indigenous peoples of the mission countries. The ruling classes, Schillebeeckx argues, thus feel betrayed by a church that exercises a preferential solidarity with the poor. Christians in missions find themselves facing the abuses of police control which is set in place to safeguard the interests of national and international capital within an ideology of "national security." The murder of Salvadoran Archbishop Oscar Romero, an event that deeply affected Schillebeeckx,[185] symbolizes the extreme situation of persecution and martyrdom that threaten people who dare speak the dangerous truth of the inbreaking Reign. Because sociopolitical engagement inevitably deals with the dangers that emanate from the centers of power, political love often entails a sacrificial dimension, a "new ascetism" for our times:

> That political form of Christian love of God and neighbor, albeit in another area of experience, knows the same conversion and metanoia, the same ascesis and detachment from self, the same suffering and dark nights, the same of one's self in the other as was the case in contemplative mysticism in times past. A difficult ascetical process of purification not inferior to the ways of purification of classical mysticism

lies in the disinterested partisanship of the poor, the oppressed, the exploited, as a demand for Christian love precisely in its societal and political dimensions.[186]

The sacrificial cost of political holiness, in whatever form that may take, is comparable to what contemplative mystics of the past described as a journey through the "dark night." The Spanish Carmelite mystic and church doctor Teresa of Avila articulated her trying experiences in the expression "*Nada*," which she took to mean "a nothingness of fullness." Schillebeeckx explains, "God's presence as a pure experience of faith, even if this is communicated in a negative way."[187] Schillebeeckx considers the mystical ascetism associated with service to God's Reign as "an experience of the real presence of God, not in the mediation of positive support but in the experience of extreme negativity, a dark night."[188] For him, the mystical "hope against hope" in political holiness is a form of negative contrast experience.

Praxis, for Schillebeeckx, is decisive, and must legitimate itself in "disinterested love." But he is also careful not to overlook the mystical component of political holiness. Since God himself is the source of authentic human liberation, prayer and liturgical celebration of "God as liberator" precede sociopolitical engagement. Both mystical and political aspects are important to the creative, dialectical process— "Politics without prayer or mysticism quickly becomes grim and barbaric; prayer or mysticism without political love quickly becomes sentimental and irrelevant interiority."[189] Schillebeeckx's own psalm prayer, in itself the articulation of a negative contrast experience, then becomes a fitting doxological illustration of the marriage of mysticism and politics in political holiness:[190]

> Do Not Fear
> Are you a God at hand
> and not a God far off?
>
> *Jer 23:23*
>
> Truly you are a hidden God.
>
> *Is 45:15*
>
> Or do you hide your face from us,
> to see what our end will be?
>
> *Deut 32:20*

And yet
you do not willingly afflict
or grieve us.

Lam 3:33

You are ready to be sought
by those who do not ask for you;
you are ready to be found
by those who do not seek you.

Is 65:1

Do I look for you in chaos?

Is 45:19c

I hear you saying, Lord:
"I, the Lord, speak salvation
and declare what is right."

Is 41:19d

But the poor and needy seek water
and there is none
and their tongues are parched with thirst.

Is 41:17

How can my soul wait in silence
for you, God, who are my salvation?

Ps 62:1

May you find people, Lord,
who work for justice.

Is 64:5

Then we shall be able to say to everyone:
You are our God.
You set people free.
You have heard my cry.
You have heard me and said:
"Do not fear!"

Lam 3:37

Behold I am doing a new thing;
now it springs forth—do you not see it?

Is 43:19

Lord I believe;
help my unbelief!

Mk 9:24b

I am a poor fool, Lord—
teach me how to pray.

(G. Gezelle)

Interview with Edward Schillebeeckx

The liberation of human beings is the golden thread of my theology[191]

ANTONIO SISON: In your essay *"Theologie als bevrijdingskunde: Enkele noodzakelijke beschouwingen vooraf"* found in *Tijdschrift voor Theologie* 24, you spoke of wanting to forge a dialogue with Third World liberation theologies. How important is this dialogue to your theological project as a whole?

EDWARD SCHILLEBEECKX: I said in an earlier article that my purpose of the moment is to have a liberation theology for the West because we are always quoting theologians of the Third World although they are contextualized in their own situation. Theirs is a theology from below because they are in solidarity with the movement of liberation. Our problem here in Europe is that theologians who try to create a liberation theology for the West have no movement in which the theology can grow from. Thus, the liberation theology in the Western context must have knowledge of what is going on in Europe, above all, the globalization of the whole Western economic system, which is one of the greatest threats to the Third World. But we are the cause of that. America and the rich states of Europe have great economic interests in globalization. Therefore, we have to analyze the causes of globalization and our relationship with the Third World. It is more difficult for us to make this analysis because that means examining the consequences of our capitalistic economic system, its consequences for the Third World, and how we can change that. I do not claim to be an expert in economic analysis but the whole tendency of my theology is in that direction.

ANTONIO SISON: Can you say that based on your work, you have achieved this goal of initiating a dialogue with Third World liberation theologians?

EDWARD SCHILLEBEECKX: I've learned more theoretically from Third World theologian Clodovis Boff who worked on his dissertation in Leuven. His theology is not only hermeneutical theology but also sociopolitical analysis and that was also my framework; I recognized my work in his research. In my time as a professor, I was always in dialogue with Gustavo Gutiérrez and the last twenty years of my theologizing has been focused on the praxis of the Kingdom of God. For me, that is the liberation theology I am working out.

ANTONIO SISON: As I understand your later theology, you always talk about salvation and liberation conjointly, you do not polarize them.

EDWARD SCHILLEBEECKX: *Via ethos* . . . from justice, solidarity with the poor and the distressed . . . theology must be a liberation theology. I always speak of the praxis of the Kingdom of God. But praxis of the Kingdom of God is human, social, societal liberation in which the ethical is assumed in our faith relationship with God. The ultimate reason why theology must be a liberation theology is mysticism as basis for the ethical or political holiness. Therefore, I talk about the central idea of negative contrast experiences, which are also disclosure experiences. When you experience indignation about something that is a negative experience because you are facing evil and you ask, "how is this possible?" But that implies positive possibilities . . . that you can change things. That is a disclosure experience. For me, this is one complete and very nuanced idea and it can be one of the key ideas of a liberation theology. We are starting with evil. The destruction of the humanity of human beings.

ANTONIO SISON: In your eschatological perspective, you talk about an eschatological proviso but in your later work, you seem to have emphasized an eschatological surplus more.

EDWARD SCHILLEBEECKX: That was a reaction to Professor Johann-Baptist Metz because he was always speaking of an eschatological proviso, and rightly so, as he was speaking of a political theology. However, with the emphasis on a divine eschatological proviso, you can neutralize the whole idea of engagement with the poor. That is the other side of it. Therefore, I said no, not only the proviso because we do not adequately know the essence of God. We must understand that God is love and God is loving justice, *Deus Humanissimus*, therefore, he is against evil and the promoter of the good. Then you have a positive element, an eschatological surplus, in order to do liberation theology.

ANTONIO SISON: Would you say that the quest for justice is the epistemological project of your later theology?

EDWARD SCHILLEBEECKX: Praxis is the emphasis of my later theology. In a recent homily, I said that you can theoretically negate the existence of God but when you are *homoiousios*, truly the home of righteousness and solidarity for people, that is the beginning of love, of caritas. Through your praxis—doing justice for people—you affirm the humanity of God. That solidarity implies the existence of

God . . . Matthew 25, when you gratuitously give a glass of water to the thirsty, implicitly, you have contact with God.

ANTONIO SISON: Why is it then that in the reception of your work in theological circles, not much attention has been given to the liberative soteriological significance of your theology?

EDWARD SCHILLEBEECKX: I do not use the term "liberation theology" too much to describe my work, that is the third world concept and I have to respect that. Otherwise, I talk about liberation theology for the West. Therefore, I use "praxis of the Kingdom of God," that is my liberation theology. The preface I wrote for Thompson's book reflects the tendency of my liberation theology,[192] however, I did not describe it as liberation theology but "critical-hermeneutical" interpretation. "Critical" is not just conceptualizing and thematizing, it is a praxis. The liberation of human beings is the golden thread of my theology. I do not understand why that is not given attention in the reception of my work.

ANTONIO SISON: Reading your work with Third World glasses, I find a very rich articulation of our situation although you do not claim to share our context. Do you think it's important for Third World theology to have a Western mouthpiece?

EDWARD SCHILLEBEECKX: I think so. The fact that the founding fathers of liberation theology—Gutierrez, Boff, Sobrino, etc.—have studied in Leuven, in Lyon, in Germany, and in America, shows that their work is also based on Western theories. At one point, Asian theologians of the EATWOT (Ecumenical Association of Third World Theologians) critiqued Latin American theology as having underplayed the mystical relationship with God too much. At that time, it was necessary to do that, but it was certainly not a denial of the mystical. There was a period when I also emphasized that direction because at that time, there was a move toward horizontalization among many theologians.

ANTONIO SISON: A new generation of incipient theologians are reappropriating your theology for varying contexts. I, for one, am trying to bridge your work with the concrete stituation of my home country, the Philippines. What is your reaction to this?

EDWARD SCHILLEBEECKX: You are right to do that. Erik Borgman says that there is something "classical" about my theology. Without my own initiative, a 23-year-old lady in China wants to translate my work from 1974 in Chinese. I think that there is indeed something "classical" about my theology that will be picked up for some time. I am not writing for eternity, but, hopefully, for some time. For me, my approach is historical—I began with the first page of the Bible down to the last theologian at the moment. But the historical is very relativizing.

PART III

Creative Crossings

CHAPTER 5

The Crystallization of Political Holiness in Third Cinema

In this chapter, I explore the points of convergence between the cinematic principle and the theological principle. It is instructive to review the two-tiered methodological structure I had described in the introductory chapter.

First, I explore the epistemological resonances between the praxis-oriented later theology of Schillebeeckx and the liberative project of Third Cinema. I argue that a more regardful consideration of the practical-critical soteriological base of Schillebeeckx's eschatology offers a parallel connection with the liberative propositions that undergird Third Cinema. The clarification of this epistemological link serves as the ground principle from which to posit a second level of convergence.

A creative examination of what I perceive as the crystallization of Schillebeeckx's conception of political holiness in the Third Cinema stylistic options embodied in Third Cinema. Grounded on the close correspondence between the epistemological project of Schillebeeckx's later theology and Third Cinema, I discuss the ways in which the main threads of Schillebeeckx's eschatological perspective find cinematic expression in the previously discussed case studies. My intention is not to draw out a one-to-one correspondence as the very intertextual nature of this project, which attempts to bring together a theological text and cinematic texts, precludes such a neat linkage. I make this qualification to emphasize that the points of convergence take on varying contours considering the polysemic quality and complex syntagmatic organizations intrinsic to the art form of cinema[1] as against the more systematic organization of arguments in written theological discourse. What I propose as the methodological and conceptual bridge in this intertextual project is Third Cinema critical theory, which is, as earlier established, posited on the use of stylistic strategies to foreground the Third World quest for liberation and equality. As such, I pay attention to what I would describe as the "creative crossings" between the two principles through the mediation of Third Cinema stylistic strategies.

This creative and open-minded exploration argues for the primacy of cinematic style as the locus for a theological hermeneutic of film over the prevailing practice of extracting the religious dimension out of the more thematic, literary bases of film.

Epistemological Resonances

The consistent epistemological project of Schillebeeckx's later theology is liberative praxis. In his "interactive soteriology,"[2] Schillebeeckx dissolves the dichotomy between salvation and sociopolitical liberation maintaining that the two concepts interrelate dialectically and are mutually implicated. Hence, he proposes that religion sees the divine manifested in humanity's search for justice and good in the world. In the light of the abiding vision of the Reign of God, Schillebeeckx's theological commitment is to present "the gospel of the poor for prosperous people."[3]

Schillebeeckx's liberative epistemological project is further evinced in his express intention of developing a Western reappropriation of liberation theology that may serve as a dialogue partner to Third World liberation theology. An investigation of his trilogy, most especially *Church: The Human Story of God*, part 4 of *Christ: The Experience of Jesus as Lord*, as well as key points in *Jesus: An Experiment in Christology*, provide clear references to this intercultural initiative. In the personal interview I conducted, Schillebeeckx himself clarifies the liberative sociopolitical trajectory of his later work:

> I said in an earlier article that my purpose of the moment is to have a liberation theology for the West because we are always quoting theologians of the Third World although they are contextualized in their own situation. Theirs is a theology from below because they are in solidarity with the movement of liberation. Our problem here in Europe is that theologians who try to create a liberation theology for the West have no movement in which the theology can grow from. Thus, the liberation theology in the Western context must have knowledge of what is going on in Europe, above all, the gobalization of the whole Western economic system, which is one of the greatest threats to the Third World. But we are the cause of that. America and the rich states of Europe have great economic interests in globalization. Therefore, we have to analyze the causes of globalization and our relationship with the Third

World. It is more difficult for us to make this analysis because that means examining the consequences of our capitalistic economic system, its consequences for the Third World, and how we can change that. I do not claim to be an expert in economic analysis but the whole tendency of my later theology is on that direction.[4]

In the same interview, Schillebeeckx underlines his efforts at maintaining a dialogue with Third World theologians. He explains

> I've learned more theoretically from Third World theologian Clodovis Boff who worked on his dissertation in Leuven. His theology is not only hermeneutical theology but also sociopolitical analysis and that was also my framework; I recognized my work in his research. In my time as a professor, I was always in dialogue with Gustavo Gutierrez and the last twenty years of my theologizing has been focused on the praxis of the Kingdom of God. For me, that is the liberation theology I am working out.[5]

From the side of Third World liberation theology, the affirmation as to whether or not Schillebeeckx's theology has proven to be a relevant dialogue partner for Third World Liberationist theologies can be drawn from the witness of Third World theologians themselves. As an appropriate case in point, I refer to the heuristic value of Schillebeeckx in the development of an inculturated theology in the work of José M. de Mesa, one of the most creative and noteworthy theologians of the Philippines. De Mesa considers the work of Schillebeeckx, grounded as it is on concrete human experience, as an important resource in his project of "theological re-rooting," the contextualization of theology within the contemporary postcolonial Philippine situation. While keeping attuned to the compounded dynamics of Philippine culture, De Mesa has maintained a respectful and meaningful critical dialogue with Western theology mainly through the mediation of Schillebeeckx's thought. De Mesa underlines the link between salvation and liberation in Schillebeeckx's theology when he discusses the concept of providence as applied to the context of the Philippine lowlands:

> God's providence, his concern for us, is not merely. a gift. It is also a task, a mission. It is our mission in the Church as much as in the world because by our entry into Christ through faith and baptism "we are not only the 'object' of divine providential care but at the same time enter into this divine concern for our fellow men."[6]

Further, when De Mesa articulates eschatological salvation in the Filipino concept of *ginhawa*, which literally means "relief from pain, sickness, straits or difficulty," he relies on part 4 of Schillebeeckx's *Christ: The Experience of Jesus as Lord*:

> Our awareness of eschatological ginhawa can be no more than a negative awareness for the time being because "our situation never allows us to define in positive terms what this will ultimately imply for human well-being, given the spiritual openness and 'self-transcendence' still to be realized in history and in view of the absolute freedom of God whose glory lies in human happiness."[7]

Here, De Mesa conceives of *ginhawa* in distinctly Schillebeeckxian terms—as fragmentary experiences of salvation in the here and now, but in view of an eschatological vision of complete well being, thus far, conceivable as a negative awareness.

The place of Schillebeeckx's thought in the enrichment of Filipino inculturated theology augurs well for the liberative epistemological project of his theology. However, while salvation and liberation are bridged decisively in Schillebeeckx's thought, the reception of his work in theological circles have often accorded marginal attention to this liberationist soteriological direction. The incisive work of Derek Simon pays due attention to this oversight. He contends

> Schillebeeckx's alignment of practical-critical soteriology with socio-political liberation and emancipative political praxis, however, continues to receive minimal development in the reception of his Christology . . . There is very little evidence in the reception of his work that a comprehensive discussion of the practical-critical orientation of Schillebeeckx's soteriology has taken place, especially with respect to the constitutive significance of emancipative praxis and structural sociopolitical transformation for the experience and interpretation of salvation . . . the comprehensive representation of the practical-critical and liberationist approaches to the interpretation of salvation in Schillebeeckx's soteriology remains incidental.[8]

Simon asserts that the depoliticization of Schillebeeckx's theology has been angled toward either of two directions:

- The first tendency dilutes Schillebeeckx's engagement with critical theory, which is taken as a "philosophical digression" detached from the development of his christology.
- Consequently, the second tendency is a representation of Schillebeeckx's christology on a theoretical-hermeneneutical level devoid of its sociopolitical implications.

To substantiate his argument, Simon criticizes the virtual omission of the practical-critical dimension of Schillebeeckx's soteriology in the research work of Tadahiko Iwashima entitled *Menschheitsgeschichte und Heilserfahrung*.[9] He notes that Iwashima's predominantly transcendental and anthropocentric hermeneutic thoroughly decontextualizes Schillebeeckx's soteriology so that the link between salvation and liberation is obscured:

> Iwashima injects a considerable distance between emancipation and the liberation of human freedom: this minimizes the soteriological significance of the concept of emancipation while leaving the concept of liberation thoroughly depoliticized in a transcendental anthropology of human freedom. Thus, the mediations of liberation through a correlation with sociocritical analysis and the critiques of ideologies are never articulated in relation to soteriology, even though Schillebeeckx insists on their constitutive role.[10]

Moreover, Simon argues that Iwashima unduly dichotomizes historical salvation and eschatological salvation when he suggests a circular exchange between them—"Worldly salvation praxis thus mediates the dimension of earthly salvation and the history transcending religious praxis (mediates) the dimension of eschatological salvation."

Simon rightly points out that in the frame of Schillebeeckx's conception of the eschatological proviso and surplus, "it is precisely the historical which mediates the eschatological in proleptic fragments."[11]

Additionally, Simon takes note of Erik Borgman's essay *Theologie tussen universiteit en emancipatie: De weg van Edward Schillebeeckx.*[12] He contends that while Borgman expressly identifies the work of Schillebeeckx as "a university theology in dialogue with and influenced by emancipation theology," it stops short of accounting for the praxis-theory correlation in the dialectical relationship between salvation and liberation, a definitive principle in Schillebeeckx's soteriology.[13]

Simon concludes that at best, the liberative, sociopolitical dimension of Schillebeeckx's practical-critical theology had been given occasional and incidental attention in existing theological discussions.

I submit that an adherence to the depoliticizing tendencies in the reception of Schillebeeckx's work as noted by Simon represents a myopic reading of Schillebeeckx and an undervaluing of the continuing intercultural relevance and impact of his later thought on the Third World situation. From my own Third World optic, I see these tendencies as missed opportunities; the inordinate muting of the prophetic-liberating voice of Schillebeeckx as a credible and significant Western mouthpiece for marginalized peoples who are still in the process of finding their own voice amid dehumanizing sociopolitical realities.

Schillebeeckx himself emphasizes the constitutive project of praxis and liberation in his theology:

> *Via ethos* . . . from justice, solidarity with the poor and the distressed . . . theology must be a liberation theology. I always speak of the praxis of the Kingdom of God. But praxis of the Kingdom of God is human, social, societal liberation in which the ethical is assumed in our faith relationship with God. The ultimate reason why theology must be a liberation theology is mysticism as basis for the ethical or political holiness.[14]

As such, Schillebeeckx points out categorically that "Human liberation is the golden thread of my theology."[15]

In the preceding chapter, I sought to contribute to the rectification of the scholarly amnesia in the reception of Schillebeeckx's work through an exploration of political holiness as the rubric of Schillebeeckx's praxically oriented eschatological perspective. Having done so, the convincing epistemological link between Schillebeeckx's conception of political holiness and Third Cinema becomes emergent.

To recall, Teshome Gabriel clarifies the liberative epistemological agenda of Third Cinema:

> The main aim of Third Cinema is to immerse itself in the lives and struggles of the people of the Third World . . . Third Cinema cineasts advocate a political cinema whose ideology is not only implied but adheres to the dialectic of traumatic changes that are engulfing the peoples of Africa, Asia, and Latin America. This cinema, therefore, is informed not only with the cultural tastes and ideological needs of the people it represents but also with the militant manifestations of their struggles.[16]

Third Cinema is not defined by geography but by its emancipative agenda. It is a cinema that seeks to raise a radical, oppositional consciousness that is consistent with the liberative vision of sociopolitical transformation. This vision integrates the representation of divine intervention alongside human agency as an empowering principle in the quest for fuller humanity amid the harsh realities of structural injustice. Third Cinema adheres to the liberationist configuration of a God-image that is sympathetic to and in solidarity with the Third World struggle for decolonization and emancipation. Conversely, a god who looks and sounds like the colonizers or neocolonizers, identifies with them exclusively, and functions as a legitimizing weapon wielded by society's powerholders to perpetuate the sociopolitical status quo, sets off the alarm bells and is met with militant resistance by the indigenous culture. From the Third Cinema standpoint, institutional religion is not exempted from ideological suspicion. A previously discussed example is the Cuban film *The Last Supper* where a black slave is ill at ease over the divinization of the neocolonial masters when he comments, "The priest says the overseers are like Jesus Christ." Similarly, in the Colombian film *One Day I Asked* (Julia Alvarez, 1970), a woman devotee praying in the church astutely pronounces, "one thing is sure, he (God) eats at the boss' table."[17]

Liberative theologies and Third Cinema reject institutional religion when it supports structures of inequity but turn to faith as a means for bringing about liberation. In the postcolonial universe of *Perfumed Nightmare*, authentic religion is a verb as much as it is a noun—it is the empowering ground principle that enables the Filipino to break free from the enslaving cocoon of colonially infused "religion" into a new, emancipative sociopolitical vision. Thus, the theology evinced in *Perfumed Nightmare* views the divine as the driving force to liberation who stands on the frontier of the historical future.

If it can be accepted that Third Cinema, grounded as it is on the praxical vision of decolonization and emancipation, shares fundamental resonances with a liberationist theological perspective, then I propose that there is legitimate basis to posit its epistemological connection with Schillebeeckx's practical-critical project; both understand salvation and liberation in the matrix of human interaction with history. I also maintain that Third Cinema, as a cinematic mirror of a Third World liberationist perspective, is responsive to Schillebeeckx's epistemological project of forging a dialogue with Third World liberation theology. Third Cinema offers a creative and revitalizing intercultural contribution to the Schillebeeckx-Liberation Theology dialogue and expands the view of such a dialogue by bringing an intertextual dimension to the equation.

In the succeeding discussion, I examine how the varying contours of Third Cinema work to express and register the epistemological resonances between Schillebeeckx's liberative eschatological perspective and Third Cinema. I explore how the stylistic options of Third Cinema work to crystallize, that is, to mirror in a truly cinematic fashion, Schillebeeckx's unique eschatological understanding of the liberationist concept of Political Holiness. I frame the discussion according to the cogent topics of Schillebeeckx's eschatological perspective insofar as I perceive them reflected in the stylistic grammar of Third Cinema.

I reiterate that the locus of the Theology-Cinema dialogue has often been limited to the thematic and literary bases of film at the expense of stylistic examination, a critical area for understanding cinema on its own terms and not as a mere adjunct to literature.

THE ECUMENE OF SUFFERING

For Schillebeeckx, the *humanum* or full, authentic humanity, escapes exact definition; it is not possible to offer a totalitarian norm of what it is to be truly human. Schillebeeckx insists that the human is the royal road to God but there is no directional map from which to base definite navigational patterns toward that direction. If anything, human history testifies to the horrific excess of suffering that defies hermeneutical verification. What is certain in Schillebeeckx's prognosis is that the unbroken thread of human suffering in history is a collective experience, an "ecumene of suffering." It is "my suffering, my evil, and my death."[18] As such, the *humanum* remains as an eschatological concept, already here fragmentarily in praxical initiatives, but not yet consummated.

The examples of Third Cinema I discussed previously all envisage people who are economically deprived, who are treated unjustly by the powers that be, who are at the mercy of ruthless economic interests, and who have no social status. The slaves of *The Last Supper*, the beggars of *Xala*, the displaced village folk of *Perfumed Nightmare*, the politically oppressed masses of *Romero*, the migrant workers of *Bread and Roses*, the Palestinians of *Divine Intervention*, the Tutsis of *Hotel Rwanda*, and the indigenous communities of *The Motorcycle Diaries*—all are co-members of the ecumene of suffering. I draw attention to some of these titles and discuss in greater detail how they represent the ecumene of suffering and the sociopolitical forces that perpetuate such a condition.

Among the dehumanizing forces that threaten the *humanum*, Schillebeeckx is stridently critical over the Western ideal of progress, buttressed as it is by Enlightenment principles, and unequivocably names the asymmetrical power structures it perpetuates as demonic. *Perfumed Nightmare* problematizes the incursion of progress and its resultant impact on the ecumene of suffering in the leitmotiv of the "phantom of progress." This symbolic rendering of the dehumanizing side of rapid, American-style progress with its sacralization of socioeconomic and technological advancement, finds stylistic expression in the film's mise-en-scène. Through the point of view of the protagonist Kidlat, the phantom of progress is portrayed surrealistically, appearing as a ghastly cloaked-figure wearing a mask with a demented expression. What is established here is that the phantom of progress conceals its true nature under the mask of universal validity. The mask itself is a leitmotiv that would reappear later in the pivotal mock farewell-party scene. Grainy, deliberately off-focus camerawork and diffused lighting add a spectral quality to the appearance of the phantom and the atmospheric space surrounding its presence. The trope of the phantom of progress works as a visual representation of the film's title *Perfumed Nightmare*, the attractively utopic but vacuous promise of the American dream. A visitation by the phantom of progress is likened to a haunting; it is, in no unclear terms, portrayed as demonic. This image conjured up by specific stylistic choices dovetails lucidly and accurately with Schillebeeckx's own denunciation of positivistic Western ideals of progress. Schillebeeckx pictures the "unbridled Western concern for self-realization," in whatever incarnation that may assume—Americanism, multinationalism, or even communist state capitalism—in vivid imagery reminiscent of the horror genre of cinema. To recall

> The programme of a total liberation of man by man at present seems to be a greatest threat to all humanity. The "modern western world" is in particular need of salvation today, for liberation and redemption precisely from those dark powers which modern man has himself called to life. The demonic in our culture and society has taken on a different name and content from the Medieval Ages, but it is no less real and just as threatening.[19]

The totalizing salvific claims of progress and technological advancement are hence judged by Schillebeeckx's argument as bogus, and, ultimately, a threat to the very humanity it purports to lead to salvation.

In *Perfumed Nightmare* the encroachment of the phantom of progress means an oppressive disruption of the characters' lives and consequently, an assault on their humanity. The guru Kaya reports to Kidlat by way of a letter that Balian, his home village located in the Philippine countryside, had been visited by the phantom of progress. Its forested environs had been denuded to give way to a new tourist-friendly road and as a result, his own mother's hut had been displaced. The film's mise-en-scène shows the hut being borne on the shoulders of the village folk who, in vain, try to relocate it to a greener spot. The scene plays out like a chaplinesque homage to a viewer unfamiliar with Philippine culture; otherwise, it presents a richer codified meaning. Employing a wide-angle, long shot of the portable house carried by the neighborhood folk, Tahimik frames the communal action in the scene and conveys its ideological significance. An informed reception attuned to cultural specificity would be able to identify in the scene the Philippine rural custom called *bayanihan* where the community literally pools manpower to help relocate a neighbor's hut. In Philippine culture, the term *bayanihan* is also understood in an expanded sense to describe the value of solidarity and love of neighbor. Context, however, changes everything and in *Perfumed Nightmare*, the phantom of progress imposes a perverted definition of *bayanihan*. Instead of an organic expression of community spirit, the concept is taken to mean forced ejection, collective displacement, and the subjection of members of the indigenous community to exploitation and humiliation; they are made to become squatters in their own land. The suffering caused by the mad scramble for development and progress is represented in the mordant image of the displaced house collectively yoked on the shoulders of the village folk who have no idea where to relocate it. Here, the pressure brought upon the Third World to keep up with economic growth at the cost of justice finds poignant cinematic expression.

The displacement and suffering brought about by progress in a postcolonial context also finds riveting depiction in *The Motorcycle Diaries*. In their road trip to various Latin American countries, Ernesto and Alberto see the common plight of a suffering humanity, be they starving miners on the slopes of the Andes or landless farmers in Machu Picchu. The chilling montage featuring various tableaux of indigenous people looking straight at the camera serves as a poetic representation of the many human faces of the ecumene of suffering. While *Perfumed Nightmare* names and exposes social injustice in the surrealistic symbol of the phantom of progress, *The Motorcycle Diaries* reveals the impact of the demonic structures as they are mirrored on the very faces of its victims. They are faces that bespeak of long-hours of hard labor, deprived of the luxury of rest and just compensation; their eyes, staring at the two protagonists and, on another level, at the audience, are windows to their toil and suffering.

Arguably, *Hotel Rwanda* has the most harrowing dramatization of the ecumene of suffering among the examples of Third Cinema cited previously. I am not even referring to the depiction of the genocide itself; as I discussed earlier, the film does not create a spectacle out of the bloodshed the way that a number of political thrillers have. I am referring to a pivotal scene when the UNAMIR forces decide to leave Rwanda and exclusively secure the safe exit of foreign nationals. Wide-angle shots effectively capture the unfolding drama as the frenzied crowd is sorted out by nationality. Orphaned Rwandan children are wrenched out from the hands of foreign missionaries, multiracial friendships are broken, and a clear line separates the Rwandans from the rest of the humanity. The exodus is reserved only for those who count in the affluent world. The Rwandans have been abandoned, not just in the film's diegetical world, but more tragically so, in the extradiegetical reality of history the film strives to signify. Here, it is difficult to ignore how the issue of race, consciously or otherwise, plays out in geopolitics. The scene ratifies what the American character Colonel Oliver had told Paul earlier:

> COLONEL OLIVER: You're black. You're not even a nigger, you're African! They're not gonna stay, Paul. They're not gonna stop the slaughter.

The irony of it all is that the former European colonizers' self-serving manipulations of tribal politics fanned the flames of hatred between the Tutsis and the Hutus; colonialism was one of the root causes of the genocide. The breaking down of social conscience and the cowardly exit of the Western forces would later mean the massacre of a million Rwandans. The scandalous scene of a predominantly Euro-American exodus and the abandonment of Rwandans essays how the ecumene of suffering is, from the perspective of geopolitics, an ecumene of Third World suffering. The imagery is forthright and dramatic in its representation of the First World-Third World divide here visually translated into political and racial binaries.

Schillebeeckx's own prophetic-liberating critique recognizes the global asymmetry in like manner:

> While two-thirds of the world population is crying out for justice and love, a powerful block made up of the remaining third, in East and West, is concentrating all its knowledge and its science, its power, its diplomacy and its tactics and means of subjugation, on keeping what it has.[20]

Sociopolitical analysis plays a pivotal role in Schillebeeckx's thought because it is the feeble and defenseless that are given epistemological privilege in his interactive soteriology. As such, the conflictual approach is meant to identify inequities and injustices within the historical situation. Evidently, the resonances with Third Cinema's emancipative conjunctures are unmistakable. I argue later that while such a critical diagnosis can be found in both Schillebeeckx's thought and Third Cinema, neither ends with it.

NEGATIVE EXPERIENCES OF CONTRAST

In Schillebeeckx's conception of negative experiences of contrast, the very experience of human suffering may offer a positive, cognitive power when it kindles creative dissatisfaction over the dehumanizing status quo. The situation of suffering is seen as a negation of the divine will, hence, fueling militancy and defiant resistance. Paradoxically, negative experiences of contrast give rise to protest, hope, and praxical initiative.

In *Perfumed Nightmare*, the sequences portraying Kidlat's protest suggest that the divine identifies with the marginalized, who face the threat of systematic exploitation and abuse. The allusion to a mysterious, divine force crystallizes during the mock farewell party scene when Kidlat comes to a clearer insight of the structural causes of his subjugation. In a stylistic shift to magic realism, the latter part of the sequence shows Kidlat toppling down the towering Western dignitaries by the sheer power of his breath. An earlier allusion pre-figures this surprising turn. There is the revisionist, mythic story of Kidlat's father, a local hero, who, prior to his unjust execution, superhumanly blows away armed American sentries in occupied Manila in the aftermath of the fraudulent 1898 Treaty of Paris. The link is drawn clearly by a flash cut showing an extreme close-up shot of the mouth of Kidlat's father, lips pursed in the act of blowing. This same frame was shown in an earlier flashback scene accompanying Kaya's storytelling of the heroic event. The magical breathpower fulfills the prophetic message of the village guru Kaya. His pithy admonition is reprised in the sequence as a voice-over:

> KAYA: Where is your true strength Kidlat? Where is your real strength? The sleeping typhoon must learn to blow again.

The metaphorical pattern is unlocked—Kidlat, as synechdochic representation of the struggling Filipino, is the sleeping typhoon who has learned to blow again. *Perfumed Nightmare* uses the concept of "breath" and "wind" in a sense consonant with the biblical *ruah*,[21] which is used when God's transformative presence is perceived to be at work, such as in prophecy. The divine presence is sublimated in Kaya's interlocution and in the liberative breathpower, both of which are eloquent expressions of Kidlat's protest.

Referring again to *Perfumed Nightmare*'s mise-en-scène, I also point to an important leitmotiv, the running theme of "creativity amid the postcolonial ruins" expressed stylistically through a unique set of symbols akin to Laura U. Marks's "recollection-objects." In their very materiality, recollection-objects function as repositories of popular and subversive collective memories and have thus been described by Marks as "radioactive."[22] While Marks emphasizes what she considers as Tahimik's fetishist portrayal of the recollection object, for example, his preoccupation with ordinary objects such as double-yolk eggs and supermarket incinerators,[23] she fails to note the more significant recollection-objects in the film, those that play a central role in providing critical comment on the Philippine postcolonial struggle. *Perfumed Nightmare* reconfigures the recollection-object by equating it with Tahimik's notion of Filipino "indio-genious," here, precisely taken to mean native creativity amid the postcolonial ruins. Aside from their irreducible materiality and radioactivity, these recollection-objects are hewn from the very weapons originally used by the colonizers to forward their imperialist agenda. The recollection-object as conceived in *Perfumed Nightmare* is a paradox; it is the implosion of a positive, defiant counter-force arising from the crucible of colonial trauma. Thus, it is easy to see *Perfumed Nightmare*'s recollection-objects as emotive of Schillebeeckx's negative experiences of contrast when the colonial trauma, an otherwise "negative mis-experience," is perceived as offering an implicit impulse toward militant praxis, and, ultimately, toward greater human flourishing. Two of these recollection-objects evoke negative experiences of contrast in symbol form: the wooden horse-figure, which Kidlat's mother carved from the butt of her late husband's U.S.-made rifle; and the jeepney, which is essentially the wreckage of a U.S. military jeep transmogrified as a useful means of public transportation—"vehicles of war which we made into vehicles of life."

The Last Supper's narrative allusions to resistance fit effortlessly into the concept of negative experiences of contrast. As I discussed previously, the representation of resistance in the film is largely character-driven; it is worked out in the portrayal of the defiant slave Sebastian. In a series of actions, he resists the manipulative overtures of his masters as he refuses to accept the legitimacy of the distorted master-slave relations. The pivotal impulse of negative experiences of contrast crystallizes in the scene when Sebastian invokes the Afro-Cuban folk religion Santeria as a means of finding legitimation for his desire for freedom. He rejects the colonial, institutional religion, which has become a weapon wielded by the powerholders to justify and perpetuate slavery, and, in a subversive act, turns to folk religion for redemptive validation. The eerie imagery produced when Sebastian lifts the head of a roasted pig over his face in mockery of the count's exploitative reference to Catholicism, is a stylistic device that reinforces this rejection. The power of the count is the power of the lie. Because he has come to an awareness of the dignity and freedom that is his patrimony, Sebastian unmasks the god of his masters as foreign, bogus, "not-God." That said, Sebastian does not see the divine in the religion of his masters. Where are the traces of an authentic divine presence from Sebastian's perspective? The divine is rarefied in his righteous anger and in his struggle for freedom. Unlike the count's god, whom he carves out of a twisted interpretation of codified religion, Sebastian's god is alive and kinetic; as unstructured and ungovernable as nature itself. We get a visceral sense of this in Sebastian's eventual escape from the clutches of slavery. The intercutting imagery of nature, formidable and untamed, accompanies his sprint to freedom. Cinematically, *The Last Supper* suggests that Sebastian's god flies with the eagle, rumbles with the river, tears down mountain rocks, and runs with the wild horses. Because slavery and any form of curtailment of freedom is anathema to this god, he or she rages against the forces that conspire to effectuate such conditions. To shackle the spirit of this god is as futile as imprisoning the wind. And it is the same spirit that inflames Sebastian's defiance.

In *Xala*, protest and indignation function as a form of sociospiritual purgation and this is where the link to negative experiences of contrast can be drawn out. I am referring specificially to the film's denouement, which features a disquieting folk ritual of spitting. To free himself from a *xala* or spell of impotence, the central character El Hadji has to go through a ritual where a band of beggars—established earlier as victims of his neocolonial snobbery and arrogance—spit on his naked body. Gabriel notes that the spitting ritual is "a symbolic social act" expressing the outrage of those marginalized by the neocolonial class:

> Its treatment in film language makes it a powerful "trope" or cinematic rhetoric to connote the bourgeoisie's spiritual and material decadence and the common people's expression of anger and outrage against that class.[24]

In the trope of the spitting ritual, the indigent of Senegalese society express their remonstration against the oppressive reality of the status quo and make a spectacle out of it. The intimation of the divine as a force made manifest in the struggle for justice lies in the spitting ritual itself as an act of purgation. The decadence of the bourgeoisie, as represented by El Hadji, is imputed to a supernatural *xala*, a spell that inflicts not just the physical but the spiritual. The spitting, which Gabriel likens to a "vomiting of bile,"[25] can then be understood as a form of exorcism where the demons of an unjust colonial past are expunged and driven out from the national psyche. The spitting ritual, therefore, sets over against the abusive neocolonial culture and offers a positive moment; there is hope for social change.

Protest is portrayed in literal, documentary fashion in the polemical *Bread and Roses*. A crew of illegal immigrants and African-Americans work as janitors in a downtown Los Angeles building, which has big-profit corporations as tenants. With the sweat of their brow, the janitors earn poverty wages under an abusive management. Here, an internal Third World congeals as the characters navigate through the compounded political economy of labor, race, culture, and gender. But the disadvantaged janitors unionize, grow in political awareness, and organize a series of protest actions against their employers. Street demonstrations calling for just wages and work benefits are the most literal expressions of protest in the film and as I noted earlier, politically charged songs accompany the janitors' struggle and give them voice. One of the most trenchant representations of protest in *Bread and Roses* takes place when the janitors' union gate-crashes an exclusive party hosted by the law firm that owns the building. Union leader Sam Shapiro hands out a "golden turkey" award to the law firm for its complicity in the unjust labor situation and the janitors, armed with noisy vacuum cleaners, make their way through the well-heeled crowd of corporate bigwigs and Hollywood glitterati and mockingly vacuum their legs. The incongruent imagery presented in the film's mise-en-scène is a satirical protest of the social inequality the janitors face in their lives. While no direct reference to the divine is found in *Bread and Roses*, the onus to form a community of equals is indexical of a vital force that is sympathetic to the striving for a more human life. God is affirmed in the longing for both "bread" and "roses." In *Bread and Roses*, the divine has not, so to speak, affixed a clear and legible signature, but is known by his or her actions in history.

A closer look at the key scenes of *Divine Intervention* also brings to view the film's connotative alliance with the concept of negative experiences of contrast. Earlier, I introduced how the motif of protest and liberating anger is worked out in the film's stylistic elements. *Divine Intervention* assembles a mosaic of startling images that portray the anxiety, desperation, and indignation arising from the Palestinian social layer in the extended Israeli occupation of Palestine. It is interesting to note that in no other stylistic option does the theme of protest take on such emblematic clarity than in the film's re-appropriation of the "David and Goliath" myth. Referring to the biblical text would be helpful here:

> When the Philistine drew nearer to meet David, David ran quickly toward the battle line to meet the Philistine. David put his hand in his bag, took out a stone, slung it, and struck the Philistine on his forehead; the stone sank into his forehead, and he fell face down on the ground. So David prevailed over the Philistine with a sling and a stone, striking down the Philistine and killing him; there was no sword on David's hand.[26]

In this biblical account, David refuses to fight Goliath using conventional weaponry; he opts to use a shepherd's sling and some stones. The statement is clear: there is a higher power on David's side on which the outcome of the battle rests.[27] Surely, a puny stone is not likely to fell a towering champion who is armed and in full battle gear. A reappropriation of the "David and Goliath" story is hinted in the opening scene of *Divine Intervention*; Palestinian youths chase after a man in a Santa Claus suit and pelt him with stones. If, as I noted earlier, Santa Claus is a symbolic rendering of American powerplay and its support for the Israeli occupation, it would seem quite absurd to have Palestinians, youths at that, use puny stones against him. Certainly, it is the representational value of the stones as symbols of protest that is underscored here.

The "David and Goliath" motif is depicted in sharper relief in another important scene. We see Israeli riflemen taking target practice at cardboard dummies of a Palestinian woman garbed in a ninja-like warrior costume. The riflemen demonstrate their shooting skills in an amusing, perfectly coordinated, choreographed display that emphasizes the systematic and professionally trained military might of Israel. When the Palestinian woman herself emerges in the flesh, she promptly faces rapid Israeli firepower as the riflemen shoot at her. At this point, the film employs the stylistic option of magic realism; the woman deflects the bullets superhumanly by levitating and spinning around like a top. As the riflemen fire at her, the bullets pause mid-air and form a striking iconic image of a crown of thorns around the woman's head. With arms outstretched, the allusion to the crucified Christ is undeniable.[28] While this image in itself can trigger ideological discussion,[29] I focus on a more relevant later turn. The woman is shown whirling a sling à la David and then pelting the riflemen with stones until they are disarmed and defeated one after another. The absurdity of the idea that a beautiful woman uses puny stones as weapons against a superior military power directs us to a connotational interpretation. The stoning, understood within the lopsided "David and Goliath" equation, de-emphasizes violence. Again, it is protest and liberating anger that is foregrounded by the use of stones; otherwise, firepower should have been met squarely with firepower. There is a divine initiative behind the stoning and it militates against the oppressive situation brought about by the Israeli occupation. A higher power has taken up the Palestinian cause. The very title *Divine Intervention* already serves as a heuristic cue that in the film's perspective, God is identified with, and imbricated in, the Palestinian quest for freedom.

Divine Intervention recasts the long-drawn Palestinian struggle for freedom at the center of a cultural text drawn from the Hebrew Bible, thus, making a particularly Semitic cultural myth stand on its head.[30] In the light of this liberative optic, the powerholders that occupy the privileged center of geopolitics inevitably face the full impact of Palestinian stones.

Interestingly, a parallel equation plays out in *Perfumed Nightmare*. The diminutive and powerless Kidlat is no match for the high and mighty phantom of progress, which is backed by the forces of the world's most powerful socioeconomic system. But at a significant turn, Kidlat plays David to the phantom's Goliath when he pelts an imposing supermarket building with stones. As in *Divine Intervention*, the collective protest of the oppressed is represented in this scene.

The representation of the divine power immersed and actively involved in the struggle for liberation quadrates with Schillebeeckx's theological understanding of the God who is experienced negatively in the militant refusal to acquiesce to dehumanizing, oppressive situations that characterize the anti-Reign. Mary Catherine Hilkert's description of Schillebeeckx's negative experiences of contrast fits effortlessly as an annotation to the protest motif in *Perfumed Nightmare*—"God is the source of a creative dissatisfaction with all that is less than God's vision of humanity."[31]

Eschatological Salvation

For Schillebeeckx, the requisite course of action in the quest for the elusive *humanum* is the positive promotion of justice and human liberation within the guiding framework of the anthropological constants; indeed, "the human is the royal road to the divine." In the face of the horrific reality of the ecumene of suffering, however, Schillebeeckx configures praxis as negative experiences of contrast. Hence, there is a converse action accompanying the positive search for the *humanum*—the praxical imperative to reject and oppose that which is evil and dehumanizing:

> [T]o fight energetically against everything which vitiates man's physical life, burdens his psychological life, humiliates him as a person, enslaves him through social structures, drives him into an irresponsible adventure through irrationality; makes the free exercise of his religious feeling impossible; and finally, to oppose everything which infringes human rights and reifies men as a result of their working conditions and the bureaucracy which shapes them.[32]

The journey toward eschatological salvation or final good is the good fight. While negative experiences of contrast ground the eschatological ethic of the present, definitive salvation is never fully realized in history. The full disclosure of the *humanum* is a future, eschatological reality.

One of the central images in *Perfumed Nightmare* is the bridge. In the opening sequence, a jeepney is shown moving back and forth of Balian's crude and archaic bridge. Kidlat notes that it is the only bridge in and out of the village and describes it as "our bridge of life." Aside from its many uses in the day-to-day life of the community, Kidlat narrates that the bridge had also been used in the past by both the Spanish and American colonizers. He is then shown pulling three jeepneys, one at a time, across the bridge. The sequence begins with a small toy jeepney and, in a progressive gradation, ends with a real, full-size version. While pulling the jeepney with a rope, Kidlat faces the camera and self-reflexively asserts:

> KIDLAT: I am Kidlat Tahimik. I choose my vehicle and I can cross this bridge.

Kidlat's affirmation of self-determination, as it is, already bespoken in his name which means "Silent Lightning," coupled with his peculiar act of pulling the jeepney instead of simply driving it, is set in motion by "crossing the bridge." Although Kidlat begins to cross a number of bridges, both literally (the Balian bridge, the bridges of Paris) and figuratively (rural to urban, tradition to modernity, local to international, Third World to First World), the film keeps the journey's end ambiguous and open-ended. Kidlat, in fact, already hints at this open-endedness in the latter part of the opening sequence. As he pulls the jeepney across the bridge in a labored manner, he exclaims:

> KIDLAT: Today I am still making that final crossing to freedom.

Perfumed Nightmare suggests a perspective congruent to that of Schillebeeckx, who emphasizes the imperative of human striving in history while understanding the actual realization of the *humanum* as a future, eschatological event. In *Perfumed Nightmare*, the bridge lends itself as the symbolic pathway from subjugation to liberation, suffering to salvation. It is also, importantly, the passage from past to future. Kidlat makes it clear that the bridge to freedom is still being crossed; the destination remains a hopeful future yet to emerge on the horizon.

The ending of *Bread and Roses* shares a similar view of salvation as fragmentary. In the film, there is an ebb and flow of salvific moments that, while present and real, do not quite reach fullness and completion. The janitors are arrested after holding a demonstration in the lobby of the building. Just as the interrogation process ensues, they receive word that management had given in to their demands for better pay and benefits. The good news is met with loud cheers and justice is served at long last. The jubilation, however, is short-lived. The police hands out a deportation order to Maya for a petty crime she had committed earlier; she stole money from a shop to support the education of one of her friends, a fellow Mexican janitor, who gained entrance to law school. Notwithstanding the ethical question triggered by her "Robin Hood" act, Maya is no criminal; she is a powerless immigrant worker who, like her friend, struggles to get by in a ruthless world that crushes the weakest links of the socioeconomic chain. Her "crime" represents her refusal to accept the inconsistencies of a society that claims to be democratic, but violates basic human rights. In the final scene, Maya is escorted to a van, which will take her back to Tijuana. As the vehicle begins to drive away, the camera assumes Maya's point of view and we see her sister Rosa against the glass window, running after the van, and waving at her. They see each other through the glass but it is also the symbol of their separation. Rosa utters reassuring words that echo faintly as the distance between the sisters widen. While the wheels of justice have turned in favor of the janitors' union, Maya still has to pay the wages of an obdurate legal system. *Bread and Roses* closes with a scene that is bittersweet; bread had been won but the roses are yet to come. Salvation is both here and not yet.

Romero also mirrors the Schillebeckxian perspective of eschatological salvation, but in a way that is less inchoative and more categorically religious than *Bread and Roses*. This is apparent in the closing sequence, which is the point in the narrative immediately following the assassination of the bishop. The masses of El Salvador are shot in frontal, wide-angle framing, in a single long take that shows them walking through a dirt road. On surface reading, we see the *gestus* of common folk as they go about their daily lives. But a deeper level of meaning emerges as soon as we hear the voice-over of the bishop:

> ROMERO:　I have often been threatened with death. If they kill me, I will arise in the Salvadoran people. Let my blood be the seed of freedom and a sign that hope will soon be a reality. A bishop will die but the church, which is the people of God, will never perish.

The death of the bishop, who was the voice of the poor, represents the myriad sufferings of the victims of political oppression and a rude awakening to the reality that salvation is fragmentary. However sobering that reality is, it is not the final word. The vision of a world of greater justice and equality "resurrects" as a promise; it is the hope that lives on in the church, the "people of God." As we take a second look at the long take, the poor are pressing on toward an exodus that is ongoing, but not yet fully realized. Praxical initiatives are fragmentary manifestations of God's Reign; eschatological salvation ultimately rests in the hands of the divine.

Schillebeeckx's conception of an eschatological proviso and an eschatological surplus also finds filmic expression in Third Cinema. Schillebeeckx clarifies that the sum total of all sociopolitical action will not precipitate definitive salvation or final good. It is, as such, free and open-ended. Schillebeeckx thus proposes a relativizing critical principle he terms as an "eschatological proviso" that bars the tendency to totalize any emancipative movement as the sole agent of final salvation. On the other hand, Schillebeeckx also proposes an "eschatological surplus" of God's transcendent love, which emphasizes the positive link between salvation and praxis, reorienting liberative initiatives in the light of the Reign. The eschatological proviso and surplus are two sides of the same coin; the creative tension that exists between them considers praxical initiatives as provisional yet essential constituents of eschatological salvation.

I return to *Perfumed Nightmare* at this juncture as it is the one film from our case study list that crystallizes the eschatological proviso/surplus analogy in truly cinematic fashion and with remarkable complexity. In the film, the American ideal of progress and technological advancement insistently hovers in the atmosphere as the way to salvation and liberation. The American dream offers itself as the closest thing to heaven on earth, a life of seemingly endless possibilities light years away from Kidlat's small rural world of bamboo huts and recycled jeepneys. The celestial allusion is already apparent in the very idea of the historical moon landing of 1969, which amazes Kidlat no end. At the point when Kidlat approaches the final leg of his journey—his trip to America and Cape Canaveral—he is shown in partial close-up with an eerie background image looming behind him. It is a backlit stained glass window adorned with the iconized face of his American boss. As the image appears, the association with religious stained glass art normally found in Catholic churches is immediate and hard to miss. Additionally, the accompanying voice-over reinforces the religious connection. With his grating voice conspicuously identical to that of then U.S. secretary of state Henry Kissinger, the American poseur offers salvation:

> AMERICAN BOSS: Right after the party we fly to America on the Concorde. You will be the first Filipino to fly supersonic. Tomorrow, Kidlat, tomorrow . . . you shall be with me in Paradise.

The paradisial ascription to America is a twisted re-appropriation of the words of Jesus Christ on Calvary, meant as a response to the repentant convict by his side.[33] The ideological jigsaw abandons all restraint—the American is the savior, Paradise is America, and Kidlat is the lost soul in dire need of salvation. Kidlat, however, deepens in insight and his suspicion comes to a boil. To recall Kidlat's words:

> KIDLAT: Is this the Paradise I longed for? Is this the Paradise I dream of?

In Kidlat's growing critical awareness, *Perfumed Nightmare* questions and rejects the proposition that a socioeconomic system, in this case, the American dream, could be the estimable agent of final salvation. I extend the argument further by submitting that the film angles this motif in a way that is effectually consonant with Schillebeeckx's notion of an eschatological proviso/surplus. Historical initiative and self-determination is affirmed in the character of Kidlat, but neither he, nor the group of people he stands for–those who struggle to cross the bridge to freedom—are presented as the sole agents of a new sociopolitical order. Through the employment of magic realism, *Perfumed Nightmare* admits the place of divine initiative in the quest for justice. After blowing away the masked guests at the farewell party, Kidlat bolts out and runs through a dark tunnel, toward its lighted end. Kidlat then boards one of the supermarket incinerators and begins to propel it to flight by the sheer force of his breath. The leit-motiv of "breath," by now well established as a signifier for liberation by divine initiative, had turned the chimney into a kind of magical space craft. The anti-positivist statement is apparent when this surprise twist is viewed in relation to the earlier allusions to the Apollo space program and the moon landing that captured Kidlat's imagination prior to his re-awakening. The vision of progress and technology had broken the boundaries of space and taken human beings to the moon, but it had proven to be shortsighted in the most proximate responsibility, that of respecting and upholding humanity here on earth. Kidlat's spacecraft, in contrast, is empowered by a force not generated by progress and technology. It defies gravity by the same mystical, liberative force that helped his father in the past and that felled the masked guests—divine intervention. As the magical space-craft soars into a night sky, Kidlat is shown in close-up, gazing toward an open-ended, future destination. He is certainly not on the same course as the astronauts in the Apollo spacecraft, there will be no moon landings for Kidlat. The self-conscious frame of magic realism suggests an eschatological, rather than a mere geographical destination.

The sequences following shift back to realism as it shows Kidlat's mother closing the window of her hut back in Balian. This is followed by the scene earlier mentioned, that of Kidlat's sister Alma driving her toy jeepney with the horse-figure mounted on its hood. As I previously pointed out, the postcolonial struggle for liberation is rooted in the past (Kidlat's father and mother), ongoing in the present (Kidlat himself), and continuing to the future (Alma), with the destination remaining open-ended. There is no attempt to map the realization of a new, emancipative sociopolitical order; what is emphasized here is the promise and possibility of that order. But just as the film seemingly leaves it at that, a small but significant reference in the closing credits pinpoints an imagined future. The whole segment of the closing credits come in the form of postal letters shuffled one at a time. Each of the letters come with a different postage stamp indicating commemorative designs from various countries. The very last one is a child's artwork featuring Kidlat, perched outside his magical spacecraft in some unspecified celestial destination. This is obviously not on the same realm of reality as the preceding Balian scenes, as such, it presents no indication of the aftermath of some sociopolitical revolution. The stamp belongs to the sphere of imaginative, utopic reality; the world of the liberating breathpower and magical space craft. It is a perspec-tive wide enough to include the possibilities offered by the workings of a divine power. Just outside the border of the stamp's design reads the word, "Philippines." As a syntagmatic organization, the image recalls the *Filipino* value of *Bathala Na*, (literally, "may God's will be done") the belief that divine intervention ultimately completes an authentic human endeavor. Liberation and salvation is seen as an eschatological reality.

The film's resonances with Schillebeeckx's eschatological proviso/surplus crystallize at this point. Resistance and protest against structural evil is a necessary course of action but it cannot bring about final good. Eschatological salvation lies in the divine will. But in turn, the divine will proffers to relativize human efforts so that they factor into the total scheme of salvation. *Perfumed Nightmare* cinematically mirrors this creative, eschatological tension in its stylistic strategies. Kidlat as synechdoche of the postcolonial Filipino is in a liberative struggle and does what is humanly possible to express resistance and protest against the dehumanization wrought by the positivism of the American dream. The final outcome, however, lies in a power bigger that Kidlat, the people of the Philippines, or other Third World cultures kept marginal by the current order. The alternative future is a divine initiative, which, in the meantime, offers a hopeful, liberating vision.

Anthropological Constants

The anthropological constants constitute a meta-concept that implicitly frames the direction of Schillebeeckx's thought; they do not evince his eschatology as such. As established in my earlier discussion of Schillebeeckx's understanding of the *humanum*, the anthropological constants work to demarcate, rather than evaluate, the concept of being human. Nonetheless, it is worth exploring how Third Cinema stylistic strategies may configure a path to human flourishing along a matrix consonant with Schillebeeckx's anthropological constants. Schillebeeckx speaks of six paradigmatic anthropological constants (the seventh being the synthesis of all six) within which salvation may be worked out in the reality of the present. Situated within his liberative eschatological perpective, the anthropological constants offer a discursive framework for a more in-depth discussion of the Third World situation as represented in Third Cinema.

It is pertinent to clarify that while the case studies mirror important facets of the anthropological constants, they do not necessarily showcase all of them. The one exception is *Perfumed Nightmare*, which notably crystallizes all six anthropological constants. As a paradigmatic example of the seventh anthropological constant emphasizing the synthesis of all six, *Perfumed Nightmare* reasonably merits more privileged space in the discussion.

The Relationship of Human Corporeality, Nature and the Ecological Environment

Schillebeeckx considers the respect for human bodiliness and ecological nature as constitutive of humanity and thus, an essential concern of salvation. The first half of *Perfumed Nightmare*, prior to Kidlat's departure for Paris, registers the outlook of this anthropological constant. The Balian community folk are portrayed as symbiotically related to their unrestricted, natural environment. I had referred earlier to the way in which the film's cinematography renders this visually through the employment of the wide-angle shot. In an uninterrupted long take of 40 seconds, *Perfumed Nightmare* features a green field flittering with hundreds of butterflies. Understood in the grammar of Third Cinema, the field of butterflies scene punctuates the thriving of nature alongside its human inhabitants. Moreover, the choice of a natural setting—the lush tropical forest of Balian—further emphasizes this respectful human closeness to nature. The forest is where community life happens. In the flashback scene featuring an adolescent Kidlat and his gang mates undergoing circumcision at the hands of one of the village elders, the crude ritual transpires in a natural, outdoor operating room canopied by trees and brush, with the flowing river serving as wash basin. Although the forest is the natural site of the community's rites of passage and daily life, there is no sign of domination and systematic exploitation by the village folk. As a study of contrast, the film reprises the idyllic Balian setting at a later turn, this time, with the forest degraded into a wasteland of tree stumps after a visitation by the phantom of progress. The relevance of this dramatic scene hits closer to home when one considers the larger reality of the precarious ecological situation in the Philippines. Described by *National Geographic* as "Galapagos times ten," the country's forests and marine parks are unparalleled virtual laboratories of biodiversity.[34] Progress, however, and its by-product of industrial wastes, has been a major culprit in putting one of the earth's "incubators of life" on life support. Additionally, *Perfumed Nightmare*'s contrasting images of cityscape epitomized by a hyper-modernizing Paris, serve to critique the ecological cost of urbanized development and progress. Kidlat's Paris is a deteriorating city in a hurry to build its concrete jungle of super malls and super chimneys at the cost of ecological and humanitarian considerations.

The Motorcycle Diaries' comparative representation of a simpler, more organic lifestyle vis-à-vis the onslaught of urbanization, expressively dramatizes Schillebeeckx's second anthropological constant in a stylistic option analogous to that of *Perfumed Nightmare*. *The Motorcycle Diaries* is replete with picturesque wide-angle shots of the Latin American countryside and the imagery meaningfully contributes to the social commentary. We return to the scene when Ernesto and Alberto reach Peru. As they engage in a conversation with an indigenous farmer, who relates how unscrupulous rich men had grabbed land from his people, the handheld camera pans left, right, and around the farmer, so that we get a view of the lush mountains and rushing streams in the background while he speaks. The camerawork suggests the farmer's oneness with the land of his heritage and this provides foil for his testimony on the avarice of the rich land-grabbers. The indigenous community, which had integrated its way of life with the natural environment, had been displaced and exploited by those blinded by the profit motive. In an obvious lack of moral restraint, the rich and powerful have convinced themselves that they have the right to exploit others and dominate the natural environment. This finds confirmation in the contrasting intercut images of Macchu Picchu, which integrates symbiotically with the mountainscape, as against the flat, bulldozed urban sprawl of Lima. The film discloses the link between the race for urbanization and the alienation of humans from nature.

Being Human Involves Fellow-Humans

The second anthropological constant advocates a relationship of mutuality between people in a society built upon inclusiveness and responsibility for the other. The transcendence of individuality and the movement toward greater involvement in an expanding "co-humanity" characterizes this anthropological touchstone. Third Cinema's stylistic option of privileging a communitarian perspective rather than individual psychology allows for an effective visual representation of this principle. As can be deduced from the previous discussions, all of the case studies unremittingly foreground the communitarian context from which the characters find identification, interaction, and accountability.

Romero offers a cinematic illustration in its second half, when the Archbishop had undergone a conversion to justice. At this point onward, he is often framed in wide-angle shots alongside the *anawim*, or God's poor, showing his solidarity with the oppressed and their struggle for justice and equality. In the scene depicting the military takeover of the town of Aguilares, Romero attempts to recover the Eucharistic bread from the tabernacle after the church had been turned into a barracks. The soldiers threaten the archbishop with gunshots and kick him out of the church. As he is about to leave, he glances upon a crowd of people quietly witnessing the unfolding drama. We see them in wide-angle framing; a sea of faces, both young and elderly, men and women, steadfastly holding their ground in front of the church, but helplessly paralyzed before military firepower. The oppressed poor, as a community of accountability, compels the bishop to return and reenter the church. Costuming plays a symbolic role here; Romero dons his priestly alb and stole, indicating that the "people of God" wage a moral battle. As he defiantly walks into the church, the crowd walks with him in a spontaneous display of people power. Shamed, the soldiers are left with no choice but to allow them entrance.

A similar scene plays out in *Hotel Rwanda*. Paul Rusesabagina's family is one of the few chosen ones granted exit visas by host countries. As family members and other lucky ones board the truck that would take them out of the hotel to safe passage, Paul takes one last look at those left behind. Through Paul's optic, we see a wide-angle shot of the faces of refugees and hotel staff, all facing a future of uncertainty, impending violence, and the shadow of death. The truck starts to drive away in haste, but at that frantic moment, Paul does the unexpected: he breaks away from his family and decides to stay. His wife and children wail in protest as the truck pulls away but Paul had made a preferential choice for his expanded family, fellow members of a co-humanity who depend on him for protection, indeed for survival, in the ongoing genocidal bloodshed.

Humanity is the center of Schillebeeckx's theology and he emphasizes that "the face is the image of ourselves for others." This entails going beyond the personal "I-thou" level and acknowledging the "we" relationship in the pursuit of human liberation.

The Connection with Social and Institutional Structures

For Schillebeeckx, the social dimension is not a mere addendum to human identity but is constituent of this identity. To conceive of structures and institutions as independent entities is to perpetuate them as natural and unchangeable when they are, in fact, contingent and mutable; both their preservation and plasticity are dependent on human action.

Religion is one of the social structures that find cinematic expression and commentary in *Perfumed Nightmare*. The Philippines carries the national trauma of three centuries of colonial rule where Roman Catholicism became a tool conveniently used by the Spanish colonizers to sacralize their imperialist agenda. The marriage of the Iberian import with indigenous folk religiosity only served to promote a culture of passivity and subservience, which the colonizers readily exploited.[35] The continuing repercussions of colonial religion are dramatized in the film's mise-en-scène when Kidlat is shown flagellating with other devotees before the image of a distinctly Spanish-looking Virgin Mary. Colonial religion also takes the form of the American civil religion, represented in the film as the American dream. The belief in "manifest destiny," the sacralizing principle that sublimates American expansionism under the cloak of divine appointment, is imaged stylistically in the critical sequence when Kidlat's American boss appears in divinized radiance on a stained glass window as he describes America as paradise. The idea that institutions do not drop from heaven and can therefore be challenged and subjected to change is evident in the film when Kidlat views the American dream with suspicion and begins to question its validity. The contingent nature of institutional religion is emphasized in the portrayal of an alternative "religion" where the divine is perceived as having taken up the emancipative cause of the weak and vulnerable. Authentic religion is metaphorized in the sleeping typhoon that must learn to blow again.

Xala deals with the new social order in post-francophone Senegal, which is steeped in neocolonialism and marked by the ascendancy of a new economic elite. Traditional institutions of home and family become subordinate to the caprices of El Hadji, who is neocolonialism personified. But it is within his family that the call for social change arises. Rama, El Hadji's daughter from his first wife, is the antithesis of her father and his voice of conscience. The value of the character of Rama can be discerned immediately in her appearance. She is a young medical student garbed in a traditional African dress. Rama stands for the future Senegalese society healed of its colonial past and proudly rerooted in its authentic identity. Her unyielding decision to address El Hadji in the native Wolof language rather than French, and her refusal to drink his favorite imported "Evian" water are ways of denouncing the neocolonial values her father swears by. Earlier on, El Hadji slaps Rama for indicting all polygamous men as "dirty dogs," just before he is set to marry his third wife. Ironically, during El Hadji's dismissal from the chamber of commerce, he quotes Rama's very words and says:

EL HADJI: Each one of us is a dirty dog. I repeat "dirty dogs" worse
     than I.

The statement, coupled with the exorcism ritual he eventually goes through, serves as indicators of his transformation. It also symbolizes the possibility of a Senegal in the brink of meaningful, structural change.

The Conditioning of People and Culture by Time and Space

In the fourth anthropological constant, Schillebeeckx underscores the fact that by our very historicity and finality, it is incumbent upon human beings to understand prevailing social realities and to critically assess and unmask the meaninglessness perpetuated in human history.

Schillebeeckx points to the responsibility of the affluent west to promote international solidarity in view of the wrenching reality that two-thirds of the global community is buckling under the weight of grave structural evil and abject poverty. Schillebeeckx does not subscribe to the idea that citizens of the First World ought to be personally guilty for the misery of the Third World. However, he is clear in denouncing unjust socioeconomic structures that only function to propel profits to trickle up to the most prosperous nations and not trickle down to the poorest.

> But we are bound to recognize that the structures are at fault- that the capitalist mode of production in the West is the cause of the disastrous situation there (in the third world) and that calls for a radical process of learning. Every critical community has to learn, reflect and analyse and encourage that learning process in others.[36]

A glimpse of the unjust dynamics driving the current freemarket gospel espoused by the World Trade Organization (WTO) concretizes and confirms the continuing validity of Schillebeeckx's fourth anthropological constant. The *International Herald Tribune* editorializes how the unfair protectionist strategies of developed countries are pushing Third World economies such as that of the Philippines on to the losing end of globalization.

> Small-scale farmers across the Philippine archipelago have discovered that their competitors in places like the United States or Europe do not simply have better seeds, fertilizers and equipment. Their products are also often protected by high tariffs, or underwritten by massive farm subsidies that make them artificially cheap. No matter how small a wage Filipino workers are willing to accept, they cannot compete with agribusinesses afloat on billions of dollars in government welfare . . . The same sad story repeats itself around the globe, as poor countries trying

to pull themselves into the world market come up against the richest nations insistence on stacking the deck for their own farmers.[37]

The editorial criticizes the deliberate, systematic defrauding of global trade rules in order to insure a "one way street" geared only to benefit and enrich the industrialized elites while crippling the weakest links of the global economy. Rightly so, the ruthless duplicity of the dominant economies is denounced as "morally depraved:"

> By rigging the global trade game against farmers in developing nations, Europe, the United States and Japan are essentially kicking the development ladder out from under some of the world's most desperate people. This is morally depraved. America's actions are harvesting poverty around the world. Hypocrisy compounds the outrage. The United States and Europe have mastered the art of forcing open poor nations' economies to imported goods and services. But they are slow to reciprocate when it comes to farming, where poorer nations can often manage, in a fair game, to compete. Globalization, it turns out, can be a one-way street.[38]

Perfumed Nightmare offers a thorough and insightful reflection of the fourth anthropological constant through a clear examination of the massive asymmetry between the First World and the Third. I had previously discussed this at length but it is instructive to review how the film portrays the global socioeconomic divide stylistically along the ideological trajectory of Third Cinema:

- The dangerous memory of the fraudulent 1898 Treaty of Paris referred to constantly in the film through flashback scenes of Kidlat's father, the deliberate choice of Paris as contrasting setting, and the synechdochic significance of the Kidlat-objects as positive expressions of defiance. These references to the Philippine colonial trauma indicate that the debilitating structures of Western domination are deeply rooted, compounded social realities. Against the frame of the current global economy, it can be seen that essentially, the phenomenon of structural injustice is nothing new; history has merely repeated itself. The Philippines is still on the short end of high-stakes First World double-dealing in new incarnations of the Treaty of Paris.
- The initial portrayal of Kidlat as a naive and vulnerable Third World bumpkin thoroughly captivated by the utopic delights of the American dream. The imagery conjured up by this portrayal is that of a starving rabbit going witless over the carrot being dangled on its face by its master.

- The mock farewell party scene employing camera angling strategies to portray Western bigwigs as towering masked figures alighting from limousines, in contrast to Kidlat, who appears to be dwarfed by them.
- The trope of the crude, recycled jeepney used for rural, day-to-day transportation as contrasted to the advanced NASA space- age technology capable of sending humans to the moon.
- The portrayal of the increasing disenfranchisement of people who are deemed dispensable by the structural demands of progress—Kidlat's parents, the Balian community, the pushcart vendors-over and above the ecological degradation caused by the phantom of progress.

Kidlat's journey of self-discovery, which confers on him a liberated consciousness and allows him to rediscover his prophetic-liberating voice, represent the unmasking and indictment of these structural inequalities.

The critical unmasking of human-induced meaninglessness in history is a core issue in *Divine Intervention*. The film's vignettes featured in the film's first half seem pointlessly amorphous–a man driving a car curses under his breath just after greeting people on the street, a man repeatedly throws garbage at the neighbor's side of the fence and berates her when she does the same, semi-catatonic patients push their I.V. stands listlessly in a hospital corridor—until we get a sense of their cumulative significance. These are images depicting the effects of a long-drawn military occupation on a human community. The Palestinians are prisoners in their own land and decades of repression had driven them to their wit's end. The line of causation begins to surface as the film progresses. The systematic humiliation Palestinian nationals have to face each day congeals in the checkpoint scenes where motorists become mere playthings in the hands of the Israeli soldiers. Palestinians are yelled at, ordered around, and submitted to all sorts of harassment by an occupying power. In one memorable scene, an armed checkpoint guard plays a sadistic game of mix-and-match with the motorists and their cars, and heckles them with a mocking song. Director Elia Suleiman notes in an interview that *Divine Intervention* represents "one one-thousandth of what actually goes on."[39] This is confirmed by Phyllis Bennis, an expert in Middle East issues who heads the Institute for Policy Studies in Washington:

Certainly the Israeli troops' use of helicopter gunships, of machine guns mounted on tanks, and so on is profoundly disproportionate when used against a Palestinian civilian population armed only with stones and some old Kalashnikov rifles. But the real issue is the Israeli military occupation of Palestine—not only that it is inherently violent and a violation of international law and contrary to United Nations resolutions. Even if Israel used only proportionate violence, it would still be absolutely illegal, because the occupation of Palestinian land is illegal . . . Unfortunately, the years of occupation have created, or have allowed to flourish, an incredibly racist vantage point among the majority of Israeli Jews. The majority of Israeli Jews are willing to accept the killing of Palestinians and collective punishment of the Palestinian population as justified state policy.[40]

Divine Intervention is but a glimpse of the Israeli occupation of Palestine through Palestinian eyes. It is, in Schillebeeckx's terms, a "hermeneutical undertaking" even as it unmasks the historical reality of a collective experience of meaninglessness inflicted on a community of human beings by fellow human beings.

Mutual Relationship of Theory and Practice

In the fifth anthropological constant, Schillebeeckx maintains that a degree of permanence is necessary if salvation is to be worked out in the shifting landscape of human culture. Herein, the mutual relationship between theory and practice plays a crucial hermeneutical role.

Kidlat's liberative journey in *Perfumed Nightmare* puts emphasis on the dynamic relationship between thought and action. No categorical distinction is drawn between the two principles; they are taken to be organically inseparable. Thus, the voice-over of Kidlat's personal declaration of independence and his magical toppling of the masked western guests are two waves emanating from the same current. They are treated as constitutive, unified expressions of the central rubric of postcolonial struggle and liberation. The mutuality between theory and practice in the film carries strong resonances with the way in which a Filipino theology of liberation is being developed. Known as the "theology of struggle," Philippine liberation theology emerged in the crucible of the Marcos dictatorship in the decade of the 1970s, the same circumstantial background as that of *Perfumed Nightmare*. The Theology of Struggle, by the denotation of its name, gives due emphasis on "lived theology" as much as it does the articulation of an inculturated theology; it is "not only an interpretation of the struggle, but is at the same time a struggle of interpretation."[41] The theology of struggle, thus, considers the very act of doing contextual theology as its method, as well as its brand of spirituality.[42]

Romero also very clearly establishes the integration of thought and action. The gradual conversion of Oscar Romero from conservative bishop to prophetic voice of the poor maps the link between his recognition of structural injustice and his eventual radical commitment to social change. This conversion process threatens the more conservative members of the Salvadoran church who find self-protection and safety in the dualistic separation of thought and action. Romero's journey toward justice resonates with the 1968 documents of the Latin American bishops at Medellín, which calls for a redistribution of Church resources and personnel as genuine expression of a "preferential option for the poor."[43] Through the prophetic character of Romero, the film exposes the grave inadequacy of a pulpit-Church whose teachings are divorced from the praxical imperative that is constitutive of the principles of the Reign of God.

The Religious and "Para-Religious" Consciousness of the Human

Schillebeeckx speaks of the utopian dimension of human consciousness as a fundamental anthropological constant. While the expressions of this utopian sensibility vary and may not necessarily take on a squarely religious nature, they are nonetheless forms of faith. The human religious or "para-religious" consciousness defies scientific, rational explanation but for Schillebeeckx, it is certain that they contribute to the wholeness of humanity.

I already pointed out how dimensions of a religious/para-religious current had been crystallized in most of the case studies. What is important to reiterate and nuance here is the way in which the divine is identified and located in situations of injustice and suffering. It is apparent in *The Last Supper*, for example, that the oppressed slave Sebastian does not see the divine in the institutional Catholic religion of his European masters because it is used as a weapon of subjugation and abuse. Instead, his religious consciousness is kindled by the subversive Afro-Cuban folk religion Santeria and the liberating life force associated with nature itself. In the case of *Divine Intervention*, the crystallization of a religious/para-religious consciousness is predicated on the reappropriation of the David and Goliath story, ironically, drawn from the normative religious text of the Israelis—the Hebrew Bible. The divine presence the Palestinians invoke is the God who liberates, whom they believe has taken up their cause. In both *The Last Supper* and *Divine Intervention*, the religious/para-religious consciousness could only accept a God who promotes human liberation and flourishing; any force to the contrary simply cannot be attributed to the divine.

To further illustrate the sixth anthropological constant, I present *Perfumed Nightmare* as a paradigmatic example because it offers a multi-layered representation of "faith" and the religious consciousness.

To recall:

- At the outset, Kidlat is shown as a devout Catholic immersed in the exuberant religious rituals of his community. The representation of religious consciousness can be seen in Kidlat's folk religiosity; the intermingling hues of Spanish colonial Catholicism and native beliefs colorfully portrayed in the film's mise-en-scène. For all the contradictions folk religion connotes here, it also works to establish that Kidlat believes in a divine being, a personal God, whom he perceives as actively involved in his life choices.

- On another level, religious consciousness is sublimated in the metaphor of "the sleeping typhoon that must learn to blow again." It is also rendered in the film as magic realism–the liberating, superhuman "breathpower" of Kidlat and his father before him–which points to a power greater than the human capabilities of the film's characters. "Wind" and "breath" is used in a sense akin to the biblical *ruah* and its allusion to God's creative spirit breathed into humans in the Genesis creation accounts. Moreover, the reappropriation of the David and Goliath motif (akin to *Divine Intervention*) in the stoning of the hulking supermarket works to strengthen the proposition that the divine is on the side of the victims of the phantom of progress.

- And then there is the eschatological dimension of the film expressed in the open-endedness of Kidlat's journey. The uninterrupted long-take of the mobile horse-figure moving against the dystopic construction rubble of Paris, Kidlat's magical flight to an undisclosed celestial destination aboard a chimney, and the reemergence of the horse-figure atop a toy jeepney being driven by Kidlat's young sister Alma, are some of the notable ways in which a critical utopian vision is worked out stylistically in the film.

In view of its consistent references to the possibility of a liberative divine presence, *Perfumed Nightmare* takes the human religious or "para-religious" consciousness as a natural given and is completely at home and unapologetic in portraying this dimension. The strong reflection of Schillebeeckx's sixth anthropological constant is no accident as the film, in the first place, is a cinematic mirror of Philippine culture where faith and robust religious experiences continue to flourish through the different contours of its history. The local Philippine Catechism describes this phenomenon:

> We Filipinos have had a long history of very sharp and colorful religious experiences: From our pre-Christian times, through the centuries of Spanish Christian evangelization, to the American Protestant influx in the Commonwealth era, and the Japanese occupation of World War II, right up past Vatican II's "Second Pentecost," to "People Power" and today's "Basic Christian Communities," and the 2nd Plenary Council of the Philippines (PCP II) . . . all these experiences have somehow defined and clarified our unique identity as *persons*, as *Christians*, as *Filipinos*, as a *nation*.[44]

As Schillebeeckx points out, authentic liberation is unrealizable without faith and hope.

Conclusion: The New Stained Glass Window

The term "crystallization" conjures up an image of something liquid metamorphosing into a more definite, conceivable structure. Indeed, at this point, we are in a better position to picture the methodological schema of this interdisciplinary project. It is germane to reiterate that our exploration of the creative crossings between Schillebeeckx's eschatological perspective and Third Cinema stands on two legs.

The first concursion is based on the epistemological resonances between the liberative soteriological frame of reference of Schillebeeckx's later theology and the film's exemplification of the critical principles of Third Cinema. Released from the depoliticizing tendency characteristic of the reception of his thought, Schillebeeckx's eschatological perspective matches convincingly with the emancipative agenda of Third Cinema. Congruently, Third Cinema's audiovisual coding of the Third World postcolonial struggle and its ascription of a praxical imperative in the representation of the divine, is receptive to Schillebeeckx's epistemological project of engaging in a mutually critical dialogue with Third World liberationist theologies.

The second point of convergence has to do with the ways in which Third Cinema stylistic strategies evinced in the case studies crystallize the essential lines of Schillebeeckx's eschatological perspective, namely, the Ecumene of Suffering, Negative Experiences of Contrast, Eschatological Salvation, and Anthropological Constants. Navigating through the grammar of Third Cinema—the ideologically determined cinematic elements such as mise-en-scène, editing, cinematography, and sound—we devoted attention to the intertextual crossings between the cinematic principle and the theological principle.

The resonances between Schillebeeckx's thought and Third Cinema, as expressed epistemologically, and through the method-ological mediation of Third Cinema stylistic strategies, do not hinge on a neat, perfectly matched correspondence, but on a creative and open-minded intertextual exploration that offers mutual enrichment to both sides of the Theology-Cinema equation. On the side of Third Cinema, the eschatological perspective of Schillebeeckx offers a rich discursive framework on which to posit a reasoned and in-depth theological interpretation of the film. On the side of Schillebeeckx's eschatological perspective, Third Cinema offers a cinematic rendering of the significance of Schillebeeckx's liberative thought to a deeper understanding of the ongoing postcolonial struggle and sociopolitical contradictions of the Third World.

Ultimately, the crystallization of Schillebeeckx's eschatological perspective in Third Cinema may be likened to a window that sheds light to the quest for the God of salvation and liberation, whose presence is rediscovered in the very endurance and protest of Third World peoples. I see it as an imaginative stained glass window depicting hope and promise as painted in light. In contrast to the shadows cast by the phantoms of our time, who remain at the service of the powers that be, this stained glass window reflects the diffused but undeniable likeness of the God of the edge, the God who is ever mindful of humanity's weakest links.

Notes

Introduction

1. Anthony R. Guneratene and Wimal Dissanayake, eds., *Rethinking Third Cinema* (New York: Routledge, 2003), 7.

2. Tillich points out the priority of style in determining the religious in artworks that bear no overt religious content at all—"Style is the over-all form, which, in the particular forms of every particular artist and of every particular school, is still visible as the over-all form; and this over-all form is the expression of that which unconsciously is present in this period as its self-interpretation, as the answer to the question of the ultimate meaning of existence." Refer to "Existential Aspects of Modern Art," ch. 7 of Carl Michalson, ed., *Christianity and the Existentialists* (New York: Scribner and Sons, 1956), 128–146.

3. "Film as Hierophany," in John R. May and Michael Bird, eds.,*Religion in Film* (Knoxville: University of Tennessee Press, 1982), 13–14.

4. Joseph Cunneen, *Robert Bresson: A Spiritual Style in Film* (New York: Continuum Press, 2003).

5. Paul Schrader, *Transcendental Style in Film: Ozu, Bresson, Dreyer* (Berkely: University of California Press, 1972).

6. Ibid., 4.

7. Peter Fraser, *Images of the Passion: The Sacramental Mode in Film* (Cincinnati, PA: Praeger Publishers, 1998).

8. The various essays on the Theology-Cinema confluence lined up in notable compilations such as George Aichele and Richard Walsh's *Screening Scripture: Intertextual Connections Between Scripture and Film* (Pasadena: Trinity Press International, 2002), Joel W. Martin and Conrad E. Oswalt Jr.'s *Screening the Sacred: Religion, Myth, and Ideology in Popular American Film* (Oxford: Westview Press, 1995), Clive Marsh and Gaye Ortiz's *Explorations in Theology and Film* (Oxford: Blackwell Publishers, 1997), John R. May's *New Image of Religious Film* (Kansas: Sheed and Ward, 1997), John R. May and Michael Bird's *Religion in Film* (Knoxville: University of Tennessee Press, 1982), as well as Lloyd Baugh's discussion of the "Christ-Figure," in *Imaging the Divine: Jesus and Christ-Figures in Film* (Kansas City: Sheed and Ward, 1997), all heavily favor analyses of

thematic and fabula considerations with hardly any regard for cinematic style.

9. Neil P. Hurley, *The Reel Revolution: A Primer on Liberation* (Maryknoll, NY: Orbis Books, 1978), 12. Emphasis mine.

CHAPTER 1   THE CONCEPT OF THIRD CINEMA

1. Ella Shohat and Robert Stam explicate, "The late 1960s were heady days for revolutionary cinema. Worldwide decolonization seemed to suggest revolution everywhere in the Third World, while First World revolutionary movements promised an overthrow of the imperial system from within 'the belly of the beast'. . . At the time, tricontinental revolution, under the symbolic egis of Frantz Fanon, Che Guevara, and Ho Chi Minh, was deemed imminent, lying in wait just around the next bend of the dialectic." *Unthinking Eurocentrism: Multiculturalism and the Media* (London: Routledge, 1996), 260.

2. Ibid., 262.

3. Ibid.

4. Ibid., 264.

5. Michael Chanan, "The Changing Geography of Third Cinema," in *Screen* 38.4 (Winter 1997). http://www.mchanan.dial.pipex.com/chanan%20third%20cinema.htm.

6. Ibid.

7. Michael T. Martin, ed., *New Latin American Cinema: Theory Practices, and Transcontinental Articulations, vol. 1,* (Detroit, MI: Wayne State University Press, 1997), 33.

8. Martin asserts that film scholars from Europe and North America "condescendingly relegated Third World Cinema to the margins of film history" until international film festival circuits began to take token notice of Latin American and Third World cinema in the 1970s. "The Unfinished Social Practice of the New Latin American Cinema: Introductory Notes," in Ibid., 15.

9. Brazilian filmmaker Glauber Rocha's brief polemical statement "The Esthetics of Hunger," (1965) is an earlier declaration noted to have lent impetus to the movement toward militant cinema in Latin America. Martin comments that Rocha "inverts the social reality of underdevelopment and dependency—the 'themes' of hunger—into a signifier of resistance and transformation where violence is the authentic and empowering expression of the oppressed; he inserts the filmmaker allied with the movement, *Cinema Novo*, in the continent's struggle against neocolonial domination." Ibid., 17.

10. As Shohat and Stam explain, " 'Dependency theory' (Latin America), underdevelopment theory (Africa), and the 'world systems theory' argue that a hierarchical global system controlled by metropolitan capitalist countries and their multinational corporations simultaneously

generates both the wealth of the First World and the poverty of the Third World as the opposite sides of the same coin." *Unthinking Eurocentrism*, 17. The term "Third World" was originally proposed in 1952 by French demographer Alfred Sauvy to describe the similarity between countries moving towards decolonization and the Third Estate in France which struggled against inequality during the French Revolution. Virginia Fabella in Virginia Fabella and R.S. Sugirtharajah, eds., *Dictionary of Third World Theologies* (Maryknoll, NY: Orbis Books, 2000), 202–203.

11. Shohat and Stam, *Unthinking Eurocentrism*, 25.
12. Fabella argues that the alternative term "Two-thirds World" refers more to numbers; it does not sufficiently indicate a quality of life. She maintains that "Third World" continues to be the preferred term— "Theological groups, for example, EATWOT, affirm the term as valid and significant for their self-identification, and maintain it for its theological and evangelical relevance as an alternative voice. Fabella and Sugirtharajah, eds. *Dictionary of Third World Theologies*, Maryknoll, NY: Orbis Books, 2000, 202–203.
13. Chanan quotes Solanas and Getino in "The Changing Geography of Third Cinema," http://www.mchanan.dial.pipex.com/chanan%20third%20cinema.htm.
14. Fernando Solanas and Octavio Getino, "Towards a Third Cinema," in Michael T. Martin, ed., *New Latin American Cinema: Theory Practices, and Transcontinental Articulations, vol. 1*, (Detroit, MI: Wayne State University Press, 1997), 34.
15. Ibid.
16. Ibid., 34–35.
17. Teshome Gabriel. *Third Cinema in the Third World: The Aesthetics of Liberation* (Ann Arbor, MI: UMI Research Press, 1979), 2.
18. Solanas and Getino in Martin, ed., *New Latin American Cinema*, 40.
19. Ibid., 50.
20. Ibid., 35.
21. Irene L. Gendzier, *Frantz Fanon: A Critical Study*, (London: Wildwood House, 1973), 197.
22. The contentious issue in Fanon's work is the endorsement of violence as a valid pathway to decolonization—"When the people have taken violent part in the national liberation they will allow no one to set themselves up as 'liberators.' " Frantz Fanon, *The Wretched of the Earth*, trans. Constance Farrington (New York: Grove Press, 1963), 94. Problematic as this proposition may be, Irene L. Gendzier qualifies that "Struggle was the critical concept and process more than the violence that might mark it." *Frantz Fanon: A Critical Study*, 201.
23. Fanon, *The Wretched of the Earth*, 37.
24. Solanas and Getino in Martin, *New Latin American Cinema*, 50.
25. Ibid., 39.
26. Ibid., 37.

27. Julio Garcia Espinosa, "For an Imperfect Cinema" in ibid., 76.
28. Ibid., 82.
29. Jorge Sanjines, "Problems of Form and Content in Revolutionary Cinema," ibid., 63.
30. Michael T. Martin in ibid., 16.
31. Paul Willemen enumerates similar manifestos elsewhere in the world. In North Africa, "*Jamaat as Cinima al jadida*" ("Movement of the New Cinema," Cairo, 1967–1968), Third Cinema arguments in the Moroccan journal *Cinema 3*, and "*Cinima al Badil*" ("Alternative Cinema," Egypt, 1972). Additionally, "The First Manifesto for a Palestinian Cinema" (Damascus Film Festival, 1972) followed by "The Second Manifesto (Carthage Festival, 1972). "The Third Cinema Question: Notes and Reflections," in Pines and Willemen, eds., *Questions of Third Cinema*, 6.
32. Frantz Fanon, *The Wretched of the Earth*, trans. Constance Farrington (New York: Grove Press, 1963), 222–223.
33. Gabriel, *Third Cinema in the Third World*, 6–7.
34. Teshome Gabriel, "Towards a Critical Theory of Third World Films" in Jim Pines and Paul Willemen, eds., *Questions of Third Cinema* (London: British Film Institute, 1991), 31–35.
35. Ibid., 32–33.
36. It can be recalled that in his manifesto, "For an Imperfect Cinema," Julio Garcia Espinosa argues that "imperfect cinema must above all show the process which generates the problems. It is thus the opposite of a cinema principally dedicated to celebrating results, the opposite of a self-sufficient and contemplative cinema, the opposite of a cinema which 'beautifully illustrates' ideas or concepts which we already process." He adds, "Imperfect cinema is no longer interested in quality or technique. It can be created equally well with a Mitchell or with an 8mm camera, in a studio or in a guerilla camp in the middle of the jungle. Imperfect cinema is no longer interested in predetermined taste, and much less in 'good taste.' " Michael T. Martin, ed., *New Latin American Cinema*, 82.
37. Chanan, "The Changing Geography of Third Cinema," http://www.mchanan.dial.pipex.com/chanan%20third%20 cinema.htm.
38. Teshome Gabriel in Pines and Willemen, eds., *Questions of Third Cinema*, 35.
39. Ibid., 35.
40. Ibid., 36.
41. Gabriel does not elaborate on his conception of "text" so I see it useful to review two notable definitions adopted by Cinema Studies that resonate in his definition. Roland Barthes describes a text as "not a line of words releasing a single 'theological' meaning (the 'message' of an Author-God) but a multidimensional space in which a variety of writings, none of them original, blend and clash." *Image/Music/Text* (New York: Hill and Wang, 1977) p. 146. Similarly, Christian Metz

considers "text" as a dynamic concept—"The system of a text is the process which displaces codes, deforming each of them by the presence of the others, contaminating some by means of others, meanwhile replacing one by another, and finally—as a temporarily 'arrested' result of this general displacement— placing each code in a particular position in regard to the overall structure, a displacement which thus finishes by a positioning which is itself destined to be displaced by another text." Christian Metz, *Language and Cinema* (The Hague: Mouton Press, 1974), 103. Robert Stam, Robert Burgoyne, and Sandy Flitterman-Lewis note that the dynamic conception proposed by Metz emphasizes that a text is not merely the "list" of a film's operative codes, "but rather the labor of constant restructuration and displacement." *New Vocabularies in Film Semiotics: Structuralism, Post-Structuralism and Beyond* (London: Routledge, 1992), 52.

42. Eric Rentschler, "Expanding Film Historical Discourse: Reception Theory's Use Value for Cinema Studies," as quoted in Judith Mayne, *Cinema and Spectatorship* (London: Routledge, 1993), 67.

43. Apparently, Gabriel's view of Reception reflects a Marxist perspective akin to Jostein Gripsrud's description in the essay "Film Audience" that "a Marxist conception of film as a medium for changing people's way of thinking in 'progressive' directions, or, on the contrary, for the reproduction and dissemination of ideology in the sense of 'false consciousness.' " John Hill and Pamela Church Gibson, eds., *The Oxford Guide to Film Studies* (New York: Oxford University Press, 1998), 202–203.

44. Bordwell and Thompson, *Film Art: An Introduction*, 411.

45. Teshome Gabriel in Pines and Willemen, *Questions of Third Cinema*, 38.

46. In a similar illustration, Alan A. Stone takes note of the contrasting reception accorded to the film *The Story of Qiu Ju* (Zhang Yimou, China 1992) in the United States and in its home country, China. American critics dismissed the film as a thin story with a bleak ending while Chinese audiences rocked with laughter as they viewed the film as a comedy; an implausible, satirical take on the national legal system and bureaucracy. "Comedy and Culture," in *Boston Review* (1993–2000). http//:www.bostonreview.net/BR18.5/alanstone.nclk

47. Reinhold Wagnleitner " 'No Commodity Is Quite So Strange As This Thing Called Cultural Exchange': The Foreign Politics of American Pop Culture Hegemony" *Amerikastudien/American Studies: A Quarterly* 46, no. 3 (2001):454.

48. Teshome Gabriel in Pines and Willemen, eds., *Questions of Third Cinema*, 40.

49. From the perspective of Cinema Studies, 'style' refers to "The repeated and salient uses of film techniques characteristic of a single film or a group of films (for example, a filmmaker's work or a national

movement).” David Bordwell and Kristin Thompson, *Film Art: An Introduction, 3rd ed.* (New York: McGraw-Hill, 1990), 412.

50. Gabriel, *Third Cinema in the Third World*, 41.

51. Ibid., 41. Gabriel does not provide a definiton of ideology so it is instructive to present one here. The term “ideology” is defined as “a system of ideas (a way of thinking, a system of logic) and a system of social representations (images, myths utopias) with which human beings identify themselves, think, and represent themselves within the world in which they live” and may be construed positively or negatively. In its Third Cinema linkage with style, ideology takes on a positive sense, akin to the manner in which Third World theologians use the term to emphasize the praxical imperative for Third World peoples “to become historic ‘agents’ who are capable of resistance within the system and who propose and design alternatives.” Refer to Paolo Richard in Virginia Fabella and R.S. Sugirtharajah, ed., *Dictionary of Third World* Theologies, 103.

52. Ibid., 42.

53. See Wayne, *Political Film*, 27–33, 68.

54. David Bordwell notes that “Along with Eisenstein’s technical innovations went an insistence that the artist must fulfill a political task.” *The Cinema of Eisenstein* (Cambridge: Harvard University Press, 1993), 12. Bordwell’s book provides a good overview of Eisenstein’s contribution to the art and history of cinema.

55. Gabriel, *Third Cinema in the Third World*, 46.

56. Ibid., 54.

57. [1]Noel Carroll, “Style in Cinema,” in *Style* 32.3 (Fall 1998): 381–534. See also Carroll, *Philosophy of Art: A Contemporary Introduction* (London: Routledge, 1999), 142–152.

58. Ibid.

59. Teshome Gabriel in Pines and Willemen, eds. *Questions of Third Cinema*, 44–50.

60. Ibid., 44.

61. Bordwell and Thompson, *Film Art: An Introduction, 3rd ed.*, 410.

62. Ibid., 408.

63. Teshome Gabriel in Pines and Willemen, eds., *Questions of Third Cinema*, 45.

64. ordwell and Thompson, *Film Art: An Introduction, 3rd ed.*, 411.

65. Teshome Gabriel in Pines and Willemen, eds., *Questions of Third Cinema*, 48.

66. Gabriel indicates that the richness of folklore is tied to the people’s relationship to the land and community; the more closely-bonded a group of people are to the land, the more folkloric tradition thrives. This holds true for the popular expression of 70–75% of the Third World population. The author does not elaborate on this assertion any further except to point out that this phenomenon is “grounded in the notion of balance and harmony between nature and humanity.” Ibid.

67. Ibid., 54.

68. Ibid.

69. It is interesting to note that Coppola's $35 million opus is said to have epitomized the crass commodification so associated with Hollywood filmmaking practices. Alluding to Gerald Sussman's 1992 essay "What 'Hearts of Darkness' Left Out?" released in *The Guardian*, E. San Juan Jr. alleges that while shooting on location in the province of Quezon in the Philippine countryside, "Coppola's 'conspicuous consumption' poisoned the local environment with prostitution, discriminatory treatment of Vietnamese and Filipino participants, and other con games that usually gravitate around Hollywood big-time spending." *After Postcolonialism: Remapping Philippines-United States Confrontations* (Lanham: Rowman and Littlefield Publishers, 2000), 85. Sussman's *Guardian* article cited above refers to *Hearts of Darkness: A Filmmaker's Apocalypse* (Bahr and Hickenlooper/US, 1991), a documentary featuring actual footage taken by Coppola's wife during the filming of *Apocalypse Now*. Among several excesses committed by Coppola and his crew as recorded in the documentary, what stands out for me as one of the most culturally damaging to the host country was the fact that the director hired an entire mountain tribe, a proud warrior people known as the *Ifugao*, transplanted them to the film location, and decontextualized their rituals to provide exoticism and eerie spectacle to the film's surreal dénouement.

70. Wayne, *Political Film: The Dialectics of Third Cinema*, 5.

71. Ibid., 6–8.

72. Ibid., 6.

73. As a case in point, Wayne argues that postmodernism "advocates a liberal multiculturalism or hybridity at the expense of understanding the material divisions that can exist irrespective of cultural exchanges, or how the struggle for resources which have been made scarce due to the social relations of production unleashes (as it did in formerly cosmopolitan Sarajevo) the fundamentalist cultural politics(nationalism and tribalism) against which advocacy of liberal hybridity is a mere straw in the wind." Ibid., 8.

74. Shohat and Stam, *Unthinking Eurocentrism*, 28.

75. Wayne adds to this exploration by introducing the cinematic character of the "bandit," an individual who goes against the grain of society's otherwise unquestioned social realities. Unlike the celluloid "gangster" who is out-of-joint with collective struggle and depoliticized, the archetypal figure of the bandit serves as an "important repository of utopian revolt." The social significance of the bandit is hazy and underplayed in First Cinema (e.g., *Pat Garett and Billy the Kid*, Peckinpah/United States, 1973) but according to Wayne, the Second Cinema incarnation of the bandit notwithstanding its romanticism (e.g., *Eskiya*, Turgul/Turkey, 1997; *Bandit Queen*, Kapur/India-UK,

1994), is a prefiguration of "future collective resistance," thus, providing an important dialectical link with Third Cinema. Wayne, *Political Film: The Dialectics of Third Cinema*, 60–61. Wayne's inquiry of the cinematic figure of the bandit is, without a doubt, a distinct contribution to the development of Third Cinema Theory as this artery in the Third Cinema-Second Cinema dialectical relationship was not previously explored. I am of the opinion though, that it is in Wayne's successful navigation of the dialectics of Third and First Cinema where he leaves an indelible mark.

76. It is not within the scope of this research to explore the arguments of these key cultural theorists. Suffice it to say that all of them had a Marxist epistemological project that anticipates the critical social resonance of Third Cinema theory. Ibid., 25.

77. Wayne derives the quote from Reiss, E., *Marx: A Clear Guide* (London: Pluto, 1997). Ibid., 61.

78. Ibid., 62.

79. Ibid., 81.

80. Ibid., 137.

81. Ibid., 2.

82. Ibid., 141.

83. However much Wayne underscores the key role of Che as contributing to the notion that *Evita* qualifies as Third Cinema, he nonetheless acknowledges the film's "gender blind spot" when it sets a revolutionary male to pronounce judgments on a woman who has to rise above her subjugated social position. Ibid., 141.

84. Ibid., 10.

CHAPTER 2   EXPLORING NATIONAL DIMENSIONS OF THIRD CINEMA

1. Ella Shohat and Robert Stam assert, "Since the 'post' in 'postcolonial' on one level suggests a stage 'after' the demise of colonialism, it is imbued, quite apart from its users' intentions with an ambiguous spatiotemporality. 'Postcolonial' tends to be associated with the 'Third World' countries that gained independence after World War II, yet it also refers to the 'Third World' diasporic presence within 'First World' metropolises . . . But given that virtually all countries have been affected by colonialism, whether as a colonizer, colonized, or both at the same time, the all inclusive formulation homogenizes very different national and racial formulations." *Unthinking Eurocentrism: Multiculturalism and the Media* (London: Routledge, 1994), 38.

2. See introduction of *Media Worlds: Anthropology on New Terrain*, ed. Faye Ginsburg, Lila Abu-Lughod, and Brian Larkin (Berkeley: University of California Press, 2002), 11.

3. For examples of Filipino films that resonate with the Third Cinema project, see my essay "*3rd World Hero*: Rizal and Colonial Clerical Power in Philippine Third Cinema," in *Senses of Cinema* 36 (July–September 2005). http://www.sensesofcinema.com/ contents/05/36/3rd_world_hero.html. See also my review of the film *Dekada 70* in *Journal of Religion and Film* 8.1 (April 2004), http://www.unomaha.edu/jrf/Dekada70.htm.

4. Allison Arnold Helminski, "Memories of a Revolutionary Cinema," in *Senses of Cinema* 2 (January 2000), www.sensesofcinema.com/ contents/00/2/memories.html.

5. Tomás Gutiérrez Alea, "The Viewers Dialectic," trans. Julia Lesage in *New Latin American Cinema: Theory, Practices, and Transcontinental Articulations*, vol. 1, ed. Michael T. Martin (Detroit, MI: Wayne State University Press, 1997), 109.

6. Ibid., 110.

7. Teshome H. Gabriel notes, "While the 'establishment' film critics have praised Memories by linking it with the film of either Antonioni or Fellini, the opinion of the 'left' has been ambivalent. The recurrent 'left' criticism has been that the film's focus on the displaced bourgeoisie is a waste of time." *Third Cinema in the Third World: The Aesthetics of Liberation* (Ann Arbor, MI: UMI Research Press, 1982), 70.

8. John Marz. "Recasting Cuban Slavery: The Other Francisco and the Last Supper," in *Based on a True Story: Latin American History at the Movies*, ed. Donald D. Stevens (Delaware: Scholarly Resources, 1997), 103–123.

9. Tomás Gutiérrez Alea, "El verdadero rostro de Calibán," Cine Cubano 126 (1989): 12–22.

10. Luke 22:49–51 (New Revised Standard Version).

11. Mark 8: 27.

12. Mark 8: 29.

13. Gen. 3: 1–24.

14. Gabriel, *Third Cinema in the Third World*, 18.

15. Josef Gugler, *African Film: Re-Imagining a Continent* (Bloomington: Indiana University Press, 2003), 126.

16. Ibid., 126.

17. Gugler explains that "Africa South of the Sahara" is preferable to the racist "Black Africa," and the Eurocentric "Sub-Saharan Africa." This is to distinguish the region from the distinctly Arabic North Africa. Ibid., 3.

18. Teshome Gabriel likens the satirical *Xala* to a form of African poetry known as "sema-enna-worq," which literally translates as "wax and gold." The term alludes to the process wherein a goldsmith pours a wax form, casts a clay mold around it, and then drains out the wax. The clay mold then serves to shape molten gold. He uses this analogy

to underscore the importance of looking beyond the superficial meaning of the text and consider the deeper "real meaning" generated by an understanding of local folk culture. See *Third Cinema in the Third World*, 78–79.

19. Francoise Pfaff notes that Sembene's open-ended films are derived from "African dilemma tales," whose endings are determined by the audience. As such, "Sembene trusts the viewer's imagination to prolong his films." See "The Uniqueness of Ousmane Sembene's Cinema," in *Ousmane Sembene: Dialogue with Critics and Writers*, ed. Samba Gadjigo, Ralph H. Faulkingham, Thomas Cassirer, and Reinhard Sander (Amherst: University of Massachusetts Press, 1993), 17.

20. Bienvenido Lumbera, *Writing the Nation/Pag-akda ng Bansa* (Quezon City: University of the Philippines Press, 2000), 45.

21. The phrase "*Nouvelle Vague*" was coined by Francoise Girard, a journalist for the magazine *L'Express*, who wrote about the ideals of French youth at the end of the 1950s. Applied to cinema, the term refers to a group of idealistic directors who had previously worked as critics for *Cahiers du cinema*—Francois Truffaut, Jean-Luc Godard, Claude Chabrol, Jacques Rivette, and Eric Rohmer. Truffaut's 1959 Cannes Film Festival victory for his first film *Les quatre cent coups* ("The 400 Blows," 1959) launched the *Nouvelle Vague* as a slogan used in the pro-Gaullist press to promote the concept of a resurgent France after the change of regime in 1958. Among the notable films of the *Nouvelle Vague* are Truffaut's *Tirez sur le pianiste* ("Shoot the Pianist," 1960), Godard's *A bout de souffle* ("Breathless," 1959), Chabrol's *Le beau serge* ("Bitter Reunion," 1959), Rivette's *Paris nous appertient* ("Paris Belongs to Us," 1960), and Rohmer's *Le Signe de lion* ("The Sign of Leo," 1959). "collectively, these films represented a significant break with *tradition de qualite* and a revolution not just in the way films were made but also in their social and aesthetic significance." Jill Forbes "The French Nouvelle Vague," in *The Oxford Guide to Film Studies*, ed. John Hill and Pamela Church Gibson (New York: Oxford University Press, 1998), 263.

22. Kidlat Tahimik details his filmmaking principles in the autobiographical "Midlife Choices: Filmmaking vs. Fillmaking," in *Primed for Life: Writings on Midlife by 18 Men*, ed. Lorna Kalaw-Tirol (Pasig City: Anvil Publishing, 1997), 14.

23. Francis Ford Coppola's Zoetrope Company, which had just shot *Apocalypse Now* in the Philippines, would soon after distribute the film in the U.S. market. Joel David, *Wages of Cinema: Film in Philippine Perspective* (Quezon City: University of the Philippines Press, 1998), 105.

24. Tahimik, *Primed for Life*, 14.

25. Ibid.

26. Tahimik recalls his encounter with noted German filmmaker Werner Herzog who witnessed Tahimik's quirky editing of *Perfumed Nightmare*—"When I was editing Perfumed Nightmare using my unschooled primitive methods, Werner Herzog, fresh from his Cannes Film Jury Prize, sat with me at the editing table for comments. "You edit your scenes so strangely" Herzog muttered in his heavy German accent. I panicked and begged for expert advice—Oh master which trees should I cut or prune to beautify my forest? "Oh no, I like your primitive style and your wild detours. You're best at your detours." Ibid., 54.

27. Ibid., 16.

28. Ibid., 15.

29. Fernando Solanas and Octavio Getino, "Towards a Third Cinema: Notes and Experiences for the Development of a Cinema of Liberation in the Third World," in *New Latin American Cinema: Theory, Practices, and Transcontinental Articulations*, vol. 1, ed. Michael T. Martin (Detroit, MI: Wayne University Press, 1997), 33.

30. Ibid., 82.

31. *Indio* was the racist tag given to Filipinos of Malay stock by the colonizing Spaniards. The designation is akin to the Euro-American naming of Afro-Americans as *niggers*. "Filipino" referred to the Spaniard or Spanish mestizo born in the Philippines while "Peninsular" was a designation for Spaniards born in Spain. In *Noli Me Tangere*, the first of two subversive novels written by Philippine national hero Dr. Jose P. Rizal, the abusive Spanish Franciscan friar Padre Damaso uses the designation to full effect when insulting the natives—"Do I believe it? As I believe the Gospel. The indio is so indolent!" Jose P. Rizal, *Noli Me Tangere*, trans. Soledad Lacson-Locsin (Makati City: Bookmark, 1996), 7.

32. Tahimik, *Primed for Life*, 41.

33. E. San Juan, *After Postcolonialism: Remapping Philippines—United States Confrontations* (Lanham, MD: Rowman and Littlefield, 2000), 155.

34. I use "Kidlat" when ascribing to the protagonist of *Perfumed Nightmare* to differentiate from the filmmaker, whom I refer to as "Tahimik."

35. Ted Lerner hints that the fascination for beauty pageants among a number of Filipinos may have been a colonial influence. "Some say it has something to do with the Philippines's Spanish heritage. The Spanish had colonized the country for nearly 400 years and in most Latin and South American countries today. Beauty pageants are also a national obsession. Some Filipinos say that the idea, like so many in their country, came from America and that Filipinos just gave their full attention to it." Observing the 1994 Miss Universe Pageant held in Manila, Lerner notes that the media that covered the event "like it was the moon landing" capitalized on this obsession. "The Eye of the

Beholder: 1994 Miss Universe Pageant in the Philippines," in *Transpacific* 9 (October 1994): 58. In *Perfumed Nightmare*, Kidlat cuts out a photo of Miss U.S.A. from a poster and frames it alongside an icon of the Blessed Virgin Mary.

36. Tahimik weaves a story out of a real historical incident. On February 4, 1899, a couple of days prior to the ratification of the Treaty of Paris by the U.S. Senate, an unarmed Filipino crossing the San Juan bridge in Manila was shot by an American soldier. The official U.S. account reported the atrocity as an unprovoked attack on the U.S. forces. Barbara S. Gaerlan and Jorge Emmanuel, "Republic or Empire: The Legacy of the 1898 Treaty of Paris" *BoondocksNet* (December 10, 1998).   http://www.boondocksnet.com/centennial/sctexts/legacy1898.html.

37. D.R. SarDesai in the chapter "Filipino Urge for Freedom from Spanish and U.S. Rule" *Southeast Asia: Past and Present* (Boulder,CO: Westview Press, 1994), 144.

38. Teshome Gabriel, "Third Cinema as Guardian of Popular Memory: Towards a Third Aesthetics," in Jim Pines and Paul Willemen, eds., *Questions of Third Cinema* (London: BFI Publishing, 1989), 53–54.

39. I devote more attention to the aspect of colonial religion and its post-colonial ramifications as represented in *Perfumed Nightmare* in my essay "Perfumed Nightmare: Religion and the Philippine Postcolonial Struggle in Third Cinema," in *Representing Religion in World Cinema: Mythmaking, Filmmaking, Culture-making*, ed. S. Brent Plate (New York: Palgrave Macmillan, 2003), 181–196.

40. It is interesting to note that the symbolization of the Filipino gift of reversing colonial damage through the value of indio-genius surfaces in another Kidlat Tahimik opus, *Turumba* (1983). Here, the village blacksmith re-models metal scrap, the wreckage of long-abandoned Japanese army trucks, into useful tools.

41. Laura U. Marks, *The Skin of the Film: Intercultural Cinema, Embodiment, and the Senses* (Durham,NC: Duke University Press, 2000), 77.

42. Marks likens the recollection-object to the Deleuzian conception of the "radioactive fossil." She notes that "Fossils acquire their meaning by virtue of an originary contact. A fossil is the indexical trace of an object that once existed." Moreover, Marks draws reference to the idea of the "fetish," which she distinguishes from the its colonial usage, to that of objects that "encode knowledges that become buried in the process of temporal or geographic displacement but are volatile when reactivated by memory." She adds that both terms are "nodes, or knots, in which historical, cultural, and spiritual forces gather with a particular intensity. They translate experience through space and time in a material medium, encoding the histories produced in inter-cultural traffic." Ibid., 85, 89.

43. Ibid., p. 91.

44. Bordwell notes that one of the fastest ASLs (Average Shot Lengths) for recent Hollywood films is that of the science fiction film *Dark City* (Alex Proyas/United States, 1998) that registers at 1.8 seconds. The slowest he had found was that of *Unbreakable* (M. Night Shyamalan/United States, 2000) at 18.2 seconds. Considering its employment of meditatively paced long-takes, the ASL of *Perfumed Nightmare* could easily double the Hollywood average. David Bordwell, "Intensified Continuity: Visual Style in Contemporary American Film," in *Film Quarterly* 55.3 (Spring 2002):16–28.

45. David Bordwell and Kristin Thompson, *Film Art: An Introduction*, 3rd edition (New York: Mgraw-Hill, 1990), 234.

46. Ibid.

47. I would liken this strategy to the clever decision of Philippine national hero Dr. Jose P. Rizal to write his subversive nineteenth century novels in Spanish, gaining for himself international readership and a wider platform for his liberative message, in the process. I also see the Filipino dialogue echoing behind the English as yet another way of expressing the theme of popular memory.

48. Tom Moylan, *Demand the Impossible:Science Fiction and the Utopian Imagination* (New York: Methuen, 1986), 213.

49. An example of a utopian vision that reflects the ideals of progress is the fictive reality created by the Disney comic books of the 1970s. According to Ariel Dorfman and Armand Mattelart, "The imaginative world of the child has become the political utopia of a social class. In the Disney comics, one never meets a member of the working or proletarian classes, and nothing is the product of an industrial process." In this socially guilt-free Disney universe, "The tribal (now planetary) village of leisure without the conflicts of work, and of the earth without pollution, all rest on the consumer goods derived from industrialization. The imaginative world of children cleanses the entire Disney cosmos in the waters of innocence." *How to Read Donald Duck: Imperialist Ideology in the Disney Comic*, trans. David Kunzle (New York: I.G. Editions, 1975), 59, 97.

Chapter 3   Films from a Virtual Geography of Third Cinema

1. For my review of the film *Kandahar*, refer to the online *Journal of Religion and Film* 6, no. 1 (April 2002), http:// www.unomaha.edu/~wwwjrf/kandahar.htm.

2. For a recent survey of the Third Cinema debate, refer to the introductory chapter in Anthony R. Guneratne and Wimal Dissanayake, eds., *Rethinking Third Cinema* (New York: Routledge, 2003), 1–28.

3. Mike Wayne, *Political Film: The Dialectics of Third Cinema* (London: Pluto Press, 2001), 6.

4. Teshome Gabriel, *Third Cinema in the Third World: The Aesthetics of Liberation* (Ann Arbor, MI: UMI Research Press, 1979), 82.

5. Wayne, *Political Film: The Dialectics of Third Cinema*, 32.

6. Ibid., 24.

7. Ibid., 1.

8. Figures from the United Nations 2005 Human Development Report indicate that the extent of world inequality is scandalous. "The world's richest 500 individuals have a combined income greater than that of the poorest 416 million. Beyond these extremes, the 2.5 billion people living on less than $2 a day–40% of the world's population–account for 5% of global income. The richest 10%, almost all of whom live in high-income countries, account for 54%." *Human Development Report 2005* (New York: United Nations Development Programme, 2005), 4.

9. Laura U. Marks, *The Skin of the Film: Intercultural Cinema, Embodiment, and the Senses* (London: Duke University Press, 2000), 6–7.

10. Ella Shohat and Robert Stam, *Unthinking Eurocentrism: Multiculturalism and the Media* (London:Routledge, 1996), 28.

11. Mbye B. Cham and Claire Andrade-Watkins, *Blackframes: Critical Perspectives on Black Independent Cinema* (Cambridge,MA: The MIT Press, 1988), 62–79.

12. Chanan, "The Changing Geography of Third Cinema" in *Screen* 38, no. 4 (Winter 1997) in the *Michael Chanan Website*. http:// www. mchanan.dial.pipex.com/chanan%20third%20cinema.htm.

13. Gabriel, *Third Cinema in the Third World: The Aesthetics of Liberation*, 2.

14. Naim Stifan Ateek, *Justice and Only Justice: A Palestinian Theology of Liberation* (Maryknoll, NY: Orbis Books, 1990), 74–75.

15. Phyllis Bennis contends that the Geneva Accord, which aimed at working toward ending the Palestinian-Israeli conflict, was "seriously undermined by its failure to recognize military occupation as the fundamental cause of the conflict." See "Talking Points on the Geneva Accord," *From Occupied Palestine*, December 11, 2003, http://fromoccupiedpalestine.org/node.php?id = 1026.

16. See Anne Thomson, "The Struggle of Memory Against Forgetting," in Terry George, ed., *Hotel Rwanda: Bringing the Story of an African Hero to Film* (New York: Newmarket Press, 2005), 52.

17. Ibid., 48.

18. Tom Moylan, *Demand the Impossible: Science Fiction and the Utopian Imagination* (New York: Methuen, 1986), 213.

19. Walter Salles in an interview with Erica Abeel, "Finding the Spirit of a Journey: Walter Salles on *The Motorcycle Diaries*," *IndieWire*, http://www.indiewire.com/people/people_040923salles.html.

CHAPTER 4   POLITICAL HOLINESS:
THE ESCHATOLOGICAL PERSPECTIVE
OF SCHILLEBEECKX

1. Edward Schillebeeckx, *The Schillebeeckx Reader*, ed. Robert J. Schreiter (Oxford: Oxford University Press, 1984), xi.

2. A number of research works provide for a panoramic view of the theology of Edward Schillebeeckx. I make mention of a few that are particularly useful to this research. *The Schilleebeeckx Reader* presents an incisively chosen sampling of the theologian's work including texts that have been previously untranslated. The concise commentary provided by the book's editor, Robert J. Schreiter, effectively introduces each section and provides a contextual framework to Schillebeeckx's writings. *The Praxis of the Reign of God: An Introduction to the Theology of Edward Schillebeeckx* (New York: Fordham University Press, 2002), another edited work by Schreiter in collaboration with Mary Catherine Hilkert, is an exposition of Schillebeeckx's contemporary theology by various authors based largely on the books *Jesus: An Experiment in Christology, (Jezus, het verhaal van een levende)* and *Christ: The Experience of Jesus as Lord, (Gerechtigheid en liefde: Genade en bervrijding)*. Two works by Philip Kennedy trace the development of Schillebeeckx's theology. His dissertation entitled *Deus Humanissimus: The Knowability of God in the Theology of Edward Schillebeeckx* (Fribourg: Fribourg University Press, 1993) gives a scholarly survey of the theologian's personal and intellectual history through a meticulous accumulation of detail. His other work that is simply entitled *Schillebeeckx* (London: Geoffrey Chapman, 1993) is a clear and straightforward attempt to make the Dutch theologian's thought more accessible to a wider readership. A similar effort can be seen in John Bowden's *Edward Schillebeeckx: In Search of the Kingdom of God* (New York: Crossroad, 1983), which focuses on the main lines of Schillebeeckx's theology. The book *God is New Each Moment*, trans., David Smith (New York: Seabury Press, 1983), while not in any way providing a sufficient exploration of Schillebeeckx's theology in context, also presents an initial sampling of his thought in the form of an interview conducted by Huub Oosterhuis and Piet Hoogeven.

3. Schillebeeckx, *The Schillebeeckx Reader*, 15.

4. Philip Kennedy, *Schillebeeckx*, 26.

5. Because conservative members of the Roman Curia already viewed the Dutch theologians with suspicion, Schillebeeckx was not granted the status of *peritus* to the Second Vatican Council. His ideas found fertile soil in the theological lectures he delivered to bishops outside of the Council sessions. Robert Schreiter, "Edward Schillebeeckx," in David F. Ford, *The Modern Theologians: An Introduction to Christian Theology*

in the Twentieth Century (Cambridge: Blackwell Publishers, 1997), 153.

6. Schreiter notes that Schillebeeckx's influence on the aforementioned constitutions was significant notwithstanding the fact that his direct involvement was confined to the "Marriage" section of the Constitution on the Church and the Modern World. *The Schillebeeckx Reader*, 4.

7. Schillebeeckx proposes the development of a western form of Liberation Theology, which could function as a dialogue partner for the seminal Third World version. Context differentiates the First and Third World—the democratic, secularized, and affluent West on one hand; the authoritarian, non-secularized, and impoverished Non-West on the other. Schillebeeckx, *"Theologie als bevrijdingskunde: Enkele noodzakelijke beschouwingen vooraf,"* *Tijdschrift voor Theologie* 24 (1984), 391–392, summarized and translated in the unpublished research by Dorothy Jacko, "Salvation in the Context of Contemporary Secularized Historical Consciousness: The Later Theology of Edward Schillebeeckx," as referred to in the dissertation of Brian D. Berry, *Fundamental Liberationist Ethics: The Contribution of the Later Theology of Edward Schillebeeckx* (Boston College, December 1995), 77.

8. For a thorough discussion on Schillebeeckx's earlier background, refer to Erik Borgman, *Edward Schillebeeckx: A Theologian in his History*, vol. 1, trans. John Bowden (London: Continuum, 2003).

9. De Petter was a "towering influence" early on in Schillebeeckx's intellectual history. Notwithstanding a prohibition forbidding candidates for Catholic priesthood to read the works of certain controversial philosophers, De Petter introduced the novice Schillebeeckx to such philosophers in the mid-1930s. Thus Schillebeeckx became acquainted with the works of Immanuel Kant, Georg Wilhelm Friedrich Hegel, Edmund Husserl, and Maurice Merleau-Ponty. De Petter made reference to these philosophers as an adjunct complement to his teaching of Thomas Aquinas. For a detailed discussion on the early influences in Schillebeeckx's theology, see Kennedy, *Schillebeeckx*, 17–24.

10. Schreiter, ed. *The Schillebeeckx Reader*, 2.

11. Ibid., 3. For an in-depth discussion of the theology of M.D. Chenu, refer to to the dissertation of A.J.M. van den Hoogen, *Pastorale Teologie: Ontwikkeling en Struktur in de Theologie van M.D. Chenu* (Katholieke Universiteit Nijmegen, 1984).

12. Kennedy, *Schillebeeckx*, 22.

13. Schreiter, ed. *The Schillebeeckx Reader*, 5–7.

14. "For Schillebeeckx, the basic problem with De Petter became one of emphasis: De Petter accorded too much significance to speculation over and against practical experiences." Kennedy expounds on Schillebeeckx's "clear break" with De Petter in *Deus*

Humanissimus: The Knowability of God in the Theology of Edward Schillebeeckx, 200–216.

15. Schreiter notes that the Jürgen Habermas' influence is shared by Latin American Liberation Theologians; their engagement with the ideas of Habermas was funneled through the work of Johannes Metz. *The Schillebeeckx Reader*, 23.

16. William B. Portier, "Interpretation and Method," in *The Praxis of the Reign of God*, 26.

17. Schreiter, *The Schillebeeckx Reader*, 5. Commenting on the vast range of resources subscribed to by Schillebeeckx, Schreiter adds, "No twentieth-century theologian (except perhaps for Wolfhart Pannenberg) ranges so widely over the philosophical territory." "Edward Schillebeeckx," in Ford, ed. *The Modern Theologian: An Introduction to Christian Theology in the Twentieth Century*, Cambridge: Blackwell Publishers, 1997, 154.

18. Schreiter, ed., *The Schillebeeckx Reader*, 5.

19. See Schreiter, "Edward Schillebeeckx," in *The Modern Theologians*, ed. Ford, 156–158.

20. Edward Schillebeeckx, *Christ: The Experience of Jesus as Lord*, trans. John Bowden (New York: Crossroad Publishing, 1980), 62. Mary Catherine Hilkert points out, "it is important to note that Schillebeeckx locates revelation as occuring within the human experience, but also that the two are not identical—revelation involves crossing a boundary. There is a dimension of givenness 'from above' or 'from beyond'—the specifically transcendent dimension (the experienced) in revelatory experience." See "Discovery of the Living God," in Schreiter and Hilkert, eds., *The Praxis of Christian Experience*, 41–42.

21. Schillebeeckx's emphasis on experience as the medium through which revelation is communicated became a contentious issue; it incurred the ire of the Roman Curia which had interpreted it as a threat to the doctrine that the magisterium (vis-à-vis the Scripture) is the normative criterion for revealed truth. Schillebeeckx's denial of absolute language categories was misconstrued by the Curia as a denial of Nicaea and Chalcedon. Schreiter makes clear that this was not Schillebeeckx's project—"But Schillebeeckx has struggled to be faithful to both, since a magisterium without the experience of grace and the Holy Spirit is a dead letter indeed. And his own historical sense is too keen to permit him to lapse into a rootless enthusiasm." *The Schillebeeckx Reader*, 14.

22. Schreiter, "Edward Schillebeeckx," in *The Modern Theologians*, 158.

23. Ibid.

24. Portier, "Interpretation and Method," in Schreiter and Hilkert, eds. *The Praxis of the Reign of God*, 25.

25. Edward Schillebeeckx, foreword to *Jesus: An Experiment in Christology*, trans. Hubert Hoskins (New York: Crossroad Publishing, 1979).

26. Portier, "Interpretation and Method," in *The Praxis of the Reign of God*, 22.

27. For Schillebeeckx, "Religious faith is human life in the world, but experienced as an encounter and in this respect as a disclosure of God." *Christ: The Experience of Jesus as Lord*. 32. "Disclosure," Schreiter explains, is a term Schillebeeckx uses when discussing divine revelation and the apprehension of meaning. The concept is drawn from the work of language philosopher Ian Ramsey. *The Schillebeeckx Reader*, 22.

28. Edward Schillebeeckx, *Interim Report on the Books Jesus and Christ* (New York: Seabury Press, 1980), 50.

29. *Theologisch Geloofsverstaan anno 1983*, 7 as translated by John Bowden, *Edward Schillebeeckx: In Search of the Kingdom of God*, (New York: Crossroad Publishing, 1983), 135.

30. Ibid.

31. Edward Schillebeeckx, *Church: The Human Story of God*, trans. John Bowden (New York: Crossroad Publishing, 1990), 37.

32. See Schillebeeckx, *Interim Report on the Books Jesus and Christ*, 3, 9, 51–52.

33. Schillebeeckx, *Church*, 36.

34. For a detailed discussion of "critical correlation" as per Tillich, see his book *Systematic Theology*, vol. 1 (Chicago, IL: University of Chicago Press, 1951), 59–68.

35. Edward Schillebeeckx, *The Understanding of Faith: Interpretation and Criticism*, trans. N.D. Smith (London: Sheed and Ward, 1974), 88. For Schillebeeckx's in-depth discussion of the "question-answer correlation" see 78–101.

36. Schillebeeckx, *Church*, 36.

37. Ibid., 37.

38. Ibid., 40.

39. Robert Schreiter explains that from a semiotic view, culture is "a vast communication network, whereby both verbal and nonverbal messages are circulated along elaborate, interconnected pathways, which, together, create the systems of meaning." He adds that the key to the production of meaning are the bearers of the message. *Constructing Local Theologies* (Maryknoll, NY: Orbis Books, 1985), 49.

40. Schillebeeckx, *Church*, 41.

41. Ibid.

42. In *Fundamental Liberationist Ethics: The Contribution of the Later Theology of Edward Schillebeeckx*, 70. Berry equates Schillebeeckx's argument on the "correspondence of relationships" between tradition and situation with the thought of liberation theologian Clodovis Boff as found in *Theology and Praxis: Epistemological Foundations* (New York: Orbis Books, 1987), 143–150. Schillebeeckx, however, has not referred to Boff in any explicit way although he includes him as a bibliographical entry in the book *Church: The Human Story of God*.

43. The term "inculturation" was coined by Protestant missionary G.L. Barney in 1973 and was used in the context of frontier missions. "The essential nature of these supracultural components should neither be lost nor distorted but rather secured and interpreted clearly through the guidance of the Holy Spirit in 'inculturating' them into this new culture." See "The Supracultural and the Cultural: Implications for Frontier Missions," as referred to in G. De Napoli, "Inculturation as Communication," in *Inculturation* 9 (1987): 71–98. Anscar Chupungco notes the eventual use of the term in the 1975 General Congregation of the Society of Jesus and by Pope John Paul II in the 1979 apostolic exhortation *Catechesi tradendae. Liturgical Inculturation: Sacraments, Religiosity, and Catechesis* (Collegeville: Liturgical Press, 1992), 25–26. Chupungco's work is devoted to a thorough exploration of the process of inculturation as a theological method in Liturgical renewal.

44. Schillebeeckx, *Church*, 42–43.

45. Schillebeeckx articulates the need for a theological critique of ideology in view of the contextual relativity of theological thought. He makes mention of the polemic between Hans Georg Gadamer and Jürgen Habermas in the 1960s as having helped catalyze the identification of this need in theology. *Theologisch Geloofsverstaan anno 1983*, 17, as translated by Schreiter in *The Schillebeeckx Reader*, 113.

46. Schillebeeckx, *Theologisch Geloofsverstaan anno 1983*, 17, in ibid.

47. I find it useful to illustrate further Schillebeeckx's conception of ideological false consciousness using a similar description offered by Feminist theologian Rosemary Radford Ruether when describing the phenomenon of androcentrism. She explains that "The authentic good self is identified with the favored center who dominates the cultural interpretation of humanness, and others are described in negative categories in contrast. This negative perception of the other is then reinforced when the favored group is able to gain power over the others, either to annihilate them or reduce them to servile status. The two elements are intertwined: the perception of the other as inferior, less capable of the good self, rationalizes exploitation of them." It is then the interrelated aspects of a false projection and exploitation that constitute the perpetuation of a false consciousness. *Sexism and God-talk: Towards a Feminist Theology* (Boston, MA: Beacon Press, 1985), 162.

48. Schillebeeckx issues a qualification on the ideological-critical hermeneutics within the church—"Although I find a self-serving neo-modern triumphalist critique of the church wrong, this does not alter the fact that theologians, 'mindful of their own situation,' may not hold back their own ideology-critical findings. A church that does not positively permit this or at least tolerate it, shows itself to be weak and little sure of the power of the gospel of the powerless. It is a form of 'little faith.' " *Theologisch Geloofsverstaan anno 1983*, 17, as translated by Schreiter in *The Schillebeeck Reader*, 114–115.

49. For a thorough discussion of the theology of hope, refer to Rosemary Radford Ruether, *The Radical Kingdom: The Western Experience of Messianic Hope* (New York: Harper and Row, 1970), 201–218.

50. Rejecting the other-worldly conception of eschatology as the "doctrine of the end," Jurgen Moltmann argues for a more practical-critical emphasis—"Eschatology was long called the 'doctrine of the last things' or the 'doctrine of the end.' By these things were meant events which will one day break upon man, history and the world at the end of time . . . But the relegating of these events to the 'last day' robbed them of their directive, uplifting and critical significance for all the days which are spent here, this side of the end, in history . . . From first to last, and not merely in the epilogue, Christianity is eschatology, is hope, forward looking and forward moving, and therefore also revolutionizing and transforming the present." *Theology of Hope: On the Ground and Implications of a Christian Eschatology*, trans. James W. Leitch (London: SCM Press, 1967), 15–16.

51. Ruether, *The Radical Kingdom*, 203.

52. Ibid., 217.

53. Schreiter makes this statement in the context of discussing God's concrete action in human history. *The Schillebeeckx Reader*, 17.

54. Schillebeeckx, *Christ*, 731.

55. According to Ernst Bloch, "Man does not yet know what he is, but can know through alienation from himself what he certainly is not and therefore does not want to, or at least should not want to, remain false." *Philosophische Aufzatse zur objecktiven Phantasie* as quoted in ibid. Wayne Hudson traces the link of this anthropological perspective to Bloch's earlier utopian project prior to the infusion of Marxist thought. "As part of his early utopian philosophy Bloch developed a philosophical anthropology based on the idea that man was still 'within,' and *incognito*, 'not yet' . . . this philosophical anthropology was essentially speculative and not clearly integrated with a social perspective, other than that provided by the degree to which the 'hidden secret of man' could not manifest himself in a humanly adequate world." *The Marxist Philosophy of Ernst Bloch* (New York: St. Martin's Press, 1982), 22.

56. Schillebeeckx, *Church*, 731.

57. Ibid.

58. Ibid.

59. Ibid., 732.

60. Ibid.

61. Berger and Luckmann emphasize that human plasticity amid divergent sociocultural determinations make humanness a variable concept—"It is an ethnological commonplace that the ways of becoming and being human are as numerous as man's cultures. Humanness is socio-culturally variable. In other words, there is no human nature in the sense of a biologically fixed substratum

determining the variability of socio-cultural formations. There is only human nature in the sense of *anthropological constants* (for example, world-openness and plasticity of instinctual structure) that delimit and permit man's sociocultural formations." They add, "But the specific shape into which this humanness is molded is determined by those socio-cultural formations and is relative to their numerous variations. While it is possible to say that man has a nature, it is more significant to say that man constructs his own nature, that man produces himself." *The Social Construction of Reality: A Treatise in the Sociology of Knowledge* (New York: Doubleday, 1966), 49. Emphasis mine.

62. See fn. 22, Roger Haight, *Jesus: Symbol of God* (New York: Orbis Books, 1999), 410.

63. In his discussion on hermeneutical method, Roger Haight sees Schillebeeckx's conception of anthropological constants as recognition of "the deep continuity in human existence that is continually mediated in history." In the fn. 28 to the passage, he adds—"I understand the 'anthropological constants' proposed by Edward Schillebeeckx to be both historically conscious and 'classical' insofar as they reflect the unity of the human species and universally relevant categories that can serve as bases for communication." See ibid., 41.

64. Schillebeeckx, *Church*, 735.

65. Ibid.

66. Ibid., 736.

67. Ibid., 737.

68. The "I-Thou" model for human encounter is expressed in the groundbreaking work of Martin Buber who wrote, "The primary word 'I-Thou' establishes the world of relation." *I and Thou, 2nd ed.*, trans. Ronald Gregor Smith (New York: Charles Scribner's Sons, 1958), 6.

69. Emmanuel Levinas describes "Totality" which follows the egocentric "Law of the I" in contrast to "Infinity" which follows the "Law of the Other" or infinite responsibility for the other. *Ethics and Infinity: Conversations with Philippe Nemo*, trans. Richard A. Cohen (Quezon City: Claretian Publications, 1997), 95–101.

70. Schillebeeckx, *Christ*, 738.

71. Ibid., 739.

72. Gustavo Gutierrez, *A Theology of Liberation: History, Politics, and Salvation, revised ed.*, trans. Caridad Inda and John Eagleson (New York: Orbis Books, 1988), xxiii.

73. Schillebeeckx, *Christ*, 739.

74. Portier differentiates the term "practice," which connotes a prior pure theory that can be applied practically, with "praxis," which is construed as "coconstitutive" of theory. In the latter concept, the ethical moment is then inextricably linked with theory. "Interpretation and Method," in *The Praxis of Human Experience*, 30. Schreiter points out that Schillebeeckx's use of the concept of praxis has sometimes been

inconsistent, "equating praxis only with action rather than the theory-action dialectic." Additionally, he notes that some critics have found it problematic that Schillebeeckx has not detailed the nuances of his use of "praxis" and "orthopraxis." This, of course, does not dent the unquestionable significance and depth of Schillebeeckx's work on the whole. "Edward Schillebeeckx," in *The Modern Theologians*, 159.
75. Schillebeeckx, *Christ*, 740.
76. Ibid., 741.
77. Ibid., 743.
78. Ibid.
79. Ibid., 725.
80. Ibid., 671. While it is not within the scope of this study to account for Schillebeeckx's detailed survey on the various perspectives of human suffering, I do provide a summation of relevant discussion points.
81. Greek thought is rooted in religious myths that paint a picture of humanity afflicted by suffering. Homer's Iliad, for example, presents a pessimistic view of humanity where certitude is provided only in the reality of death. The Greeks, however, did not exempt their own Gods from suffering. Schillebeeckx thus concludes that in Greek thought, "Human and divine suffering are part of the universe: there is no summer without winter." Ibid., 682.
82. Ibid., 719.
83. Ibid.
84. Ibid., 695.
85. Ibid.
86. Ibid., 698.
87. Schillebeeckx quotes Pope's "An Essay of Man" in ibid., 704.
88. Ibid., 706.
89. Ibid., 709.
90. Ibid., 714.
91. Ibid., 727.
92. Ibid., 727–728.
93. Ibid., 728.
94. Ibid.
95. Edward Schillebeeckx, *For the Sake of the Gospel*, trans. John Bowden (New York: Crossroad Publishing, 1990), 93.
96. Schillebeeckx acknowledges the influence of Dutch theologian Hendrikus Berkhof. Philip Kennedy, *Schillebeeckx*, 91–92.
97. Schillebeeckx, *Christ*, 907.
98. Derek J. Simon expounds on Schillebeeckx's conception of vertical soteriologies in "Salvation and Liberation in the Practical-Critical Soteriology of Schillebeeckx," *Theological Studies* 63.3 (September 2002): 496. He writes "Vertical theologies flee the difficulties of life on earth by attaching to and identifying with an idealized or post-historical narrative."

99. Ruether points out that a romanticized view of poverty is indigenous to soteriologies of this sort. "Poverty stands for many kinds of withdrawal from inauthentic states of existence as 'having' to the authentic state of 'being.' She cites the idealized Franciscan mendicant lifestyle as a case in point—." With only a tunic and cloak as garment by day and a bed by night, walking the dusty roads, without destination, without duties, singing as they go, in intimate communion with sun and wind, flower and beast, serving whomever they meet, sleeping wherever they may be when night falls, begging for their simple frugal meals: this is the classical Christian model for salvation by economic dropout." She adds, "In the mendicant ideal there is a strong direction toward service to the poor, yet this impulse has generally carried very little suggestion of a need to alter the conditions that make people poor." *The Radical Kingdom: The Western Experience of Messianic Hope*, 11–12.

100. Schillebeeckx, *Christ*, 744.

101. Ibid., 745. Moreover, he speaks in a similar vein when he discusses the acceptance of God's offer of grace in the person of Jesus, "To speak of God's work of grace is to speak in the language of religious affirmation about the human mystery of trusting someone." Schillebeeckx, *Jesus*, 673.

102. Schillebeeckx, *Christ*, 907.

103. Ruether, *The Radical Kingdom*, 9.

104. "Communities and biospheres become instruments sacrificed to the attitudes and ideals of the dominant ideological elite." Simon, "Salvation and Liberation in the Practical-Critical Soteriology of Schillibeeckx," *Theological Studies*, 97.

105. According to Simon, "Religious transcendence and sociopolitical immanence are in a mutually productive tension with each other, allowing their various fields of practice and interpretation to confront and develop each other. An interactive soteriology strives to articulate how religious transcendence and sociopolitical liberation are distinct yet mutually implicated aspects of both divine gift and human activity in history." Ibid.

106. This is noted by Kennedy in *Schillebeeckx*, 68.

107. See Schillebeeckx, *Christ*, 646–835.

108. Kennedy, *Schillebeeckx*, 68.

109. For an in-depth discussion of the soteriological project of Liberation Theology, see Jon Sobrino, "Central Position of the Reign of God in Liberation Theology," in Ignacio Ellacuria and Jon Sobrino, eds., *Systematic Theology: Perspectives from Liberation Theology* (Maryknoll, NY: Orbis Books, 1993), 40–45.

110. Schillebeeckx, *Church*, 54.

111. Ibid., 54–55.

112. The term appears in the heading of the Puebla documents and is described in sections 1134–1165. See ch. 10, fn. 6 of Donal Dorr,

Option for the Poor: A Hundred Years of Vatican Social Teaching (Dublin: Gill and Macmillam, 1983), 209.

113. In the years following its proposal, the term "preferential option for the poor" elicited controversy in the larger Church. Conservative quarters viewed the concept as an uncritical use of Marxist categories where the Church is made to take sides in a class struggle thus sabotaging the universality of the gospel message. In a speech delivered in Mexico, Pope John Paul II was prompted to re-state the concept in a more prudent fashion, "Medellin was a call of hope showing 'preferential yet not exclusive' love for the poor." For a more thorough discussion of the contentious debate on "preferential option for the poor," see ibid., 209–213.

114. Ibid., 55.

115. Sobrino in Ellacuria and Sobrino, eds., *Systematic Theology*, 45.

116. Schillebeeckx, *Jesus*, 140–141.

117. Ibid.

118. Ibid.

119. Ibid.

120. Schillebeeckx, *Jesus*, 142–143.

121. Ibid., 143.

122. Ibid., 146.

123. Sobrino in Ellacuria and Sobrino, *Systematic Theology*, 51.

124. Jon Sobrino, *Christology at the Crossroads: A Latin American Approach*, trans. John Drury, (Maryknoll, NY: Orbis Books, 1978), 65.

125. Schillebeeckx, *Jesus*, 156.

126. Paul Ricoeur explains that while the immediacy of belief as found in precritical hierophany is no longer accessible, hermeneutics can aim at a postcritical second immediacy or second naivete. The hermeneutical process exists not in a vicious cycle but in a "living and stimulating circle." He notes, "Such is the circle: hermeneutics proceeds from a prior understanding of the very thing that it tries to understand by interpreting it. But thanks to that circle in hermeneutics, I can still today communicate with the sacred by making explicit the prior understanding that gives life to the interpretation." *The Symbolism of Evil*, trans. Emerson Buchanan (New York: Harper and Row, 1969), 351.

127. See Schillebeeckx, *Jesus*, 156.

128. Ibid., 157.

129. Ibid., 158.

130. Ibid.

131. Ibid., 162.

132. Ibid., 172.

133. Ibid., 173–174.

134. Ibid., 177–178.

135. Commenting on the book *Jesus: An Experiment on Christology*, Rosemary Radford Ruether issues a sweeping criticism of

Schillebeeckx's Christology. She argues that Schillebeeckx presents a benign Jesus who is neither left nor right—"Schillebeeckx's Jesus is apolitical. He brings no judgments against the religious and social establishments of his day. He does not set righteous against unrighteous. His message is one of gratuitous acceptance of all equally." *To Change the World: Christology and Cultural Criticism* (New York: Crossroad Publishing, 1981), 2. Schillebeeckx does emphasize that Jesus preached an eschatological revolution rather than an overturning of existing sociopolitical structures. Jesus does not banner any particular sociopolitical movement; the salvation he preaches goes profoundly deeper than just a programmatic agenda to overturn social structures. From the optic of her own feminist project, this is probably where Ruether locates the bone of contention. But it cannot be denied that the Jesus of Schillebeeckx's christology has a partisan bias for the poor and oppressed. He is definitely not, as Ruether puts it, "apolitical." The epistemological project of Schillebeeckx's later theology has always bridged the religious with the political. The clear praxical focus of the next two books of his trilogy, *Christ* and *Church* validates that the soteriology Schillebeeckx proposes has serious sociopolitical implications that demand protest and resistance against social forces that perpetuate human oppression and suffering, "In other words, the gospel inspires Christians to a particular political action." See *Christ*, 731–839.
136. Ibid., 178.
137. Ibid., 184–185.
138. Sobrino, *Systematic Theology*, 49.
139. Schillebeeckx, *Jesus*, 191.
140. Ibid., 193.
141. Ibid., 203.
142. Ibid., 206.
143. Ibid., 211–212.
144. Ibid., 217–218.
145. Ibid., 171–173.
146. Ibid., 814.
147. Schillebeeckx, *Christ*, 768–770.
148. Ibid., 793.
149. Ibid., 776.
150. Schillebeeckx, *Christ*, 776–777.
151. Schillebeeckx issues a critique of "conservative and progressive utopias" which advocate a return to *la belle epoque*, a mystified past golden age; and "critical-rational utopias" where the future is the product of rational and deliberate human action through critical science. For a detailed discussion, refer to ibid., 662–670.
152. Ibid., 778.
153. Ibid., 779.
154. Ibid.

155. Edward Schillebeeckx, "Terugblik vanuit de tijd na Vaticanum II: De gebroken ideologieën van de moderniteit," in *Tussen openheid en isolement: Het voorbeld van de Katholische theologie in de negentiende eeuw*, ed. E. Borgman and A. van Harskamp (Kampen: Kok, 1992), 153–72, and 170–171 as translated by Simon, "Salvation and Liberation in the Practical-Critical Soteriology of Schillebeeckx," in *Theological Studies*, 517. Simon notes that "For Schillebeeckx, definitive eschatological salvation—as a salvation that completely heals the ruptures of finitude that eliminates all suffering from history, that even reconciles the living with the dead, and that permanently secures the sociopolitical and ecological integrity of life for one and for all—remains an unpredictable and excessive gift." See page 518.

156. Schillebeeckx, *Interim Report on the Books Jesus and Christ*, 123.

157. Schillebeeckx, *Christ*, 791.

158. Ibid.

159. Ibid., 838.

160. Mary Catherine Hilkert, " 'Grace-Optimism': The Spirituality at the Heart of Schillebeeckx's Theology," in *Spirituality Today* 3 (Fall, 1991): 220. In related manner, Philip Kennedy underscores the link between revelation and negative contrast experiences, "Schillebeeckx is effectively propounding, although not overtly, a new understanding of revelation in terms of historical experiences of the suffering, and not in terms of extrinsically imparted messages of an exclusively supra-historical provenance." *Deus Humanissimus: The Knowability of God in the Theology of Edward Schillibeeckx*, 246.

161. Kennedy observes, "Once the notion of negative contrast experiences gained foothold in Schillebeeckx's theology in 1968, it remained a permanent fixture of his explanation of faith's cognitive access to God in the context of ethics." *Deus Humanissimus*, 142. It is also worth noting Patricia McAuliffe's assertion in her Ph.D. research *A Liberationist Ethic: Some Fundamental Elements and Their Logic* (Regis College, 1990) that the concept of negative experiences of contrast occupies such a central place in Schillebeeckx's thought that it merits inclusion among his list of anthropological constants. Schillebeeckx confirms McAuliffe's proposition in a personal interview in 1986. See chapter 2, fn. 165, Berry, *Fundamental Liberationist Ethics: The Contribution of the Later Theology of Edward Schillebeeckx*, 141.

162. See Schillebeeckx, "Naar een 'definitief toekomst': belofte en menselijke bemiddeling," 45–47 as translated by Schreiter in *The Schillebeeckx Reader*, 55–56. See also *Christ*, 818.

163. Schillebeeckx, *"Naar een 'definitief toekomst': belofte en menselijke bemiddeling,"* 45–47 as translated by Schreiter in ibid., 55.

164. Edward Schillebeeckx, *God the Future of Man*, trans. N.D. Smith (New York: Sheed and Ward), 341–344.

165. Schillebeeckx, *Christ*, 821.
166. While Schillebeeckx draws from Theodor Adorno's notion of "critical negativity" to describe the epistemological power in human suffering, his conception of negative contrast experiences deviates radically from Adorno in that it puts forth a positive moment innervated by hope. Adorno's negative dialectics takes a decidedly negative perspective as can be seen in his reference to the Holocaust experience— "After Auschwitz, our feelings resist any claim of the positivity of existence as sanctimonious, as wronging the victims; they balk at squeezing any kind of sense, however, bleached, out of the victims' fates. And our feelings do have an objective side after events that make a mockery of the construction of immanence as endowed with a meaning radiated by an affirmatively posited transcendence." Theodor Adorno, *Negative Dialectics*, trans. E.B. Ashton (New York: Seabury, 1973), 361.
167. Schillebeeckx, *Church*, 6.
168. Ibid., 7.
169. Jon Sobrino draws from Gustavo Gutierrez's *Beber en su Propio Pozo* (Lima: CEP, 1971) in *Spirituality of Liberation: Toward Political Holiness*, trans. Robert R. Barr (Maryknoll, NY: Orbis Books, 1988), 54.
170. Mary Catherine Hilkert cites Jon Sobrino as the proponent of the concept of "political holiness." See " 'Grace Optimism': The Spirituality at the Heart of Schillebeeckx's Theology," in *Spirituality Today* 44.3 (Fall 1991): 220–239. For more discussions on political holiness and political love, see Sobrino, *Spirituality of Liberation: Toward Political Holiness*, 80–86.
171. Schillebeeckx, *Jerusalem of Banares? Nicaragua of de Berg Athos?*, 336–338 as translated by Schreiter in *The Schillebeeckx Reader*, 272.
172. Sobrino, *Spirituality of Liberation: Toward Political Holiness*, 81–82.
173. Schillebeeckx's emphasis is not on personal or collective "guilt" over the global socioeconomic divide but responsibility for the structural reasons of inequality—"You can say for example: The situation is very different here (in the Netherlands) from what it is in Latin America. But my reply would be: But we are to blame for what is happening here . . . I can't agree that it is right to feel personally guilty for the situation in the Third World or even accept collective guilt for it. But what we are bound to recognize is that the structures are at fault—that the capitalist mode of production in the West is the cause of the disastrous situation there and that this calls for a radical process of learning." He adds, "Every critical community has to learn, reflect and analyse and encourage that learning process in others." *God is New Each Moment*, 94.
174. Ibid., p. 169. Schillebeeckx's project is to initiate the formation of a western theology of liberation that may serve as a dialogue partner to

liberation theologies in the Third World. Refer to "Theologie *als bevrijdingskunde: Enkele noodzakelijke beschouwingen vooraf,*" *Tijdschrift voor Theologie* 24 (1984): 391–392.

175. Schillebeeckx, *Jeruzalem of Banares? Nicaragua of De Berg Athos?* as translated by Schreiter in *The Schillebeeckx Reader*, 272–273.

176. Ibid.

177. Schillebeeckx, *Christ*, 647.

178. Ibid.

179. Schillebeeckx expounds on his definition of the term "positivism"— "Positivism is a trend in scientific study which is at least an implicit philosophy. It puts forward the view that the only truth is scientific truth, which is empirically verifiable. Thus no communication of truth is really possible outside the sciences. It also argues that the sciences are 'value-free'; in other words, in scientific investigation it only accepts intrinsically scientific values, and leaves external values out of account. It in no way denies that the choice of the object for investigation and the use of the results achieved imply values (or non-values) extrinsic to science. However, positivists overlook that the facts that are called scientifically established 'hard facts' and 'basic propositions' are governed (a) by the historical character of the object achieved, and (b) by the historical and social position of the percipient. In other words, positivists forget that all scientific theories are also subject to historical hypothesis." Ibid., 905.

180. Schillebeeckx, "Speech of Thanks on Receiving the Erasmus Prize," in *God Among Us: The Gospel Proclaimed*, trans. John Bowden, (New York: Crossroad Publishing, 1980), 250–253.

181. Ibid.

182. As quoted in Schillebeeckx, *Church*, 648.

183. Ibid., 185.

184. For a listing of notable political saints who worked in Central America and a discussion on a "spirituality of persecution and martyrdom," refer to chapter 5 of Sobrino, *Spirituality of Liberation: Toward Political Holiness*, 87–102.

185. See Schillebeeckx, *God is New Each Moment*, 108.

186. Schillebeeckx, *Jeruzalem of Banares? Nicaragua of De Berg Athos?* as translated by Schreiter in *The Schillebeeckx Reader*, 273.

187. Schillebeeckx, *Christ*, 814.

188. Ibid., 814.

189. Schillebeeckx, *The Schillebeeckx Reader*, 273.

190. Schillebeeckx's psalm-prayer was written with the help of Dutch poet Huub sterhuis. See God *is New Each Moment*, 127–128. Refer also to Edward Schillebeeckx, *I am a Happy Theologian: Conversations with Francesco Strazzari*, trans. John Bowden (New York: Crossroad Publishing, 1994), 82–83.

191. Interview with Edward Schillebeeckx, July 11, 2003, Nimegen, The Netherlands.

192. Schillebeeckx writes, "The reality of suffering and threatened humanity, is, in my view, the central problem for us as we enter the third millennium . . . we are ultimately forced to speak of a 'history of suffering' affecting most of the world's population. In a world subject to the unavoidable sources of globalization—where the suffering of many lonely people, even in western countries, is often concealed and silenced—this history raises a central and difficult question for us." See Daniel Speed Thompson, *The Language of Dissent: Edward Schillebeeckx on the Crisis of the Authority in the Catholic Church* (Notre Dame: University of Notre Dame Press, 2003), vii–viii.

Chapter 5 The Crystallization of Political Holiness in Third Cinema

1. I reiterate that I use the term "polysemic" in a sense akin to the cultural studies definition of Michael R. Real who described the term as "the multiplicity of meanings or sign (*sema*) values inherent in a text, just as *polyphony* refers to two or more melodic lines sung simultaneously over another." *Super Media: A Cultural Studies Approach* (London: Sage Publications, 1989), 57.
2. Interactive soteriologies avoid the fideistic withdrawal into the personal and the instrumental totalization of the political; it emphasizes the political meaning of the religious and seeks for the transformation of the political.
3. See William L. Portier, "Interpretation and Method," in Robert J. Schreiter and Mary Catherine Hilkert, eds., The Praxis of Christian Experience: *An Introduction to the Theology of Edward Schillebeeckx* (New York: Harper and Row, 1989), 34.
4. Refer back to "'The Liberation of Human Beings is the Golden Thread of my Theology': An Interview with Edward Schillebeeckx" in chapter 4 of this book, 189–190.
5. Ibid., 190.
6. JosÈ M. De Mesa refers to Schillebeeckx's *God and Man* (London: Sheed and Ward, 1969), 240, in this quote. See *In Solidarity with Culture: Studies in Theological Re-rooting* (Quezon City: Maryhill School of Theology, 1991), 173. Additionally, in his attempt at "re-rooting" Jesus' resurrection in inculturated terms, De Mesa cites Schillebeeckx's *Jesus: An Experiment in Christology* a number of times. See chapter 7 "The Resurrection in the Filipino Context," in Ibid., 102–146. Stephen B. Bevans classifies De Mesa's methodological approach as belonging to the "synthetic model" of contextual theology. Bevans clarifies that "synthetic" is not understood in the sense of "artificial" but rather of "synthesis." The synthetic model is culturally immersed and open to resources from other

cultures and theological expressions, synthesizing these elements in a creative dialectic. It shares fundamental similarities with the "dialogical model," the "conversation model," and the "analogical model," which derive from David Tracy's conception of the analogical imagination. See *Models of Contextual Theology* (Maryknoll: Orbis Books, 1992), 81–96.

7. De Mesa draws from Edward Schillebeeckx's discussion of eschatological salvation in *Christ: The Experience of Jesus as Lord*, in Solidarity with Culture: Studies in Theological Re-rooting (Quezon City: Maryhill School of Theology, 1987), 91.

8. Derek Simon, "Towards Consolidating the Practical-Critical Soteriology of Edward Schillebeeckx," in *Theoforum* 3 (2002), 339.

9. Tadahiko Iwashima, *Menschheitsgeschichte und Heilserfahrung: Die Theologie von Edward Schillebeeckx als methodisch reflektierte Soteriologie* (Dusseldorf: Patmos, 1982) as cited in Ibid., 340–341.

10. Ibid., 342.

11. Ibid.

12. Erik Borgman, "*Theologie tussen universiteit en emancipatie: De Weg van Edward Schillebeeckx*," in Tijdschrift voor theologie, 26 (1986):, 388–402, as cited in Ibid., 343.

13. Simon also comments on Borgman's delimitation of Schillebeeckx's *ouvre* as just a university theology, a description which does not take into consideration the ecclesial community of ordinary believers. Such a community factors into Schillebeeckx's theological context in varying ways, interlinking with the university milieu and liberative movements. Ibid., 344.

14. Refer back to "'The Liberation of Human Beings is the Golden Thread of My Theology': An Interview with Edward Schillebeeckx," chapter 4 of this book, 190.

15. Ibid., 192.

16. Teshome Gabriel, *Third Cinema in the Third World: The Aesthetics of Liberation* (Ann Arbor: UMI Research Press, 1979), xi.

17. Ibid., 18.

18. Schillebeeckx, *Christ: The Experience of Jesus as Lord*, 725.

19. Edward Schillebeeckx, "Speech of Thanks in Receiving the Erasmus Prize," in *God Among Us: The Gospel Proclaimed*, trans. John Bowden (New York: Crossroad Publishing, 1980), 250–253.

20. Edward Schillebeeckx, *Christ: The Experience of Jesus as Lord*, 647.

21. Ellison Banks Findly writes, "*Ruah* is also the spirit of man that gives him character; because this spirit is created and preserved by God, it is thus understood to be God's spirit (the *ruah elohim* of Genesis 1:2), which is breathed into man at the time of creation." *The Encyclopedia of Religion*, vol. 2, ed. Mircea Eliade (New York: Macmillan Publishing, 1987), 303.

22. Laura U. Marks explains that unlike metaphors, which rely on mental associations, recollection-objects encode popular memory on the level of physical contact as in fossils, fetishes, or transnational objects. For a detailed discussion, refer to chapter 2, "The Memory of Touch," in *The Skin of the Film: Intercultural Cinema, Embodiment, and the Senses* (London: Duke University Press, 2000), 78–126.

23. Ibid., 99.

24. Teshome Gabriel, *Third Cinema in the Third World: The Aesthetics of Liberation*, 82.

25. Ibid.

26. I Sam. 17:48–50 (New Revised Standard Version).

27. As D.W. Gooding comments on the text of I Samuel 17:45–47 "David is going to win . . . but to match Goliath's sword with another sword, his spear with another spear, would obscure both what the real issue at stake is and the power by which victory is achieved . . . . But God will do it in such a way as to make it evident that the battle is won not by David's superior use of sword and spear, but by direct divine intervention: 'the battle is the Lord's and he will give you into our hand' . . . ." See "An Approach to the Literary and Textual Problems in the David and Goliath Story: 1 Sam 16–18," in Dominique Barthèlemy, et. al., *The Story of David and Goliath: Textual and Literary Criticism* (Fribourg: Editions Universitaires/Göttingen: Vandenhoeck & Ruprecht, 1986), 67–68.

28. For a discussion on the Israeli occupation of Palestine from a Palestinian-Christian perspective, consult chapter 3 "Being Palestinian and Christian in Israel," in Naim Stifan Ateek, *Justice and Only Justice: A Palestinian Theology of Liberation*, (Maryknoll Orbis Books, 1989), 50–73.

29. Bennis notes that the oppression of Palestinians in Israel is a gendered oppression. "It is Palestinian women who figure out how to cope with closures of cities and towns, the blocking of roads and the economic siege . . . how to feed their families when even flour and cooking oil run low, how to care for traumatized children, how to look after the not-really-fearless young men confronting the soldiers. It's the women who must hold their families together." See *Palestinian Women Suffer Under the Occupation* in http://www.fromoccupiedpalestine.org/

30. According to Ateek, there has been a "political abuse of the Bible" by Israel. He contends that "the emergence of the Zionist movement in the twentieth century is a retrogression of the Jewish community into the history of its very distant past, with its most elementary and primitive forms of the concept of God Zionism has succeeded in reanimating the nationalist tradition within Judaism. Its inspiration has been drawn not from the profound thoughts of the Hebrew Scriptures but from the portions that betray a narrow and exclusive concept of a tribal god." *Justice and Only Justice: A Palestinian Theology of Liberation*, 101.

31. Mary Catherine Hilkert, "'Grace-Optimism': The Spirituality of Schillebeeckx's Theology," in *Spirituality Today* (Fall, 1991), 220.

32. Schillebeeckx, *Christ, The Experience of Jesus as Lord,* 779.

33. See Luke 23:39–43.

34. The Philippines is counted among the earth's ecological "hotspots," in a list of the richest and most threatened reservoirs of plant and animal life. The country's 7,107 islands boast of a bounty of 12,000 species of plants; 1,100 land vertebrate species; and more than 500 coral species. Priit J. Vesilind, "The Philippines" *National Geographic* (2002 July issue), 62–81.

35. For a detailed examination of religion in the stylistic strategies of *Perfumed Nightmare,* refer to my essay, "Perfumed Nightmare: Religion and the Philippine Postcolonial Struggle in Third Cinema," in S. Brent Plate, ed., *Representing Religion in World Cinema: Filmmaking, Mythmaking, Culture-Making,* (New York: Palgrave McMillan, 2003), 181–196. For an in-depth discussion of the blending of folk religion and official religion, consult the chapter "Popular Religion and Official Religion," in Robert J. Schreiter, *Constructing Local Theologies* (Maryknoll: Orbis Books, 1985), 122–143.

36. Edward Schillebeeckx, *God is New Each Moment,* trans. David Smith (New York: Seabury Press, 1983), 94.

37. The editorial entitled "Trade Rigged Against the Poor" notes that the plea for the levelling of the global economic playing field issued by the Third World, home to an overwhelming majority of 96 percent of the world's farmers, "needs to be heeded before it is too late." *International Herald Tribune online* (July 21, 2003), 1. http://www.iht.com.

38. Ibid., 2. For a related editorial detailing the continuing effects of ruthless U.S. protectionism on the Third World, specifically its crippling onslaught against struggling Vietnamese catfish fishermen, see Seth Maydans, "Americans and Vietnamese Fighting Over Catfish," in the *New York Times,* November 3, 2002. http://www.globalpolicy.org/socecon/ffd/2002/1103catfish.htm.

39. Richard Porton, "Notes from the Palestinian Diaspora: an Interview with Elia Suleiman," *Cineaste,* (June 22, 2003).

40. Max Elbaum, "For Jews Only: Racism Inside Israel: an Interview with Phyllis Bennis," ColorLines Magazine (2000). http://www.zmag.org/meastwatch/for_jews_only.htm.

41. Eleazar S. Fernandez in Virginia Fabella and R.S. Sugirtharajah, eds., *Dictionary of Third World Theologies* (Maryknoll: Orbis Books, 2000), 201.

42. Fernandez qualifies that a "method is not simply a set of principles, a *depositum fidei,* frameworks, and techniques to be applied at specific contexts and revised when not workable; a method, as understood in

the theology of struggle, is inextricably bound with the act of struggling, interpreting, and theologizing." *Toward a Theology of Struggle* (Maryknoll: Orbis Books, 1994), 183.

43. Donal Dorr, *Option for the Poor: A Hundred Years of Vatican Social Teaching* (Dublin: Gill and Macmillan, 1983), 159.

44. Catholic Bishop's Conference of the Philippines (CBCP), *Catechism for Filipino Catholics* (Manila: ECCCE/Word and Life Publications, 1997), 12.

$$\text{B}\small{\text{IBLIOGRAPHY}}$$

Abaya, Hernando J. *Betrayal in the Philippines.* New York: A. A. Wynn, 1946.

Adorno, Theodor. *Negative Dialectics,* trans. E.B. Ashton. New York: Seabury Press, 1973.

Aichele, George, and Richard Walsh. *Screening Scripture: Intertextual Connections Between Scripture and Film.* Pasadena: Trinity Press International, 2002.

Arato, Andrew, and Eike Gebhardt, eds. *The Essential Frankfurt School Reader.* New York: Urizen Books, 1978.

Armes, Roy. *Third World Film Making in the West.* Berkeley: University of California Press, 1987.

Ateek, Naim Stifan. *Justice and Only Justice: A Palestinian Theology of Liberation.* Maryknoll: Orbis Books, 1989.

Barthelemy, Dominic, et al. *The Story of David and Goliath: Textual and Literary Criticism.* Fribourg: Editions Universitaires/Gottingen: Vandenhoek & Ruprecht, 1986.

Barthes, Roland. *Image, Music, Text,* trans. Stephen Heath. New York: Hill and Wang, 1977.

Baugh, Lloyd, S. J. *Imaging the Divine: Jesus and Christ-Figures in Film.* New York: Sheed and Ward, 1997.

Bennis, Phyllis. "Talking Points on the Geneva Accord," *From Occupied Palestine* (December 11, 2003). http://fromoccupiedpalestine.org/node.php?id=1026.

Berger, Peter L., and Thomas Luckmann. *The Social Construction of Reality.* Middlesex: Penguin Books, 1971.

Berry, Brian David. "Fundamental Liberationist Ethics: The Contribution of the Later Theology of Edward Schillebeeckx," Dissertation. Boston College, 1995.

Bevans, Stephen B. *Models of Contextual Theology.* New York: Orbis Books, 1992.

Bordwell, David. *The Cinema of Eisenstein.* Cambridge, MA: Harvard University Press, 1993.

———. *Making Meaning: Inference and Rhetoric in the Interpretation of Cinema.* Cambridge, MA: Harvard University Press, 1996.

———. "Intensified Continuity: Visual Style in Contemporary American Film," in *Film Quarterly* 3, no. 55 (Spring 2002):16–28.

Bordwell, David, and Kristin Thompson. *Film Art: An Introduction, 3rd ed.* New York: McGraw-Hill, 1990.

Borgman, Erik. *Edward Schillebeeckx: A Theologian in His History* vol. 1., trans. John Bowden. London: Continuum, 2003.

Bowden, John. *Edward Schillebeeckx: In Search of the Kingdom of God.* New York: Crossroad Publishing, 1983.

Buber, Martin. *I and Thou, 2nd ed.* trans. Ronald Gregor Smith. New York: Charles Scribner's Sons, 1958.

Buck-Morss, Susan. *The Origin of Negative Dialectics: Theodor Adorno, Walter Benjamin, and the Frankfurt Institute.* Hassocks: The Harvester Press, 1977.

Burton, Julianne. "Marginal Cinemas and Mainstream Critical Theory," in *Screen* 26.3–4 (May–August 1985):2–21.

Carroll, Nöel. *Philosophy of Art: A Contemporary Introduction.* London: Routledge, 1999.

Catholic Bishop's Conference of the Philippines, *Catechism for Filipino Catholics.* Manila: ECCE / Word and Life Publications, 1997.

Chanan, Michael. "The Changing Geography of Third Cinema," in *Screen* 4 (Winter 1997): 38.

Chow, Rey. *Primitive Passions: Visuality, Sexuality, Ethnography, and Contemporary Chinese Cinema.* New York: Columbia University Press, 1995.

Chupungco, Anscar J. *Liturgical Inculturation: Sacramentals, Religiosity, and Catechesis.* Minesotta: The Liturgical Press, 1992.

Cohen, Robin. *Global Diasporas: An Introduction.* London: UCL Press, 1997.

Constantino, Renato. *Neocolonial Identity and Counter-Consciousness: Essays on Cultural Decolonization,* ed. Istvan Meszaros.. London: Merlin Press, 1978.

Cunneen, Joseph. *Robert Bresson: A Spiritual Style in Film.* New York: Continuum Press, 2003.

David, Joel. *Wages of Cinema: Film in Philippine Perspective.* Quezon City: University of the Philippines Press, 1998.

De Mesa, Jose M. *In Solidarity with Culture: Studies in Theological Re-rooting.* Quezon City: Maryhill School of Theology, 1987.

———., and Lode L. Wostyn. *Doing Theology: Basic Realities and Processes.* Quezon City: Claretian Publications, 1990.

Del Mundo, Clodualdo. *Philippine Cinema and Colonialism: 1898–1941.* Manila: De La Salle University Press, 1998.

Deleuze, Gilles. *Cinema 2: The Time Image,* trans. Hugh Tomlison and Roberta Galeta. London: The Athlone Press, 1989.

Denzin, Norman K., and Yvonna S. Lincoln. *Handbook of Qualitative Research.* Thousand Oaks: Sage Publishing, 1994.

Dorfman, Ariel, and Armand Mattelart. *How to Read Donald Duck: Imperialist Ideology in the Disney Comic.* New York: I.G. Editions, 1975.

Dorr, Donal. *Option for the Poor: A Hundred Years of Vatican Social Teaching.* Dublin: Gill and Macmillan, 1983.

Downing, John D. H., ed., *Film and Politics in the Third World.* New York: Praeger Publishers, 1987.

Eliade, Mircea, ed., *The Encyclopedia of Religion*, vol. 2. New York: Macmillan Publishing, 1987.

Fabella, Virginia M. M., and Sugirtharajah R. S., eds., *Dictionary of Third World Theologies*. Maryknoll, NY: Orbis Books, 2000.

Fanon, Frantz. *Black Skin, White Masks*, trans. Charles Lam Markmann. New York: Grove Press, 1967.

———. *The Wretched of the Earth*, trans. Constance Farrington. New York: Grove Press, 1963.

Fernandez, Eleazar S. *Toward a Theology of Struggle*. Maryknoll: Orbis Books, 1994.

Fiske, John. *Introduction to Communication Studies, 2nd ed.* London: Routledge, 1991.

Flagg, Michael. "Philippine Film Industry Suffers Amid Ailing Economy, Competition" in *The Wall Street Journal* (September 25, 2001).

Fraser, Peter. *Images of Passion: The Sacramental Mode in Film*. Westport, CT: Praeger Publishers, 1998.

Gabriel, Teshome H. "Third Cinema as Guardian of Popular Memory: Towards a Third Aesthetics," in Jim Pines and Paul Willemen, eds. *Questions of Third Cinema*. London: British Film Institute, 1989, 30–52.

———. Third Cinema in the Third World: *The Aesthetics of Liberation*. Ann Arbor: UMI Research Press, 1982.

———. "Thoughts on Nomadic Aesthetics and the Black Independent Cinema: Traces of a Journey," in *Blackframes: Critical Perspectives on Black Independent Cinema*, ed. Mbye B. Cham and Claire Andrade-Watkins. Cambridge, MA: MIT Press, 1988.

———. "Towards a Critical Theory of Third World Films," in, *Questions of Third Cinema*, ed., Jim Pines and Paul Willemen. London: British Film Institute, 1989.

Gabriel, Teshome H., and Hamid Naficy, eds. *Otherness and the Media: The Ethnography of the Imagined and the Imaged*. Langhorne, PA: Harwood Academic Publishers, 1993.

Gadamer, Hans-Georg. *Truth and Method*, ed. Garret Barden and John Cumming. New York: Seabury Press, 1975.

Gadjigo, Samba, et al. "The Uniqueness of Ousmane Sembene's Cinema," in *Ousmane Sembene: Dialogue with Critics and Writers*. Amherst: University of Massachusetts Press, 1993.

Gendzier, Irene L. *Frantz Fanon: A Critical Study*. London: Wildwood House, 1973.

Ginsburg, Faye, et al., eds. Media Worlds: Anthropology on New Terrain. Berkeley: University of California Press, 2002.

Griffith, Keith M., ed., *The Brechtian Aspect of Radical Cinema: Essays by Martin Walsh*. London: BFI Publishing, 1981.

Guerrero, Rafael Ma. *Readings in Philippine Cinema*. Manila: Experimental Cinema of the Philippines, 1983.

Guneratne, Anthony R., and Wimal Dissanayake, eds. *Rethinking Third Cinema*. New York: Routledge, 2003.

Gutierrez, Gustavo. *A Theology of Liberation: History, Politics and Salvation,* revised ed., trans. Caridad Inda and John Eagleson. New York: Orbis Books, 1988.

Hadjor, Kofi Buenor. *Dictionary of Third World Terms.* London: Penguin Group, 1992.

Haight, Roger. *Jesus: Symbol of God.* Maryknoll: Orbis Books, 2000.

Hall, Stuart, and Bram Gieben, eds. *Formations of Modernity.* Cambridge: Polity Press, 1995.

Heath, Stephen. *Questions of Cinema.* London: McMillan Press, 1981.

Helminski, Allison Arnold. "Memories of a Revolutionary Cinema," in *Senses of Cinema* 2, (January 2000). www.sensesofcinema.com/contents/00/2/memories.html.

Hendrickx, Herman. *Social Justice in the Bible.* Quezon City: Claretian Publications, 1985.

Hilkert, Mary Catherine. " 'Grace-Optimism': The Spirituality at the Heart of Schillebeeckx's Spirituality," in *Spirituality Today* 44.3 (Fall 1991): 220–239.

Hill, John, and Pamela Church Gibson, eds. *The Oxford Guide to Film Studies.* Oxford: Oxford University Press, 1998.

Hoogen, A. J. M. van den, *Pastorale Teologie: Ontwikkeling en Struktur in de Theologie van M.D. Chenu.* Katholieke Universiteit Nijmegen, 1984.

Hudson, Wayne. *The Marxist Philosophy of Ernst Bloch.* New York: St. Martin's Press, 1982.

Hurley, Neil P. *The Reel Revolution: A Film Primer on Liberation.* New York: Orbis Books, 1987.

IDOC. "The Future of the Missionary Enterprise, An Asian Theology of Liberation: the Philippines," *IDOC International* (1973).

Jameson, Fredric. *The Geopolitical Aesthetic: Cinema and Space in the World System.* Bloomington: Indiana University Press, 1992.

Kegley, Charles W., and Eugene R. Wittkopf. *American Foreign Policy, 5th ed.* New York: St. Martin's Press, 1996.

Kennedy, Philip. "*Deus Humanissimus:* The Knowability of God in Edward Schillebeeckx." Dissertation. Fribourg University, 1993.

———. *Schillebeeckx.* London: Chapman Press, 1993.

Kolker, Robert. *Film Form and Culture.* Boston, MA: McGraw-Hill, 1999.

Lacaba, Jose F. *The Films of Asean.* Pasig: The ASEAN Committee on Culture and Information, 2000.

Lent, John A. *The Asian Film Industry.* Kent: University of Texas Press, 1990.

Lerner, Ted. "The Eye of the Beholder: 1994 Miss Universe Pageant in the Philippines," in *Transpacific* 9 (October 1994).

Levinas, Emmanuel. *Ethics and Infinity: Conversations with Philip Nemo,* trans. Richard A. Cohen. Quezon City: Claretian Publications, 1997.

Levitas, Ruth. *The Concept of Utopia.* Hertfordshire: Philip Allan, 1990.

Lumbera, Bienvenido. *Writing the Nation/Pag-akda ng Bansa.* Quezon City: University of the Philippines, 2000.

Lynch, William, S. J. *The Image Industries*. New York: Sheed and Ward, 1959.

MacLuhan, Marshall. *Understanding Media: The Extensions of Man*. Cambridge, MA: MIT Press, 1999.

Maltin, Loenard. *2002 Movie and Video Guide*. Middlesex: Penguin Books, 2001.

Marks, Laura U. *The Skin of the Film: Intercultural Cinema, Embodiment, and the Senses*. Durham, NC: Duke University Press, 2000.

Marsh, Clive, and Gaye Ortiz, eds. *Explorations in Theology and Film*. Oxford: Blackwell Publishers, 1997.

Martin, Joel W., and Conrad E. Oswalt, eds. *Screening the Sacred: Religion, Myth, and Ideology in Popular American Film*. Boulder, CO: Westview Press, 1995.

Martin, Michael T., ed., *New Latin American Cinema: Theory, Practices, and Transcontinental Articulations, vol. 1.*, Detroit, MI: Wayne State University Press, 1997.

Martin, Thomas M. *Images and the Imageless: A Study in Religious Consciousness and Film*. East Brunswick, NJ: Bucknell University Press, 1992.

Marz, John. "Recasting Cuban Slavery: The Other Francisco and the Last Supper," in *Based on a True Story: Latin American History at the Movies*, ed. Donald D. Stevens. Delaware: Scholarly Resources, 1997.

Mast, Gerald, and Marshall Cohen, eds. *Film Theory and Criticism: Introductory Readings, 2nd ed*. New York: Oxford University Press, 1979.

May, Glenn Anthony, Glenn. "America in the Philippines: The Shaping of Colonial Policy, 1898–1913," New Haven, Yale University, 1975.

May, John R., ed. *New Image of Religious Film*. Kansas City, MO: Sheed and Ward, 1997.

May, John R., and Michael Bird, eds. *Religion in Film*. Knoxville: University of Tennessee Press, 1982.

Maydans, Seth. "Americans and Vietnamese Fighting Over Catfish," in *The New York Times*, November 3, 2002. http://www.globalpolicy.org/socecon/ffd/2002/1103catfish.htm.

McKnight, George, ed., *Agent of Challenge and Defiance: The Films of Ken Loach*. Wiltshire: Flicks Books, 1997.

McLellan, David. *The Thought of Karl Marx: An Introduction*. London, McMillan Press, 1971.

Mercado, Leonardo M. *Elements of Filipino Theology*. Tacloban City: Divine Word University, 1994.

Metz, Christian. *Film Language: A Semiotics of the Cinema*, trans. Michael Taylor. New York: Oxford University Press, 1974.

Michalson, Carl, ed., *Christianity and the Existentialists*. New York: Scribner and Sons, 1956.

Miles, Margaret. *Seeing is Believing: Religion and Values in the Movies*. Boston, MA: Beacon Press, 1996.

Moltmann, Jurgen, et al. *The Future of Hope: Theology as Eschatology*, ed. Frederick Herzog. New York: Herder and Herder, 1970.

Moylan, Tom. *Demand the Impossible: Science Fiction and the Utopian Imagination*. New York: Methuen, 1986.

Myerson, Michael, ed., *Memories of Underdevelopment: The Revolutionary Films of Cuba*. New York: Grossman Publishers, 1973.

Orr, John. *The Art and Politics of Film*. Edinburgh: Edinburgh University Press, 2000.

Pines, Jim, and Paul Willeman, eds. *Questions of Third Cinema*. London: British Film Institute, 1989.

Pratt, Mary Louise. *Imperial Eyes: Travel Writing and Transculturation*. New York: Routledge, 1982.

Real, Michael R. *Super Media: A Cultural Studies Approach*. London: Sage Publications, 1989.

Ricouer, Paul. *The Symbolism of Evil*. Boston, MA: Beacon Press, 1967.

Rizal, Jose P. *El Filibusterismo*, trans. Soledad Lacson-Locsin. Makati City: Bookmark Publishers, 1996.

———. *Noli Me Tangere*, trans. Soledad Lacson-Locsin. Makati City: Bookmark Publishers, 1996.

Rony, Fatimah Tobing. *The Third Eye: Race, Cinema, and Ethnographic Spectacle*. Durham: Duke University Press, 1986.

Roosevelt, Nicholas. *The Philippines*. London: Faber and Gwyer, 1926.

Rosen, Philip. *Narrative, Apparatus, Ideology: A Film Theory Reader*. New York: Columbia University Press, 1986.

Ruether, Rosemary Radford. *The Radical Kingdom: The Western Experience of Messianic Hope*. New York: Harper and Row, 1970.

———. *Sexism and God-Talk: Towards a Feminist Theology*, Boston, MA: Beacon Press, 1985.

———. *To Change the World: Christology and Cultural Criticism*. New York: Crossroad Publishing Co., 1981.

Russell, Catherine. *Experimental Ethnography: The Work of Film in the Age of Video*. Durham, NC: Duke University Press, 1999.

Salles, Walter. "Finding the Spirit of a Journey: *The Motorcycle Diaries*," an interview with Erica Abeel in *IndieWire*. http://www.indiewire.com/people/people_040923salles.html.

San Juan, E. Jr. "*Perfumed Nightmare*: Cinema of the Naïve Subaltern," in *After Postcolonialism: Remapping Philippines-United States Confrontations*. Lanham, MD: Rowman and Littlefield, 2000.

SarDesai, D. R. *Southeast Asia: Past and Present, 3rd ed.* Boulder, CO: Westview Press, 1994.

Schillebeeckx, Edward. *Christ: The Experience of Jesus as Lord*, trans. John Bowden. New York: The Crossroad Publishing Co., 1980.

———. *Church: The Human Story of God*. New York: The Crossroad Publishing Co., 1993.

———. "Critical Theories and Christian Political Commitment," in *Concilium* 9.4 (1973): 48–61.

———. *For the Sake of the Gospel*, trans. John Bowden. New York: Crossroad Publishing, 1990.

———. *God Among Us: The Gospel Proclaimed*, trans. John Bowden. New York: Crossroad Publishing, 1980.

———. *God is New Each Moment*, trans. David Smith. New York: SCM Press, 1983.

———. *God the Future of Man*, trans. Edward Fitzgerald and Peter Tomlinson. New York: Sheed and Ward, 1969.

———. Foreword to Daniel Speed Thompson, *The Language of Dissent: Edward Schillebeeckx on the Crisis of Authority in the Church.* Notre Dame: University of Notre Dame Press, 2003.

———. *I am a Happy Theologian: Conversations with Francesco Strazzari.* New York: Crossroad Publishing, 1994.

———. *Interim Report on the Books Jesus and Christ.* New York: Crossroad Publishing, 1980.*c*

———. *Jesus: An Experiment in Christology*, trans. Hubert Hoskins. New York: The Crossroad Publishing Co., 1979.

———. *The Language of Faith: Essays on Jesus, Theology, and the Church.* Maryknoll, NY: Orbis Books, 1995.

———. "Some Thoughts on the Interpretation of Eschatology," in *Concilium* 5.1 (1969): 22–29.

———. *The Understanding of Faith: Interpretation and Criticism*, trans. N. D. Smith. London: Sheed and Ward, 1974.

———. *World and Church*, trans. N. D. Smith. London: Sheed and Ward, 1971.

Schillebeeckx, Edward, and Boniface Willems, eds. *The Problem of Eschatology.* New York: Paulist Press, 1969.

Schoof, Ted, and Jan van de Westelaken. *Bibliography 1936–1996 of Edward Schillebeeckx.* Nijmegen: H. Nelissen, Baarn/Edward Schillebeeckx Foundation, 1997.

Schrader, Paul. *Transcendental Style in Film: Ozu, Bresson, and Dreyer.* Berkely: University of California Press, 1972.

Schreiter, Robert J. *Constructing Local Theologies.* Maryknoll, NY: Orbis Books, 1985.

———. "Edward Schillebeeckx," in David F. Ford, ed., *The Modern Theologians: An Introduction to Christian Theology in the Twentieth Century.* Cambridge: Blackwell Publishers, 1997.

———., ed., *The Schillebeeckx Reader.* New York: The Crossroad Publishing Co., 1984.

Schreiter, Robert J., and Mary Catherine Hilkert, eds. *The Praxis of the Reign of God: An Introduction to the Theology of Edward Schillebeeckx.* New York: Fordham University Press, 2002.

Shohat, Ella, and Robert Stam. "The Cinema after Babel—Language, Difference, Power," in *Screen* 26.3–4 (May–August 1985): 45–58.

Shohat, Ella, and Robert Stam. "Third Cinema," in *Unthinking Eurocentrism: Multiculturalism and the Media*. London: Routledge, 1996.

———

Siebert, Rudolf J. *The Critical Theory of Religion: The Frankfurt School*. Berlin: Walter de Gruyter and Co., 1981.

Simon, Derek J. "Salvation and Liberation in the Practical-Critical Soteriology of Schillebeeckx," in *Theological Studies* 63.3 (September 2002): 494–520.

———. "Towards Consolidating the Practical-Critical Soteriology of Edward Schillebeeckx," in *Theoforum* 33.3 (2002): 337–363.

Sison, Antonio D. "*Perfumed Nightmare*: The Philippine Postcolonial Struggle in Third Cinema," in S. Brent Plate, ed., *Representing Religion in World Cinema: Mythmaking, Culturemaking, Filmmaking*. New York: Palgrave Macmillan, 2003.

———. "Dekada 70," in *Journal of Religion and Film* 8.1 (April 2004). http://www.unomaha.edu/jrf/Dekada70.htm.

———. "Divine Intervention," in *Journal of Religion and Film* 7.1 (April 2003).http://www.unomaha.edu/~wwwjrf/Vol7No1/divineintervention.htm.

———. "Kandahar," in *Journal of Religion and Film* 6.1 (April 2002). http://www.unomaha.edu/~wwwjrf/kandahar.htm.

———. "Perfumed Nightmare and Negative Experiences of Contrast: Third Cinema as Filmic Interpretation of Schillebeeckx," in *Journal of Religion and Film* 6.1 (April 2002). http://www.unomaha.edu/~wwwjrf/perfumenght.htm.

———. "*3rd World Hero*: Rizal and Colonial Clerical Power in Philippine Third Cinema," in *Senses of Cinema* 36 (July–September 2005). http://www.sensesofcinema.com/contents/05/36/3rd_world_hero.html.

Sobrino, Jon. *Christology at the Crossroads: A Latin American Approach*, trans. John Drury. Maryknoll, NY: Orbis Books, 1978.

———. *Spirituality of Liberation: Toward Political Holiness*, trans. Robert R. Barr. Maryknoll, NY: Orbis Books, 1988.

Sobrino, Jon, and Ignacio Ellacuria. *Systematic Theology: Perspectives from Liberation Theology*. London: SCM Press, 1996.

Stam, Robert, et al. *New Vocabulary in Film Semiotics: Structuralism, Post-Structuralism, and Beyond*. London: Routledge, 1992.

Tahimik, Kidlat. "Midlife Choices: Filmmaking vs. Fillmaking," in *Primed for Life: Writings on Midlife by 18 Men*, ed. Lorna Kalaw-Tirol. Pasig City: Anvil Publishing, 1997.

Thompson, Daniel Speed. *The Language of Dissent: Edward Schillebeeckx on the Crisis of Authority in the Catholic Church*. Notre Dame: University of Notre Dame Press, 2003.

Thompson, Kenneth. *Auguste Comte: The Foundation of Sociology*. London: Thomas Nelson and Sons Ltd., 1976.

Tillar, Elizabeth Kennedy. "Suffering for Others in the Theology of Edward Schillebeeckx," Dissertation. Fordham University, 1999.

Tillich, Paul. *Theology of Culture*, ed. Robert C. Kimball. New York: Oxford University Press, 1967.

———. *Systematic Theology, vol 1*. Chicago, IL: University of Chicago Press, 1951.

Tiongson, Nicanor G. "The Imitation and Indigenization of Hollywood," in *Pelikula: A Journal of Philippine Cinema* (March–Aug 2000): 23–30.

Tolentino, Rolando B. "*Inangbayan*, the Mother-Nation, in Lino Brocka's *Bayan Ko: Kapit sa Patalim* and *Orapronobis*," in *Screen* 37:4 (Winter 1996): 368–388.

———., ed., *Geopolitics of the Visible*. Quezon City: Ateneo de Manila Press, 2000.

Tracy, David. *Plurality and Ambiguity: Hermeneutics, Religion, Hope*. London: SCM Press, 1988.

"Trade Rigged Against the Poor" editorial in the *International Herald Tribune* (July 21, 2003). http://www.iht.com.

Turvey, Gerry. " 'Xala' and the Curse of Neo-Colonialism: Reflections on a Realist Project," in *Screen* 26.3–4 (May–August 1985): 75–91.

United Nations Development Program, *Human Development Report 2005*. New York: UNDP, 2005.

Vees, Ulrike. " 'Just Making Pictures': Hollywood Writers, The Frankfurt School, and Film Theory," Vees: Leinfelden-Echterdingen: 1996.

Vergara, Benito M. Jr., *Displaying Filipinos: Photography and Colonialism in Early 20th Century Philippines*. Quezon City: University of the Philippines Press, 1995.

Vesilind, Priit J. "The Philippines," in *National Geographic* (July 2002).

Wagnleitner. " 'No Commodity Is Quite so Strange as this Thing Called Cultural Exchange': The Foreign Politics of American Popular Culture Hegemony" *Amerikastudien/American Studies: A Quarterly* 46.3 (2001): 443–470.

Watkins, Greg. "Being Seen: Distinctly Filmic and Religious Elements in Film," in the online *Journal of Religion and Film*.

Wayne, Mike. *Political Film: The Dialectics of Third Cinema*. London: Pluto Press, 2001.

Williams, Patrick, and Laura Chrisman. *Colonial Discourse and Post-Colonial Theory: A Reader*. New York: Colombia University Press, 1994.

Wimmer, Roger D., and Joseph R. Dominick. *Mass Media Research: An Introduction, 2nd ed*. Belmont, CA: Wadsworth Publishing, 1987.

Yau, Esther C.M. "*Yellow Earth:* Western Analysis and a Non-Western Text," in *Film Quarterly* XLI.2 (Winter 1987–1988): 22–33.

Zulueta, Lito B. "Metro Filmfest Shows Wages of 'Global Cinema' " in *The Philippine Daily Inquirer* (January 7, 2002).